Business and Management Practices in South Asia

Arijit Sikdar · Vijay Pereira
Editors

Business and Management Practices in South Asia

A Collection of Case Studies

Editors
Arijit Sikdar
University of Wollongong in Dubai
Dubai, United Arab Emirates

Vijay Pereira
University of Wollongong in Dubai
Dubai, United Arab Emirates

ISBN 978-981-13-1398-1   ISBN 978-981-13-1399-8   (eBook)
https://doi.org/10.1007/978-981-13-1399-8

Library of Congress Control Number: 2018949311

Cover credit: Bengal at a glance/Getty Images
Cover design: Ran Shauli

This Palgrave Macmillan imprint is published by the registered company Springer Nature Singapore Pte Ltd.
The registered company address is: 152 Beach Road, #21-01/04 Gateway East, Singapore 189721, Singapore

FOREWORD

It gives me great pleasure to pen this foreword for a very significant and opportune collection titled *Business and Management Practices in South Asia: A Collection of Case Studies* edited by Dr. Arijit Sikdar and Dr. Vijay Pereira, both from the Australian University of Wollongong, Dubai Campus. Following on from a spate of recent work on business and management in South Asia region by Dr. Pereira,[1] this collection adds to the emergent body of literature needed on this important topic.

It has long been argued that business and management practices differ not only across countries but also within countries among heterogeneous groups of firms. More recently, studies have shown the dynamic nature of how firm adjust to their business environment in order to improve their performance. However, much less is known about how organizations have addressed the intricate complexities in operating in the South Asian context, especially through their unique business models and approaches. Sikdar and Pereira aim to fill this gap. This book represents the authors' long standing research interests, in explaining the complexities of doing business in South Asia. In this comprehensive collection of

---

[1] *East is East? Understanding aspects of Indian culture(s) within organisations* (Pereira and Malik, 2013); *Making Sense and Identifying Aspects of Indian Culture(s) in Organisations: Demystifying through Empirical Evidence* (Pereira and Malik, 2015a); *Investigating Cultural Aspects in Indian Organizations: Empirical Evidence* (Pereira and Malik, 2015b); *Indian culture and work organisations in transition* (Malik and Pereira, 2016); and *National Business Systems in Asian countries* (Pereira, Malik and Jintae Froese, 2017).

case studies, they offer a set of credible theoretical explanations, backed up by empirical evidence on this topical issue.

The context of South Asia is important to understand; given it has a long and rich history of conducting business globally, as is evident when not long ago the Indian sub-continent (South Asia) along with China controlled up to 62% of world GDP and this domination of global GDP continued until around the 1870s. Today, these countries are re-emerging from this past glory by being the two largest and fastest growing economies globally. In terms of global population too, one-fourth of the world's human population reside in the Indian sub-continent collectively, largely in India, Pakistan, and Bangladesh. Besides, economic expatriates from these countries live and work across the globe. Multinational Enterprises (MNEs) also find these destinations in South Asia a viable strategic business option to transfer jobs, popularly known as offshore outsourcing. Further, given the buying capacity and growing purchasing power parity (PPP) of people in these emerging countries, MNEs have also found a lucrative market as a growing middle class clientele and customers for their products and services.

These are thus reasons enough for a greater understanding through case studies when it comes to scholarship, research, and understanding of the business and management practices in the South Asian region. In this collection, the editors Sikdar and Pereira contribute by seeking to map through research and practice, topical- and business- relevant case studies from the sub-continent. This book has a variety of key international contributors who ardently identify the issues and traditions through which South Asian countries conduct and manage business. The contributors not only tackle such critical questions broadly but also provide innovative and indigenous approaches to understanding business and management practices within South Asian organisations.

As we move toward a highly volatile, multifaceted and ever-evolving global business landscape, what we need is more such "regional" and context specific case studies within the business and management discipline. The case studies capture the institutional mosaic of the region and provide a rich understanding of how firms are responding to the changes taking place locally and globally. I commend Dr(s) Sikdar and Pereira on this novel initiative.

Coventry, UK

Prof. Kamel Mellahi
Professor of Strategic Management
Warwick Business School

REFERENCES

Malik, A., and Pereira, V. (2016). *Indian Culture and Work Organisations in Transition*. London: Routledge (Taylor and Francis).

Pereira, V., & Malik, A. (2013). "East is East?: Understanding Aspects of Indian Culture (s) Within Organisations: A Special Issue of Culture and Organization Volume 21, issue 5 (2015)", *Culture and Organization*, vol. 19, no. 5, pp. 453–456.

Pereira, V., & Malik, A. (2015a). "Making Sense and Identifying Aspects of Indian Culture (s) in Organisations: Demystifying Through Empirical Evidence", *Culture and Organization*, vol. 21, no. 5, pp. 355–365.

Pereira, V., & Malik, A. (2015b). *Investigating Cultural Aspects in Indian Organizations*. Springer International Publishing: Imprint: Springer, New York.

Pereira, V., Malik, A., Froese, F. J., & Merchant, H. (2017). *National Business Systems in Asian Countries: Impact on Human Resource Management, Employment Relations Practices and Organisation Behaviour*. V. Pereira (Ed.). Emerald Publishing.

CONTENTS

EDITORS AND CONTRIBUTORS

About the Editors

Dr. Arijit Sikdar is Associate Professor at University of Wollongong, Dubai. He has exposure in industry, consultancy and academia. He has published and presented papers in international journals such as *ETP*, *BPMJ*, *JoE*, *JDE*, *IJBE* and at international conferences. His teaching and research interests are related to strategic management, entrepreneurship and international business. Coming from the IIM Ahmedabad background, his teaching approach is focused on using case studies in classroom discussion for building strong conceptual and critical thinking skills in students. He has also served as academic reviewer for international journals and conferences.

Dr. Vijay Pereira is Associate Professor and Associate Dean (Research), at University of Wollongong, Dubai. He has exposure in industry, consultancy and academia. He has published and presented over 85 papers worldwide including in A and A* international journals such as *HRM*, *JWB*, *IJHRM*, *JBR*, *SI*, *JIM*, *OD* and *IJM* and at international conferences including the *AOM*, *AIB*, *BAM* and *INDAM*. He is currently the Associate Editor (Strategic Management and OB) for the 'A' ranked *Journal of Business Research* and on the editorial board of the FT listed A* *Production and Operations Management Society (POMS) Journal* and *Asia-Pacific-Journal-of-Management*.

Contributors

Maimuna Akter Department of Banking and Insurance, University of Dhaka, Dhaka, Bangladesh

Farrah Arif Lahore University of Management Sciences, Lahore, Pakistan

Bipasha Barua Department of Banking and Insurance, University of Dhaka, Dhaka, Bangladesh

Suborna Barua Department of International Business, University of Dhaka, Dhaka, Bangladesh

Malavika Desai King's College, Kathmandu, Nepal

Perry Haan Tiffin University, Tiffin, OH, USA

Muhammad Naiman Jalil Suleman Dawood School of Business, Lahore University of Management Sciences, Lahore, Pakistan

Payyazhi Jayashree University of Wollongong, Dubai, UAE

Kiranpreet Kaur Birla Institute of Management Technology, Greater Noida, India

Sadia Noor Khan Department of Banking and Insurance, University of Dhaka, Dhaka, Bangladesh

Swati A. Kulkarni SIES College of Management Studies, Navi Mumbai, India

Natasha Mahawar Birla Institute of Management Technology, Greater Noida, India

Sushmera Manikandan Swiss Business School, Zurich, Switzerland

Md. Mohshin Uddin Institute of Business Administration, University of Dhaka, Dhaka, Bangladesh

Tonmoy Ananda Paul Institute of Business Administration, University of Dhaka, Dhaka, Bangladesh

Vijay Pereira Faculty of Business, University of Wollongong, Dubai, UAE

K. Prakash Vel University of Wollongong, Dubai, UAE

Nikhil Raval Duke Corporate Education India Private Limited, Ahmedabad, India

Abha Rishi Birla Institute of Management Technology, Greater Noida, India

Sarah Suneel Sarfraz Lahore University of Management Sciences, Lahore, Pakistan

Eesha Shah Suleman Dawood School of Business, Lahore University of Management Sciences, Lahore, Pakistan

Arijit Sikdar Faculty of Business, University of Wollongong, Dubai, UAE

Ajay Srinivasan Aditya Birla Capital Ltd., Mumbai, India

Balan Sundarakani Faculty of Business, University of Wollongong in Dubai, Dubai, UAE

Savitha Suri Pravaaha Communications LLP, Mumbai, India

Shamima Yesmin Institute of Business Administration, University of Dhaka, Dhaka, Bangladesh

Fahad Zeya Department of Banking and Insurance, University of Dhaka, Dhaka, Bangladesh

LIST OF FIGURES

LIST OF TABLES

Business and Management Practices in South Asia—A Prelude

Arijit Sikdar and Vijay Pereira

INTRODUCTION

The main objective of this book is to unbundle the complexities in the context of South Asia and how organisations have addressed these through their business models and approaches. The case studies that have been included to be a part of this book have been selected from the case studies that were presented at the 7th Asian Management Research and Case (AMRC) conference held at University of Wollongong in Dubai during January 2016. The case studies presented at the conference were selected based on a double blind review. From the case studies presented at the conference, the editors reviewed and shortlisted a set of cases that would reflect the essence of the book. In addition, we also invited other authors to provide case studies that captured the unique perspective of doing business in South Asian context. As editors, we wanted to have a compilation of varied perspectives of doing business

A. Sikdar (✉) · V. Pereira
Faculty of Business, University of Wollongong, Dubai, UAE
e-mail: arijitsikdar@uowdubai.ac.ae

V. Pereira
e-mail: vijaypereira@uowdubai.ac.ae

A. Sikdar and V. Pereira (eds.), *Business and Management Practices in South Asia*, https://doi.org/10.1007/978-981-13-1399-8_1

in South Asia and thus shortlisted ten case studies that captures the key areas of relevance in the South Asian context. In this introductory chapter, we briefly describe the case of South Asia and the need for such a contribution and then briefly introduce each of the 10 cases.

THE CASE OF SOUTH ASIA

Technically, South Asia includes the countries Afghanistan, Bangladesh, Bhutan, India, the Maldives, Nepal, Pakistan, and Sri Lanka. These countries collectively encompass one-fourth of the world's human population. Further, geographically, these seven South Asian countries expanse is about 1.7 million square miles, wherein a total population of 1.3 billion people reside. Economically, India is seen as the second largest growing economy of the world after China (Budhwar and Varma 2011). The economic forecasts currently for South Asian countries for the period 2017–2018 (Asian Development Bank Outlook 2017 Update), has an average GDP growth (%, year) of 6.7% (2017)–7% (2018).

As a collective association, the South Asian Association for Regional Cooperation (SAARC) was established with the signing of the SAARC Charter in Bangladesh in December 1985. As per the charter, the objectives of SAARC are to promote the welfare and improve the quality of life of the people of South Asia through collaboration, mutual assistance and collective self-reliance in economic, social, cultural and technological domains. To strengthen and promote regional cooperation, according to the SAARC website (http://saarc-sec.org/about-saarc), these following centres are established for the socio-economic-cultural development of the SAARC countries:

1. SAARC Agriculture Centre (SAC), Dhaka (established in 1989)
2. SAARC Energy Centre (SEC), Islamabad (established in 2006)
3. SAARC Cultural Centre (SCC), Colombo, Sri Lanka (established in 2009)
4. SAARC Tuberculosis and HIV/AIDS Centre (STAC), Kathmandu (established in 1992)
5. SAARC Disaster Management Centre (SDMC), India (re-established in November 2016)

However, it can be said that much more can be done to further the socio-economic-cultural aspects of the South Asian countries through associations such as SAARC. One way in which cases from South Asian countries can be portrayed is through such mediums where a selection of cases in this contribution represents key issues that business operations in South Asia grapple with. The growth of internet technology has led to the development and growth of ecommerce-based business models in South Asia. An ASSOCHAM-Forrester study reported that Indian ecommerce is growing at 51% annually, the highest in the world, and is expected to grow from $30 billion to $120 billion between 2016 and 2020. A major factor behind the growth of ecommerce has been facilitated by increasing mobile penetration in South Asian countries. South Asia has one of the largest populations of poor whose livelihood need to get connected to the formal economy. This presents challenge of how to find the right combination of philanthropy in the business model. This presents challenge of serving the 'bottom of pyramid' population with approaches that are different from the conventional approaches. South Asia is also the host to a growing middle class population that is aspirational but at the same time cost conscious. Poor transport and communication networks in South Asia present infrastructural challenges for business to perform effective and efficient logistic operations. Each of the selected case studies address one or more of these issues, which is depicted in the introduction of each of the selected case studies.

SUMMARISING EACH CONTRIBUTION

Chapter "Road to Growth: House of Brands, Branded House or House Blend" is the case study contributed by Nikhil Raval, Duke Corporate Education India and Ajay Srinivasan, Aditya Birla Capital Ltd, focusing on the possible choices of business expansion confronting Aditya Birla Financial Services Group (ABFSG). This interesting case portrays the changing landscape of the Indian financial services industry bought about by advent of technology, changing regulations and a growing younger population underserved in their financial needs. Indian financial services industry is represented by commercial banks, insurance companies, non-banking financial companies, co-operatives, pension funds, mutual funds and other smaller financial entities offering a spectrum of services across life and general insurance, asset and wealth management, housing finance, risk management and online money management. ABFSG was created as an umbrella brand to provide the wide spectrum of financial services and work towards achieving its 'Vision 2020' goal of being the single integrated provider of choice for the customer. The case discusses the shaping of the competitive landscape of the Indian financial services industry brought about by changing customer needs, focus on brand image, marketing efforts and service delivery differentiation. The case presents the dilemma that confronts ABFSG on how to develop a successful cross-selling program, selling all services under one umbrella (Branded House), or continue operating under different entities (House of Brands) or adapt something in between (House Blend). The case has been written to bring forth the decision making process that confront senior executives who often fall prey to their own biases of the past when making decisions and provides a useful learning tool for decision making under VUCA (Volatile, Uncertain, Complex, and Ambiguous) context.

The contribution in chapter "Leading Change in the Social Sector: A Bottom-up Revival of Two Weaving Clusters in India" is by Savita Suri, Pravaaha Communications LLP, India and Payyazhi Jayashree, University of Wollongong in Dubai, UAE. The case study focuses on the successful revival of two weaving clusters in India through a process of entrepreneurial leadership and social change. South Asia has a rich tradition of various indigenous crafts which are being lost with the advent of urbanisation and globalisation. The case highlights the challenges that two traditional handloom weaving clusters faced that prevented them from making a profitable business out of their produce and thus affecting their livelihood. The case discusses the role entrepreneurial leadership in developing a sustainable business model driven by financing, marketing and distribution, without multiple layers between the weaver and end user. The case study also provides a very successful example of bringing about social through bottom-up reorientation wherein the lost art of the weavers is rejuvenated to build a business out of their traditional skill. This case study provides lessons for how the social sector can be made more sustainable in an emerging market context. This case study provides a different perspective of doing business in South Asia away from the corporate way by specifically focusing on how creating value-based and purpose driven approaches are fundamental to successful social entrepreneurship ventures.

The next contribution (chapter "Internationalization of Bangladesh Banking Sector: Lessons from an Emerging Economy") is the case study by Suborna Barua and Bipasha Barua, University of Dhaka,

Bangladesh, related to the banking industry and focusing on the internationalisation of Bangladeshi banks. Bangladesh's banking sector is experiencing limited growth opportunities in the domestic market resulting in unhealthy competition and thus exploring foreign markets for greater growth and business opportunities appears to be a promising alternative for Bangladeshi banks. The case discusses the challenges in the internationalisation process faced by banks and how banks have responded to those challenges. A case study carried out a survey of 41 banks which showed that most of the banks have international banking activities in countries driven by the presence of growing Bangladeshi communities (in UK and US) and presence of Bangladeshi migrant labour (in Malaysia and Saudi Arabia). However, the banks consider differences in regulatory and compliance requirements faced in the host country as a challenge. Also most banks lack both international experience and quality human resources, which make it difficult to enter or expand in international markets. Interestingly, the challenges faced have different impact on performance of State Owned Banks (SOBs) versus Private Commercial Banks (PCBs). Internationalisation has an overall negative impact on profitability of SOBs while PCBs are performing significantly better in terms of improvement in profitability. This provides a meaningful insight into the impact of bank management approach on performance; PCBs tend to be dynamic in finding new markets with considerable profit opportunity, while contrastingly SOBs are generally short of dynamism and driven by the government's political agenda, which prevent them to function efficiently and effectively with whatever international outreach they have. The case highlights the opportunities and challenges faced in internationalisation of Bangladeshi banks and throws open the debate of how regulators and policy-makers can help facilitate a smoother internationalisation process for the banks. The case has been written with the objective to provide the reader a comprehensive understanding on how bank internationalisation has taking off in emerging economies and managerial challenges in advancing bank internationalisation in a fast-growing economy.

The next two contributions (chapters "Bangladeshi Banking Innovations: A Case Study on Mobile Banking" and "bKash: Revolutionizing Mobile Financial Services in Bangladesh?") are focused on the mobile banking industry of Bangladesh. Bangladesh has become a pioneer in the use of mobile banking services in South Asia and its extensive usage has played an important role in providing banking access and financial inclusion to 'bottom of the pyramid' population. Chapter "Bangladeshi Banking Innovations: A Case Study on Mobile Banking" is the case study contributed by Sadia Noor Khan, Maimuna Akter and Fahad Zeya, University of Dhaka, Bangladesh. The main objective of the case study is to discuss the factors, demographic variables and users' perception that influence the adoption of mobile banking in Bangladesh. The case study presents the historical development of mobile banking idea and its adoption in Bangladesh. Based on a survey of 400 users of mobile banking services in Bangladesh, the case highlights the various purposes for which mobile banking is preferred. An interesting aspect is the preference for mobile banking usage amongst the younger population due to its convenience. With South Asia having a large young population, the mobile banking usage case presents opportunities to understand what business models would be preferable in South Asia. Though mobile banking scores high on convenience, however, the case study also highlights the concerns of mobile banking users towards security of their money, complexity to use due to lack of technical skills and problems of network availability. The case highlights the opportunities and challenges that confront mobile banking and possibly would leave the reader with the thought whether the Bangladesh experience can work as a role model for the rest of South Asia.

Building on the theme of mobile banking in Bangladesh, the next contribution (chapter "bKash: Revolutionizing Mobile Financial Services in Bangladesh?") is a case study by Shamima Yesmin, Tonmoy Ananda Paul and Md. Mohshin Uddin, University of Dhaka, Bangladesh, focusing on the emergence of bKash as m-banking pioneer in Bangladesh. The case highlights the launch of bKash service by BRAC Bank to provide mobile banking services to the unbanked in Bangladesh. Considering the scenario of Bangladesh where majority of the rural population is illiterate or has little academic knowledge, conventional banking system is neither useful nor user friendly for them. The growth of bKash got a boost due to the rise of readymade garments sector, whereby population migrating from rural areas to work in cities like Dhaka and Chittagong started facing difficulties of sending money home on a regular basis. bKash has become so generic that it is synonymous to mobile money payments and people uses phrases like 'bKash me' instead of saying 'send me money.' Though bKash has established itself as the undisputed leader in Bangladesh's mobile financial services industry, there is increasing competition snapping at bKash's heels. The case throws open challenges for bKash, how to promote its services amongst target population, what additional services to add, moving from the rural class to targeting the urban class and addressing concerns of fraudulent activities surrounding bKash. The case has been written with the objective to provide an understanding of how to an industry leader can extend its competitive advantage to grow and beat the competition.

The next two contributions focus on the creation of ecommerce based business models, which is a growing trend being used by companies in the South Asian context to reach the wider population in a cost effective manner and build on the propensity of the population to increasingly embrace ecommerce technology. Chapter "Pakwheels.com—A Period of Transition!" is a case study contributed by Farrah Arif and Sarah Sarfraz, Lahore University of Management Sciences, Pakistan, focusing on ecommerce-based business model that helped millions of Pakistanis to buy and sell automobiles, and finding solutions to their automotive needs. Pakwheels.com was a vertical automotive portal, founded in 2003 and acquired by entrepreneurs Raza Saeed and Suneel Munj in 2008. Despite the competition from classifieds websites like OLX and carmudi.com, PakWheels had managed to grow its market share due to the cult-like following of its loyal user base. The case provides a comprehensive overview of the conventional 'used' car trade in Pakistan which was affected by the lack of transparency and reliability. With the rise of mobile and connected technology, PakWheels developed a comprehensive vertical automotive portal that created value for customers by facilitating interactions between vehicle buyers and sellers, primarily by reducing search and transaction costs. The case discusses the various actions undertaken by PakWheels, especially, in the areas of on-site advertising and promotional activities to enhance community engagement. However, the development of their growth strategy could get hampered by the possibility of a discriminating cyber-crime prevention bill called Prevention of Electronic Crimes Act (PECA), and OLX's mega media campaign to introduce its used car section. Having obtained venture capital investment in 2014, PakWheels has to decide the best way to scale up their business by utilising the investor money in an efficient manner. The case is written to highlight the issues involved in managing a business that is experiencing a changing competitive environment and explore the different ways by which value can be created and appropriated in the digital setting.

Continuing on the theme of ecommerce business model, the next contribution (chapter "The Expansion of Online Travel Portal—MakeMyTrip") is a case study by Abha Rishi, Kiranpreet Kaur and Natasha Mahawar, Birla Institute of Management Technology, New Delhi, India, focusing on its journey of growth since its inception in 2000. MakeMyTrip revolutionised the perception of Indian customers when it came to travel booking and reservation. In the past, most travel bookings had to be done physically. As internet penetrated the Indian market, MakeMyTrip developed an online portal to become a one stop solution for reservation of flight and train tickets, hotel bookings, tour and travel packages etc., in India. Building upon its success in India, MakeMyTrip crossed the national boundaries and established its roots in other countries such as Singapore, UAE and USA. Understanding the fact that MakeMyTrip is not the sole online travel portal and that it faces huge competition from various global companies in this fiercely competitive sector, MakeMyTrip needs to define its future working based on the fact that how much can it differentiate itself from its competitors. This case study is written with the objective to analyse what factors MakeMyTrip need to improve upon for its growth trajectory and success.

Building on the agenda of chapter "Road to Growth: House of Brands, Branded House or House Blend", the next contribution (chapter "Reliance Jio—Late, but the Latest and Later?") is the case study by Swati A. Kulkarni, SIES College of Management, Navi Mumbai and Prakash Vel, University of Wollongong in Dubai that focuses on analysing whether the current strategy of Reliance Jio Infocomm Limited (RJIL) is sustainable in the face of the dynamics changes in the Indian telecom industry. This case portrays the revolutionary launch of RJIL's telecom service by providing free unlimited outgoing voice calls and data at low cost to successfully grab 150 million subscribers within a short period of time. The case discusses the marketing mix adopted by RJIL in launching its telecom service. Indian telecom industry has undergone a rapid change in the last two decades and is now dominated by private Indian and foreign players fighting intensely to maintain their market position. However, future competition is being rapidly shaped by growing internet penetration, online shopping, use of mobile wallets, young population with higher disposable income, growing use of smartphones and launch of new generation of technology. The competition from RJIL has led existing players trying to consolidate their position through mergers and acquisitions so as to able to present a befitting challenge to RJIL. In this context, the case focuses on analysing whether the strategy of RJIL is sustainable to provide for long term success. The case has been written with the objective to provide an understanding of how to leverage the industry drivers to create business advantage in the face of hyper competition.

The next contribution (chapter "Overseas Courier Services, Pakistan: Logistics Operations at Central Region") is a case study by Muhammad Naiman Jalil and Eesha Shah of Lahore University of Management Sciences, Pakistan. The case focuses on the challenges of planning operations at the ground level in the South Asian context, where overcoming such challenges become a daunting task given the poor infrastructural facilities. This case involves balancing the operational cost and customer service issues that Overseas Courier Services (OCS), a major player in parcel and cargo services industry in Pakistan. With 212 pick-up locations throughout Pakistan, OCS network operations have become inefficient and costly while customers were increasingly demanding greater efficiency and timeliness for parcel and cargo delivery services. At the same time, rising fuel costs and increased competition were worrisome as these had resulted in smaller industry-wide profit margins. The case provides a background of the current logistics network operations of OCS and its services, and the challenges faced in last-mile transportation or intra-city transportation. Based on data provided, the case highlights the routing decision for effective inter-city and intra-city operations for the central region of OCS, which is the most challenging in terms of infrastructural issues. The case is written with the objective to understand how managers need to tread carefully between the conflicting objectives of operational cost and customer service considering the strategic, tactical and operational aspects of network planning and transport fleet planning within transportation and logistics industry.

In line with the earlier chapter, the challenges of managing the supply chain in pharmaceutical industry is the focus of the next chapter "SUN Rises from RANBAXY: Supply Chain Strategy of an Indian Pharmaceutical Company" is a case study, contributed by Sushmera Manikandan and Balan Sundarakani, University of Wollongong in Dubai. This case portrays the acquisition of Ranbaxy in 2014 by Sun Pharmaceutical Industries Limited (Sun Pharma) to become the largest pharmaceutical company in India and ranked 4th among the global generic and specialty pharmaceutical company with $25 billion market capital in the US pharmaceutical market. This global aspiration is a challenge as Indian companies historically were used to sell in unregulated markets but now a large part of the business is coming out of regulated markets. The case discusses following the merger how Sun Pharma integrates the operations of Ranbaxy to create and operate their supply chain footprint across the globe strategically. The merger with Ranbaxy increases the complexity in supply chain operations due to integration of Ranbaxy's global manufacturing operations, different systems, marketing and regulatory challenges. But could Sun Pharma despite its current challenges achieve its vision of becoming a global lead player? The case has been written with the objective to critically examine the supply chain strategy of 'Sun pharma' company move forward from its local acquisition towards their global expansion strategy.

Chapter "Hope in Their Hands: Seeing Hands Nepal" is a contribution from Nepal by Perry Haan, Tiffin University, US and Malavika Desai, ADAMAS University, India. This case study portrays the social entrepreneurship venture of massage clinics in Kathmandu that is operated by blind message therapists. The case focuses on the challenge that is faced by Poudel, a blind business owner, on how to expand the business considering the economic conditions of Nepal and the availability of talent. The case provides an interesting aspect of social entrepreneurship of providing gainful employment to blind who would otherwise be unemployed. The case also provides a challenge to create business opportunities without sacrificing the principle of social entrepreneurship. The case also would induce a debate on what should government and society do to support disabled people to embark on creating mainstream business ventures. Disabled being seen by society as unproductive, is an important social problem for South Asian countries, and this case shows the way how support would help disabled people to generate economic potential.

CONCLUSION

This chapter sets the scene by highlighting the South Asian context in terms of the challenges faced and future opportunities. Considering this narrative, the chapter presents a set of ten case studies of organisations that are of South Asian origin and operating in the said environment. Each of the case studies highlight the unique challenges that are being faced by the organisation and discusses the possible solutions or approaches that could be used to address such challenges. We hope these case studies of South Asian organisations would provide learning and knowledge to current and future practitioners, educators and scholars an understanding of the challenges and opportunities present to deal with operations in the South Asian context, and possibly extend the learning to similar context in other parts of the world.

REFERENCES

Asian Development Bank Outlook 2017 Update Report. https://www.adb.org/data/south-asia-economy. Accessed 20 Jan 2018.

Budhwar, P. S., & Varma, A. (Eds.). (2011). Doing business in India: Building research-based practice. London (UK): Routledge. https://doi.org/10.4324/9780203840931.

SAARC. Website. http://saarc-sec.org/about-saarc. Accessed 25 Jan 2018.

Road to Growth: House of Brands, Branded House, or House Blend

Nikhil Raval and Ajay Srinivasan

INTRODUCTION

There is a sea change which is currently undergoing the Indian Financial services industry. With the advent of technology and changing regulations, a growing younger population which is underserved in their financial needs is creating opportunities to go forth and capture the customer's additional share of the wallet for firms in this space. However, the point of differentiation is becoming more and more difficult with huge commoditization happening, which are making both the product life cycle and innovation life cycles shorter. Added to this, a growing organization creates its own challenges of collaborating which becomes increasingly difficult with size, scale, and different cultures and sub cultures that exist under a firm. In these conditions, how leader takes decision becomes the key differentiating factor.

N. Raval (✉)
Duke Corporate Education India Private Limited, Ahmedabad, India
e-mail: Nikhil.raval@dukece.com

A. Srinivasan
Aditya Birla Capital Ltd., Mumbai, India
e-mail: Ajay.srinivasan@adityabirla.com

13

While there is a lot of material on the topic of Decision Making and the importance and relevance of how key decisions are taken, much of this focuses on the classical approach to decision making—i.e., using decision trees, looking at probabilities, and arriving to a conclusion. This reliance on data has worked well in the past decades; however, given the rapid pace of change and uncertainty businesses face today, of what is often called the Volatile, Uncertain, Complex, and Ambiguous (VUCA) impact, this approach alone is not enough. In the recent years, a lot of work has been done on behavioral biases which also impact the decision-making process and how the success or methods of past cannot guarantee same results in future.

The case has been written to bring forward the decision making process in senior executives who often fall prey to their own biases of past when making decisions. The focus of the case is to have students and participants apply a process rather than the accuracy or pros and cons of a particular solution.

An Evening at the Club

It was a Sunday evening and Ajay had just finished his weekly tennis game at the club. He was excited as he had a win in straight sets. With an ice cold drink in hand, he and his friends headed towards the lounge to relax and watch some television. What not surprisingly, and as is prevalent in talking circles these days in India, "discussion about Brand India" was on one of the channel. In the news was the mention of India's recent climb on the Global "Ease of Doing Business" report, the Reserve Bank of India (RBI) Chief's decision to reduce the repo rate, the government's decision on relaxing foreign direct investment (FDI) norms on 15 key sectors, and how India has become the top destination for FDI in 2015. In 2016, the government made some key reform changes like introducing the Jan Dhan Yojna (Prime Minister Modi's scheme of India's mission for financial inclusion to ensure access to financial services, namely, banking, savings and deposits, remittance, credit insurance, pension in an affordable manner) for the unbanked and "Demonetization" (which is the act of stripping currency unit of its status legal tender and done often to combat inflation, corruption, and discourage a cash system). And in 2017, the government imposed an all-important introduction of one flat structure of taxes called "Goods and Services Tax" (GST). At the table with some snacks, all these news items got Ajay thinking of the implications and opportunities it posed for his own business. This included all the different products and services: Insurance, Asset Management, Mutual Funds, Home Loans, etc. He shared the thoughts on his mind and went on...

Understanding the Indian Economy, Financial Services Landscape, and the Opportunities

When India achieved independence in 1947, India was primarily an agricultural country with a weak industrial base. The national consensus was in favor of rapid industrialization of the economy which was seen as the key to economic development, improving living standards and economic strength. Until the early 90s, the era is often known as the "License Raj" period where companies were given licenses by the government to operate and compete which came to an end. This was a fairly protectionist view, and companies survived despite remaining unproductive, inefficient, and without competition.

After 90s, the Indian government made a sea change in its approach and opened the Indian shores to what is commonly called as: LPGization—Liberalization, Privatization, and Globalization of Indian economy. This move primarily led to domestic companies being more global in their outlook, competing with their western multinationals and making products which are acceptable beyond the Indian borders. These key reforms also lead to building of strong institutional infrastructure which would provide the base for trade within and across borders. Among many such institutions, the government also put in the regulatory and control framework for a robust banking system and more broadly the financial services sector.

Today India's financial services sector consists of capital markets, non-banking financial companies, and insurance sector. India, however, remains an underserved country when it comes to meeting financial needs of the individual. There is a huge opportunity in urban, semi-urban, and rural areas of the country where financial inclusion is still required. Prime Minister Narendra Modi recently introduced the "Jan Dhan Yojna" which allows the population below the poverty line to be part of the financial system. Despite this, one witnesses a rapid growth in the sector as individual citizens increase savings to create more disposable income. Some of the data that suggest this trend include the following:

- The asset management industry in India is among the fastest growing in the world. The AUM of the mutual fund industry stood at US$299.04 billion.
- Corporate investors accounted for around 43%, while High Net-Worth Individuals and retail investors account for 29 and 25%. In the Asia-Pacific, India is among the top five countries in terms of HNWIs.
- The insurance penetration in India is roughly at only 4% of the population. Schemes like Pradhan Mantri Fasal Bima Yojana are introduced to bring uninsured population in the ambit.
- Raising capital is a strategic priority and the rising FII inflows indicate there is a huge potential for capital markets as right now only 2–4% of population account for retail investors and the lowest strata of the pyramid remains still untapped.
- For the financial services sector, relaxation of foreign investment rules has received a positive response from, with many companies announcing plans to increase their stakes in joint ventures with Indian companies.

Foray in Financial Services

Given all the macro trends, the decision to be part of this growing sunrise sector was fully justified by ABG. Aditya Birla Financial Service Group was created and it offered services across the spectrum starting with debt, investing, and advisory products (Life Insurance, Housing Finance, Broking, Wealth Management). But as Ajay recalled some of these reforms, he knew the game was only going to get intensified. Further, with the recent advent of payment banks on the horizon, it put more pressure on existing players and incumbents to increase their share of the pie.

Conquering the Key Success Factors

Financial Service businesses offer a slew of products and services. Whether one does a small boutique firm or a large operator, understanding the key factors that shape the success of its industry are very critical. For ABFSG, these included being on top of their game with the following four points as follows:

1. *Focus on Needs*

   In India, the market place is not only large but also the demographics are very diverse. This means, catering to each segment is not just important but equally challenging, for example, sensitizing the young population on the need to grow and invest; providing the necessary working capital needs for the unorganized and small-medium sector; for many of the home grown companies which wish to expand also require support in trade financing as they expand their foot print outside India.

2. *Brand Image and Communicating Brand*

   With a slew of providers entering the market, how one creates a distinct brand is very important for customer pull and retention. The customer has the switching power and the need to build service innovations and communicating them strongly is vital in a commoditized market. Companies have to create tangible, intangible, and total value propositions to separate themselves in the market place.

3. *Measuring Marketing Efforts*

   Given the rapid commoditization of product and services, the innovation cycles in the market places are becoming shorter and shorter. When companies use marketing money to communicate their brand and services, it is essential to track spend being made against the return they get. Though a lot is being said and written about the potential of big data and analytics and how customer data can be used to create segments, the use of promotion and outreach strategies will only be as successful as the return on such initiatives. Companies will have to be both cautious and nimble at the same time.

4. *Differentiation Through Service Delivery*

   All players in the financial services industry today realize that the advantages companies want to establish through their core products are quickly copied and they operate in an environment which is highly commoditized. In such a scenario, excellence in customer service is emerging as a valuable way to differentiate oneself from competitors. Great firms whether in financial services or others make customer service experience as the backbone and commitment by providing value added services to both internal and external customers including attitude, knowledge, technical support, and quality of service in a timely manner. One can have the best service philosophy in the world, but if you don't have a unified organizational mindset, processes, and systems to deliver service excellence, you have lost the game.

An Opportunity to Go Deep "Vertically" in the New Business Landscape

Financial Services Industry had seen its share of crisis dating back to the 80s with the Savings and Loan failures to the most recent 2008 global crises which completely shook the consumer confidence in the companies. In the Indian context, however, the regulator had done a good job of laying the rules which shielded the banks and the financial services industry as a whole. In many instances, there has been more than one regulator (such as in insurance, structured finance, investments) which laid strict guidelines companies had to comply with. This was a double edged sword. It was necessary to keep consumer confidence and trust high but it also often posed more compliance requirements for companies in the business.

Well such was the reality of the companies competing in this space, but the market was rife for picking. For ABFSG which was a part of India's most iconic brand—a $42 Billion behemoth in 36 countries, there was a lot going for them. A group known to set audacious goals ABFSG had its mandate clear. A Vision "2020" strategic document was created which spelled out the aspirations of ABFSG. This included INR 25,000 Crores of top line, 20 Million Customers, 4× products per customer, and Service in advance. The road to achieving "Vision 2020," however, was not easy. ABFSG wanted to be single integrated provider of choice "The Power of One." The customer base was growing but more needed to be done as the objectives it had set for them were clearly distinct and high from their competitors:

- *Every customer to be an ABGFSG Customer*
- *Once with ABGFSG always with ABGFSG*
- *Maximize revenue from customers*
- *Minimize cost of Acquisition*

In financial services, it is an open secret that commoditization of services was leading to client attrition and high customer acquisition rates.

Numerous studies have shown that the cost of acquiring customers is generally estimated at five times the rate of retaining existing ones. Also known is that reduction in customer churn can boost net profits significantly.

What this means is companies have be smart on monetizing customer churn and consistently touch clients to keep them connected to the brand. Some external benchmarking of successful brands such as Wells Fargo in the US and HDFC in India indicated there were gaps which the company can plug to be the best. One such metric was the ratio of cross sell of products.

Cross Selling is the concept of selling additional products and services to existing clients to increase sales. If a firm uses its customer data wisely, cross selling can be become a huge revenue generator for the company. Most companies understand the concept but are poor implementers. The reason could be many for this, but primarily, it is the lack of understanding customer better and the need to work collaboratively if a firm is selling individual products separately. Companies that have done this successfully do this by making customer centricity as their core philosophy and not necessarily increase the cross-sell ratio, as in the long run, the company loses out and customers would leave.

Globally, Wells Fargo was the benchmark who is able to sell 6.5 products per customer. In India, HDFC has the best number with 4 products per customer. For ABFSG this number was at 1.5. Ajay knew even the 1.5 was not a result of a conscious effort, but more a number which has come by chance. Specifically, he had few questions which weighed on his mind which needed to be answered if cross selling was to happen successfully?

(a) *Leveraging Technology and Its ROI*
   With digitization gaining prominence, customers want instant access and prefer transacting online versus the traditional brick-n-mortar format of doing business. For this to happen, companies have to make substantive technology investment to serve the need of the customer while ensuring they protect the customer safety and privacy. The investment in technology is not only imperative, but also has to be done carefully as each new wave of technology makes the older one obsolete. Proactive anticipation of technology trends and training customers to become savvy with this are critical part of gaining and retaining customers.

Technology also provides and generates new sets of data of the customers. Firms today also use sophisticated predictive analytics techniques to predict customers likely to churn and taking action that prevent churning from occurring. Through these data, companies can segment those customers by profitability, volume, and length of engagement. Through this segmentation, firms can optimize marketing campaigns ensuring correct incentives are offered to each class of clients resulting in higher retention at lower cost, improving customer experience, by offering promotions that appeal to them. For example, Bank Itau had created several segments using technology successfully.

Additionally, firms also use analytics for risk management on things like non-compliant trading, creditworthiness, valuations, and volatility. Altogether, analytics presents a 360-degree forward looking view of the customer and is a quick reliable tool for checking ROI in the business.

While all this made sense on the front end for a seamless customer experience, how much would this cost the firm internally? There were instances where small firms had managed this by using basic existing technology and yet one could argue as a firm grew in size and scale IT had to be looked differently. Investments would need to be made in IT systems, which ensured it carried through client data across entities and the technology would serve ABFSG its mission in the coming years. If one does invest in such a technology, how much is the investment, what is the technology and what would be the payback period for such investment.

(b) *Creating a Ready Sales Bench*

One of the key pivots of cross selling underscores the notion of providing the customer a "one-stop" product and service experience. A sales rep who is traditionally trained and expected to sell a particular product (say insurance, annuity) will now also recommend and sell a mutual fund, pension, or other investment product as needed by the customer. Successful firms not only spent significant time and money in training their sales reps on understanding the features and benefits of products but also all aspects of customer servicing and relationship management. With more and more product offerings coming into the market place, continuous investment in sales and service can become a key differentiator. If a firm has to consciously adopt cross-selling, how do you go about getting your sales bench ready which is able to sell not only the products of its own entity but also across entities. A quick market entry with a trained sales team may provide a competitive advantage against incumbents. The question looming of course was do we do this in-house (which can be quite time consuming and exhaustive) or do we source ready talent from market. If we do the latter, will the new sales force assimilates quickly to ABFSG culture and systems? What is the cost and what are the pros and cons to this route?

(c) *Overcoming Regulatory Hurdles*
Financial services globally are a highly regulated industry. Regulatory bodies play a critical role in ensuring compliance and customer safety and trust elements. In India, tight regulation by the various agencies has served the country generally well— withstanding all the financial scams, scandals one has seen over the years in North America and Europe. ABFSG which has eleven independent entities offering different products has to deal with multiple agencies. For the insurance business, one has to comply with rules laid by Insurance and Regulatory and Development Authority (IRDA). The Mutual Funds business is overseen and regulated by Securities and Exchange Board of India (SEBI). The Home Finance and NBFC business need to comply with RBI guidelines. The Regulatory framework in India is one of the most complex and strict. Rules are fairly water tight yet there are rules and conditions which allow firms to cross sell if done correctly. For example, Mutual fund houses have offered term life insurance as an add-on free product to cover customer's insurance needs. It is complex maize and requires careful treading. A deep understanding of rules and adhering to all the right guidelines is a must. If one were to cross sell, how do you navigate through the various regulatory hurdles, be legally compliant, and yet give customer the options. Please see Appendix.

(d) *Equitable Compensation*
Globally, most financial services firm adopt a commission or a variable pay model to increase the sales of products. The advisory and financial planning parts of the business normally are fee based; however, product implementation is attached to commissions based on the products sold. The industry has often suffered

bad reputation when wrong sales practices have been adopted (often known as churning) in lure of higher commissions. If successful cross sell has to occur—it implicitly assumes a great fiduciary responsibility on part of the sales rep for not selling products which fetch higher commissions, but selling the "right services" which is best in the interest of customer. Further, if a sales rep now sells a product beyond its own entity (a mutual fund rep selling insurance)—how do you reward him? The rep could be an employee of one entity but may end up selling more products of another entity. How do you justify the fixed compensation from the originating entity and what is an equitable compensation for cross selling other services. This is a vital element and a careful study would need to be done as high performance and motivation are quite clearly linked to compensation in a big way.

Ajay knew the immense potential that lay in a successful implementation of cross sell programs. However, the execution of this wasn't as simple as is the concept of the idea. Successfully managing and balancing regulatory boundaries, overcoming compensation issues, cross training the sales force, managing the attrition, responding quickly to new market innovations, and creating a deeply customer centric mindset above was a tall order to achieve. It could be done, but the road to success would require persistence as it was the road often less travelled.

Conclusion

Ajay knew it was time to go deep in cashing the existing customer base. There were many questions, many answers, and a few unknowns. He knew strategy should not be made any more complex than it is but just a good swipe at improving cross sell ratio would mean a sea change in numbers, profit, and brand reach.

Several factors were swaying in Ajay's head given all the different options, its advantages, and disadvantages. A careful evaluation was required. Each choice had its trade-offs and what would be the best way to make this decision. A good decision making framework would help clear the options. He shared the options with his tennis mates at the club as they closed out the night knowing this is a match which will have a few more rounds with a winner undecided.

APPENDIX I

Decision Making Framework

- **Leading in Context**: Decision Making: Process Trumps Analysis
  - The case for Adhering to Process Organizing Framework
  - Presenting the Framework: Define, Gather, Develop, Select
- **De-biasing the Decision Making Process**: Overcoming Bias in Defining the Problem and Clarifying Decisions
  - Widen the Frame
  - Align Mental Models
  - Reduce Anchoring/Stability Bias
  - Promote Diversity of Perspective
- **De-biasing the Decision Making Process**: Overcoming Bias in Gathering and Analyzing Data:
  - Challenge your Assumptions
  - Remove Confirmation Bias
  - Avoid Availability/Recency Bias
  - Pick Unknowns to Convert to Knowns
- **De-biasing the Decision Making Process**: Overcoming Bias in Developing and Evaluating Alternatives:
  - Attain Distance,
  - Beware of Loss Aversion
  - Counterbalance Commission Regret
  - Decide on Selection Criteria
- **De-biasing the Decision Making Process**: Overcoming Bias in Selecting and Agreeing on Most Beneficial Cause of Action:
  - Prepare to be Wrong
  - Ostracize Over Confidence and Optimism
  - Watch for Social Bias
  - Reel in Influencers
- **Conduct a Process Audit and Debrief**:
  - What Biases got in the Way the Most?
  - What can you do to avoid this in the Future?

Appendix II

Decision Choice 1: Take the "House of Brands" Route

ABFSG has created separate entities for the 11 different lines of business and offering it makes. Each entity has grown and positioned itself as a unique brand in the market. Continuing to offer services in the current set up means customers deal with a familiar product, brand and service structure. Internally for ABFSG sales forces and advisors serving these customers would be clear about the product knowledge, compliance, and their target audience. They would also know the commission structure associated with the products they sell and the clear KPIs laid by the firm to achieve their targets.

The down side of this set up is multiple (ABFSG) brands are etched in the minds of one common customer. The company misses out on the opportunity to cross sell and there is no holistic advice given to the client. Each company would work in isolation and resulting in potential "conflict of interest" as multiple channels sell a product.

Decision Choice 2: Take the "Branded House" Approach

ABGFSG takes a branded house approach with focus and emphasis on cross selling. Cross selling will allow the firm:

- A great opportunity to increase the revenue.
- Benefits of efficiency in serving one account over many.
- With more services the customers are less likely to be displaced by competitors.
- The more a customer stays with ABFSG the higher the switching cost.

Benefits of Cross Selling to Customers

- Efficiency and Leverage by using a single provider for multiple products.
- Finger pointing is eliminated. One firm reduces the finger pointing which is often a common problem which can often straddle between two firms.

Downside and Barriers to Cross Selling

- Ineffective control and monitoring of cross-sell activities affects every stage of value chain: enrollment, benefit fulfillment, servicing and billing.
- Lack of process will lead a feeling of deceptive marketing practice and miserable customer experience.
- Lack of internal communication and product knowledge.
- Different purchasing points within an account, which reduce the ability to treat the customer like a single account.
- The fear of the incumbent business unit that its colleagues would botch their work at the client, resulting with the loss of the account for all units of the firm.

Decision Choice 3. Take a "House Blend" Option

ABFSG creates a separate entity in which key customer segments are created which can give "bundled products". This would be a hybrid of option 1 and 2. The bundled product gives customer the choice of key products under one offering which saves the time of dealing with multiple agents and advisors. The cost of transaction would become smaller and the servicing to be easier.

The downside of this approach would be the regulatory hurdle of creating and managing another entity and ensuring all compliance rules of different products are intact and adhered to. This would also throw the question of consolidating some entities. This approach also calls for cross product training and advisors willing to sacrifice their own targets to do what is right for the customer.

APPENDIX III

Image 1

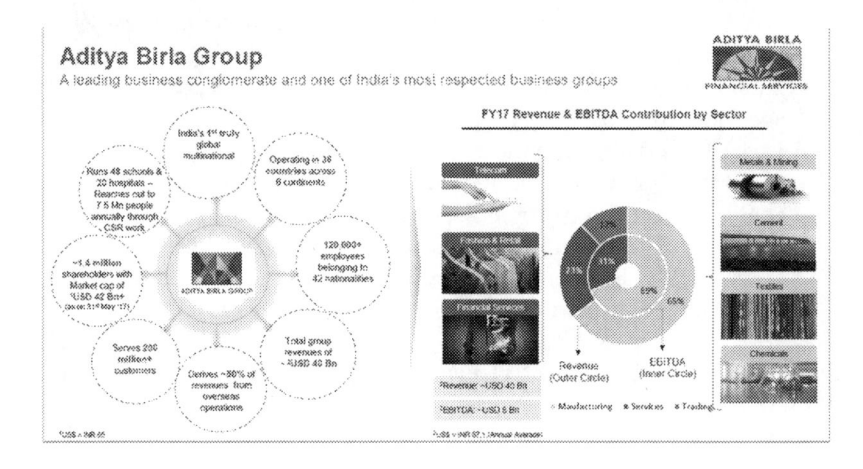

Image 2

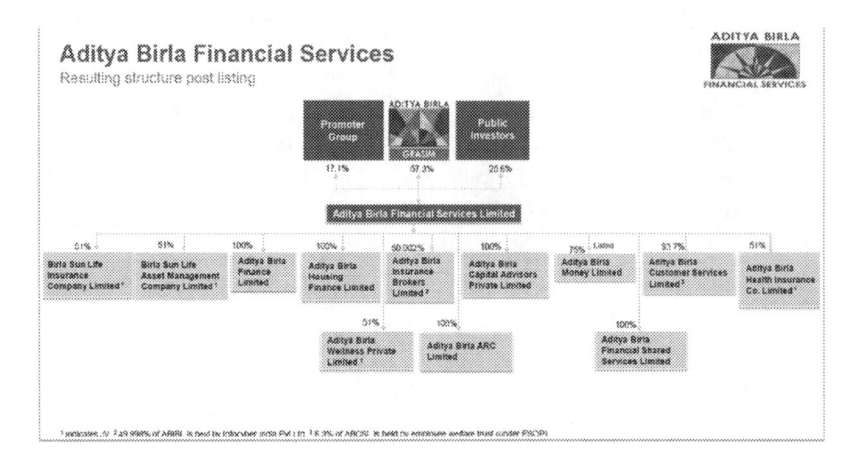

Image 3

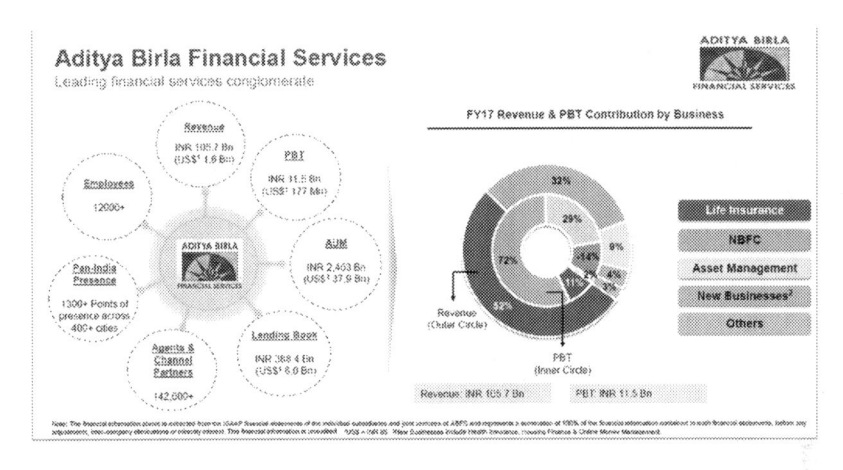

Image 4

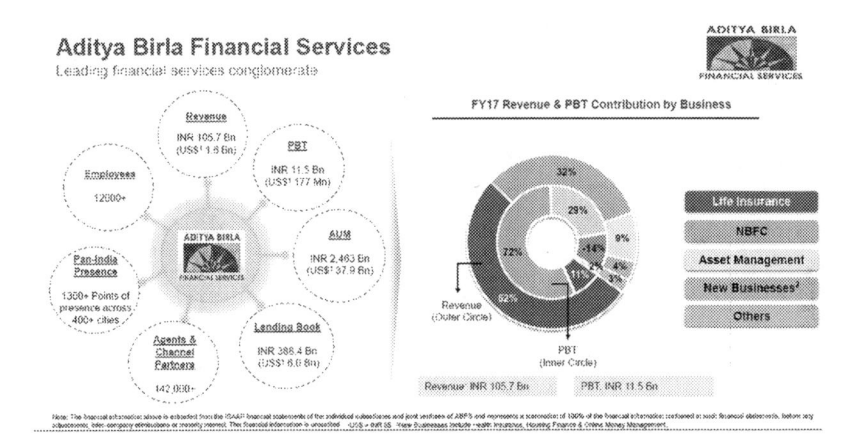

Image 5

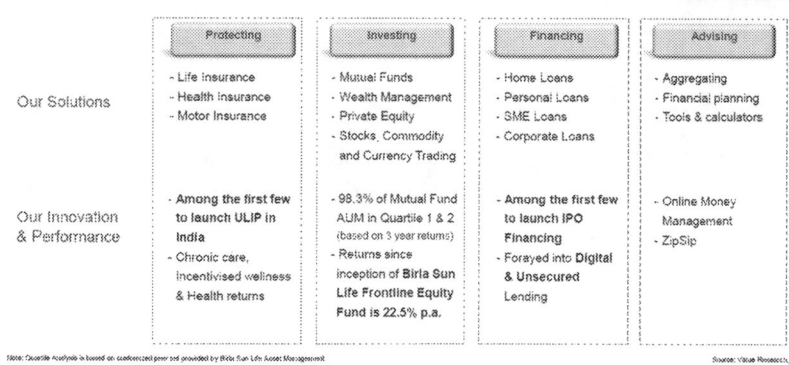

Image 6

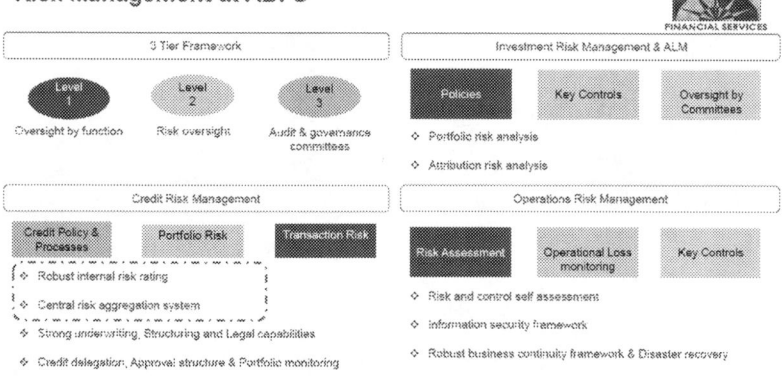

Image 7

Key Business Segments Snapshot

Image A

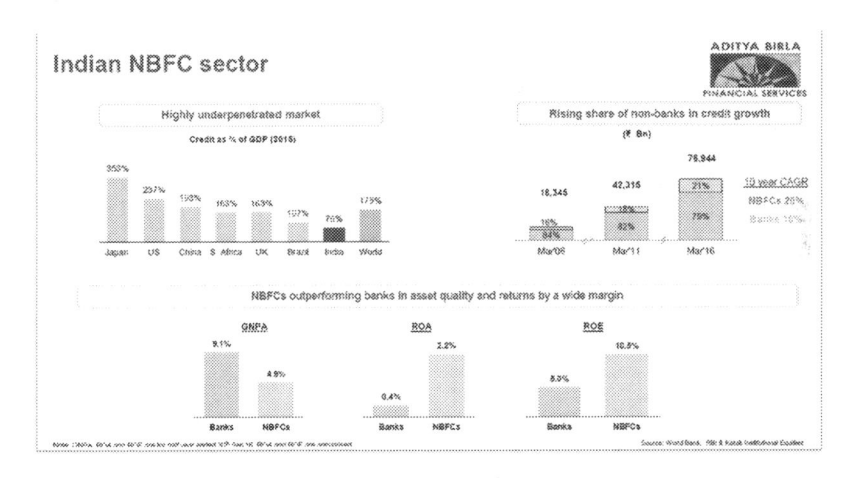

Image B

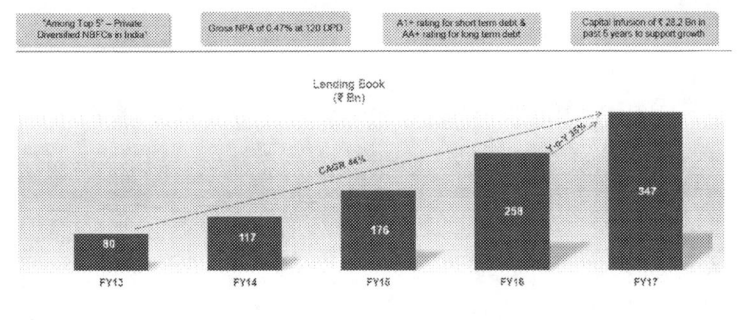

Image C

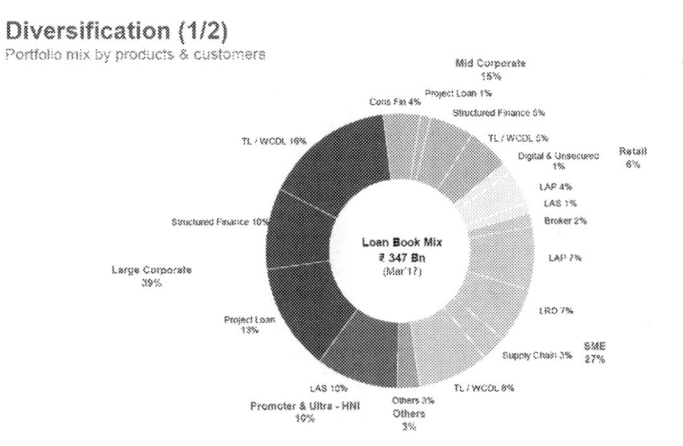

Image D

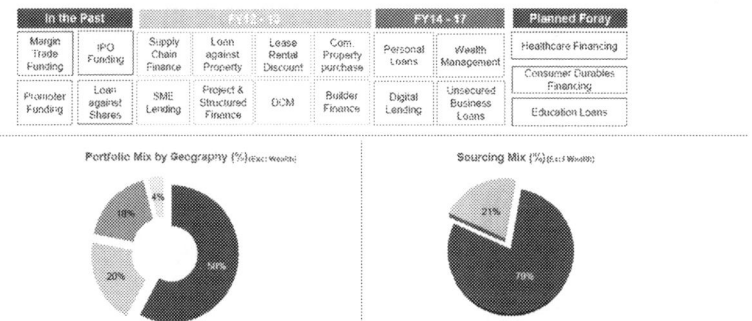

Image E

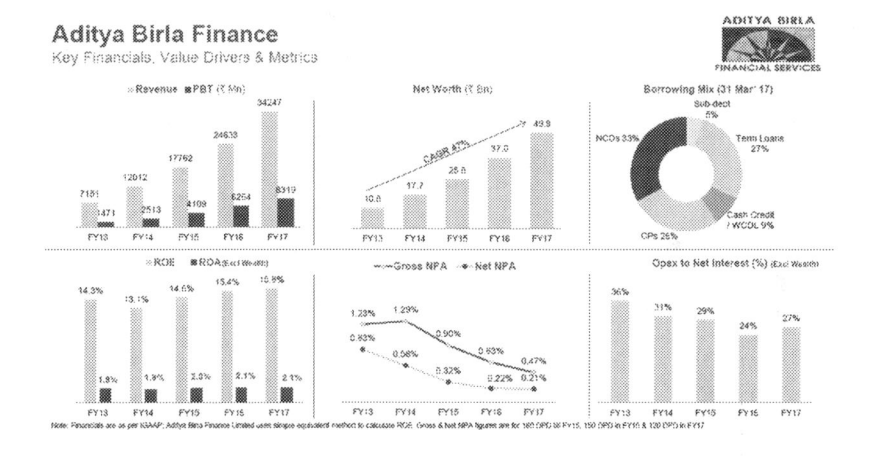

Image F

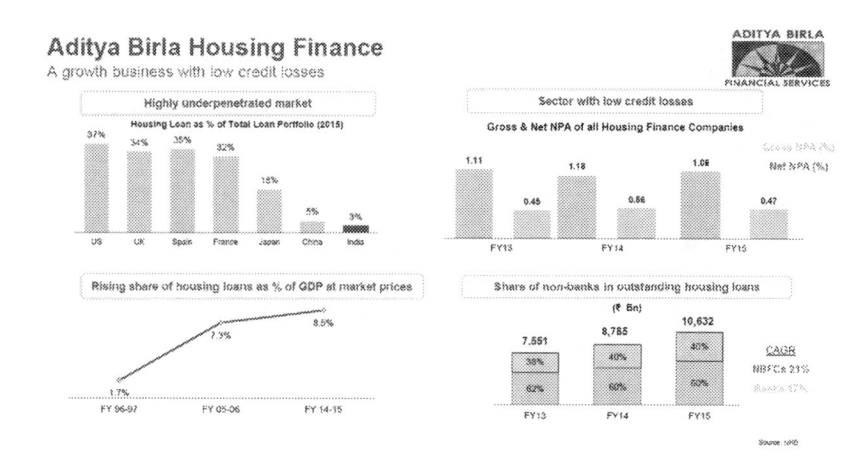

Image G

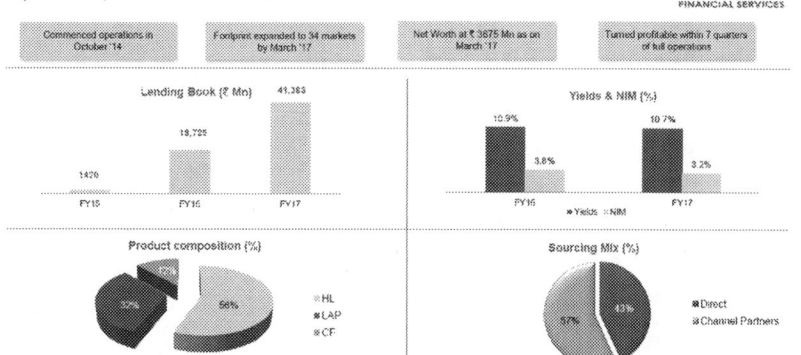

Image H

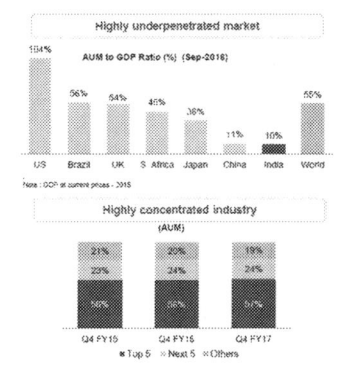

Image I

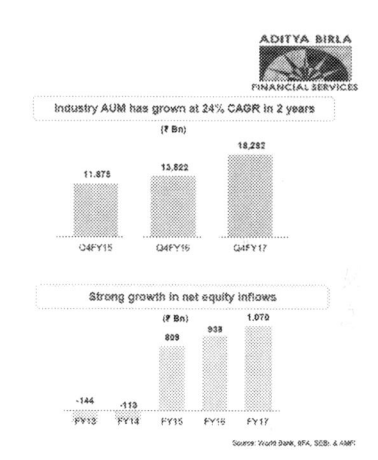

Image J

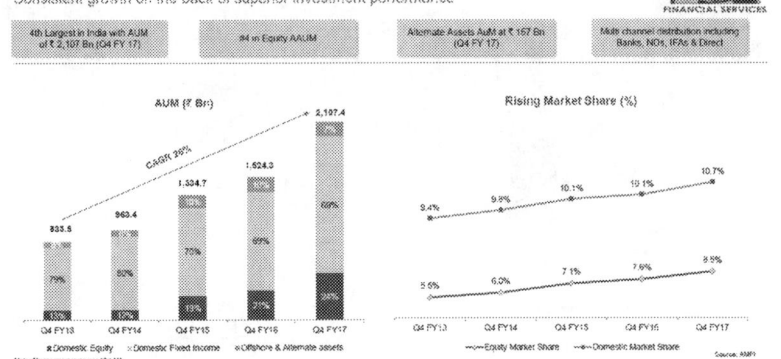

Image K

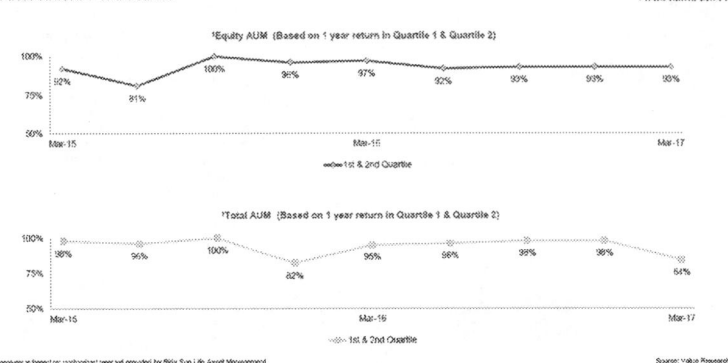

Image L

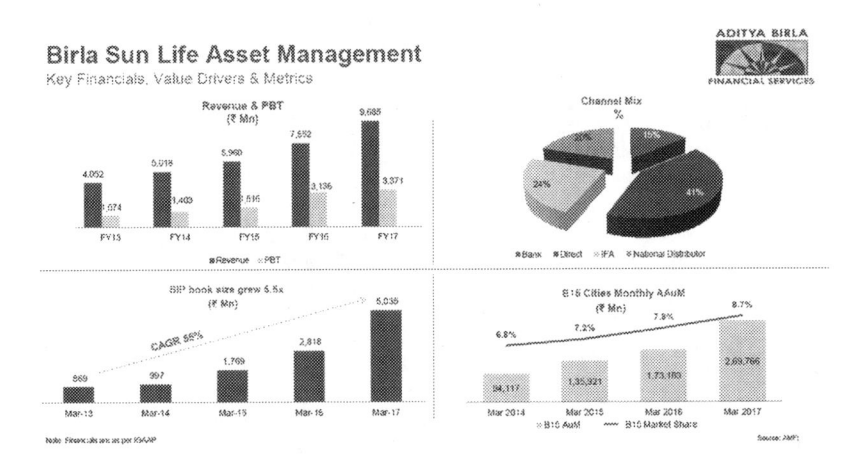

Image M

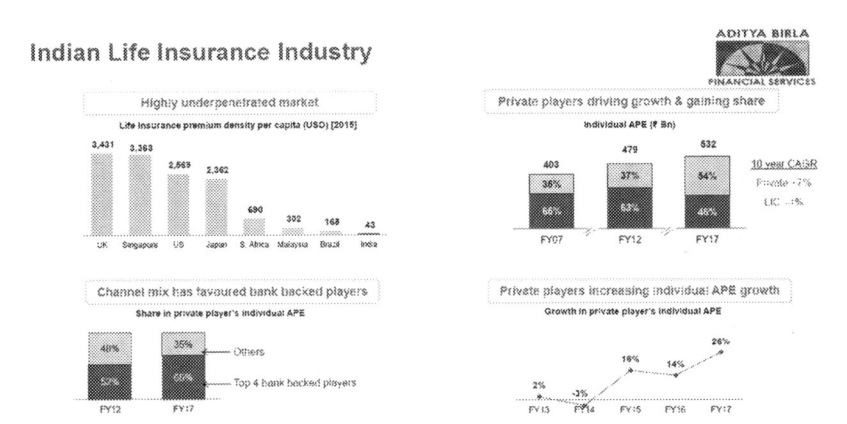

Image N

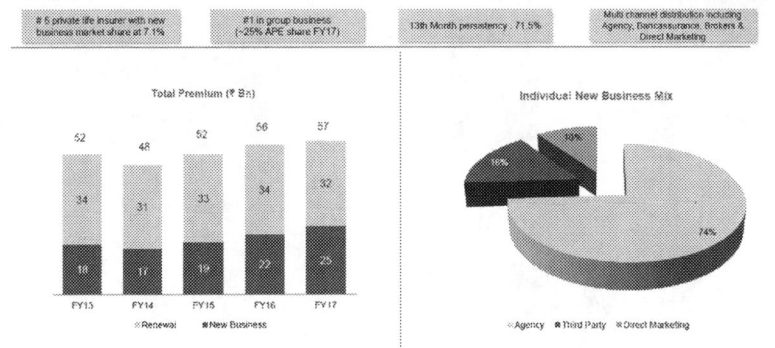

Image O

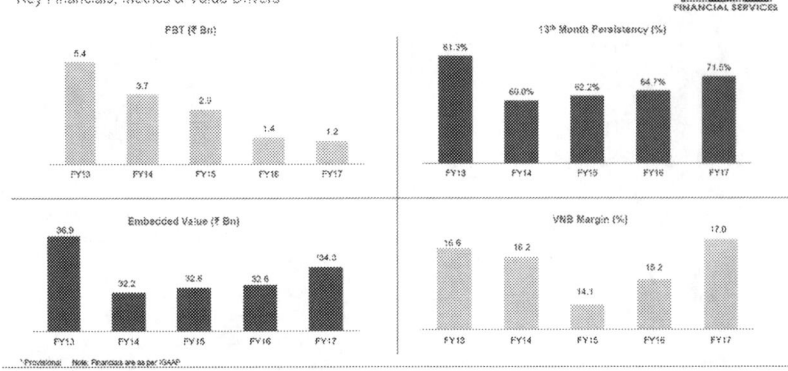

Image P

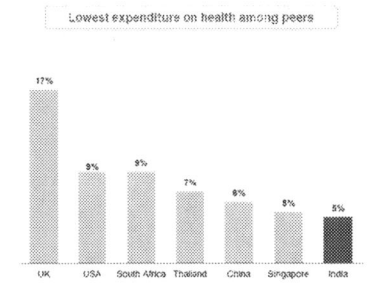
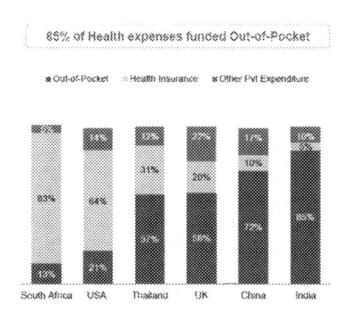

Image Q

Image R

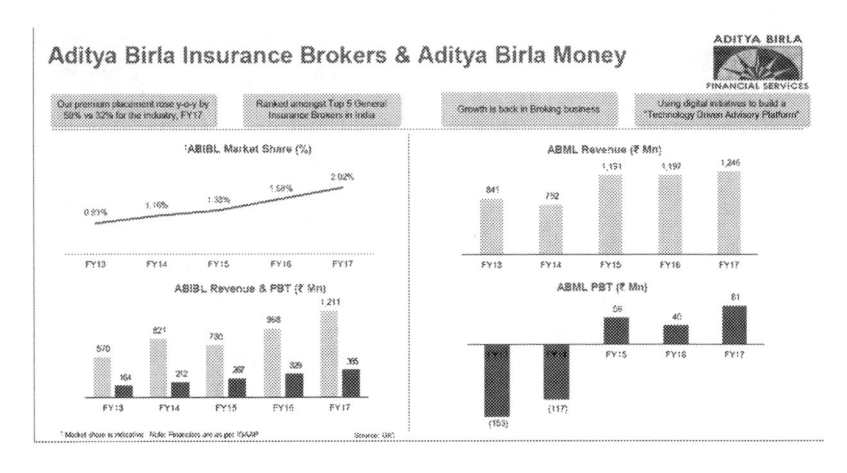

Image S

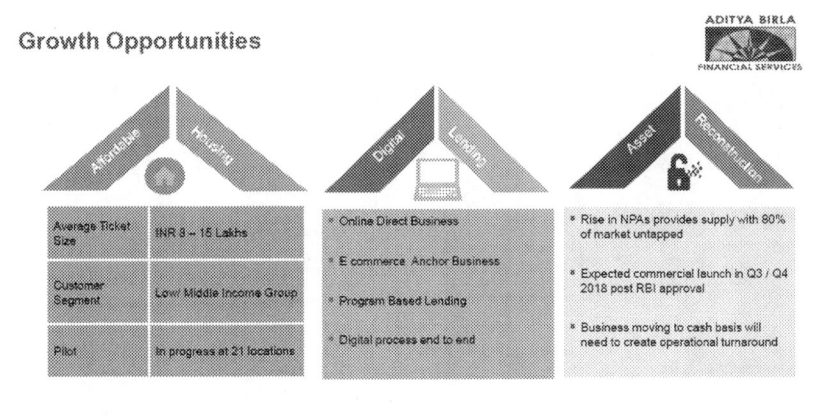

Image T

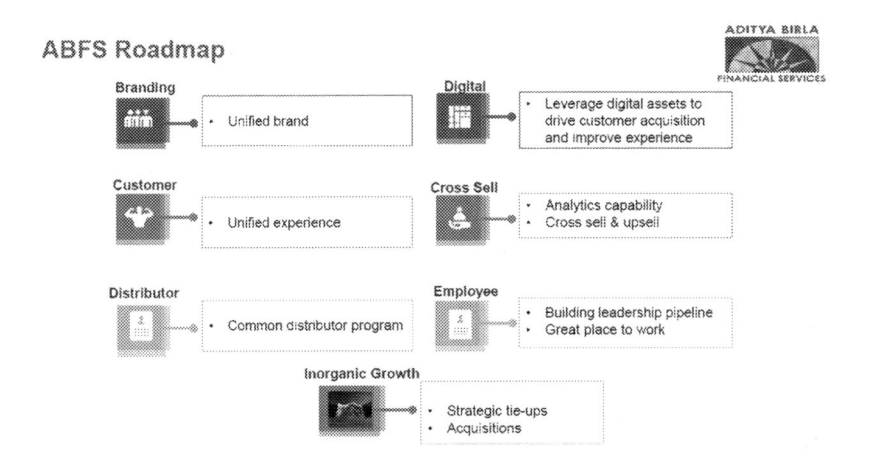

ABFS Roadmap

References
Definitions and Glossary

Abbreviation	Definition	Reference
FDI (Foreign Direct Investment)	Foreign direct investment (FDI) is an investment made by a company or individual in one country in business interests; in another country, in the form of either establishing business operations or acquiring business assets; in the other country, such as ownership or controlling interest in a foreign company. Foreign direct investments are distinguished from portfolio investments in which an investor merely purchases equities of foreign-based companies. The key feature of foreign direct investment is that it is an investment made that establishes either effective control of, or at least substantial influence over, the decision making of a foreign business	http://www.investopedia.com/terms/f/fdi.asp

(continued)

Definitions and Glossary (continued)

Abbreviation	Definition	Reference
RBI (Reserve Bank of India)	The Reserve Bank of India (RBI) is India's central banking and monetary authority. RBI regulates loans offered by banks and non-banking financial institutions to government entities, businesses, and consumers and controls the availability of funds in the financial system for credit. RBI sets the direction for interest rates and price stability and conducts fund raising activities for the central and the state governments through the auction of government securities. Reserve Bank is also responsible for monitoring the foreign exchange flows into the Indian economy, managing currency exchange rates, and supervising how banks and non-banking financial institutions function	http://whatis.techtarget.com/definition/Reserve-Bank-of-India-RBI
GST (Goods and Service Tax)	Goods and Services Tax (GST) is an indirect tax which was introduced in India on 1 July 2017 and was applicable throughout India which replaced multiple cascading taxes levied by the central and state governments. It was introduced as The Constitution (One Hundred and First Amendment) Act 2017, following the passage of Constitution 122nd Amendment Bill. The GST is governed by a GST Council and its Chairman is the Finance Minister of India	https://en.wikipedia.org/wiki/Goods_and_Services_Tax_(India)
GDP (Gross Domestic Product)	Gross Domestic Product (GDP) is the broadest quantitative measure of a nation's total economic activity. More specifically, GDP represents the monetary value of all goods and services produced within a nation's geographic borders over a specified period of time	http://www.investinganswers.com/financial-dictionary/economics/gross-domestic-product-gdp-1223

(continued)

Definitions and Glossary (continued)

Abbreviation	Definition	Reference
CAGR (Compounded Annual Growth Rate)	The compound annual growth rate (CAGR) is a useful measure of growth over multiple time periods. It can be thought of as the growth rate that gets you from the initial investment value to the ending investment value if you assume that the investment has been compounding over the time period	http://www.invest-inganswers.com/financial-dictionary/ratio-analysis/compound-annual-growth-rate-cagr-1096
SEBI (Securities Exchange Board of India)	The Securities and Exchange Board of India (SEBI) is the regulator for the securities market in India. It was established in the year 1988 and given statutory powers on 30 January 1992 through the SEBI Act, 1992	https://en.wikipedia.org/wiki/Securities_and_Exchange_Board_of_India
IRDA (Insurance Regulatory Development Authority of India	The Insurance Regulatory and Development Authority of India (IRDAI) is an autonomous, statutory agency tasked with regulating and promoting the insurance and re-insurance industries in India. It was constituted by the Insurance Regulatory and Development Authority Act, 1999, an Act of Parliament passed by the Government of India	https://www.irdai.gov.in/Defaulthome.aspx?page=H1
AMFI (Association of Mutual Funds in India)	The Association of Mutual Funds in India (AMFI) is an industry standards organization in India in the mutual funds sector. It was formed in 1995. Most mutual funds firms in India are its members. The organization aims to develop the mutual funds market in India, by improving ethical and professional standards. AMFI was incorporated on 22 August 1995	https://en.wikipedia.org/wiki/Association_of_Mutual_Funds_of_India
Repo rate	Repo rate is the rate at which the central bank of a country (Reserve Bank of India in case of India) lends money to commercial banks in the event of any shortfall of funds. Repo rate is used by monetary authorities to control inflation	http://economic-times.indiatimes.com/definition/Repo-rate

(continued)

Definitions and Glossary (continued)

Abbreviation	Definition	Reference
Cross selling	Cross-selling is the action or practice of selling an additional product or service to an existing customer. In practice, businesses define cross-selling in many different ways. Elements that might influence the definition might include the size of the business, the industry sector it operates within, and the financial motivations of those required to define the term	https://en.wikipedia.org/wiki/Cross-selling
Demonetization	Demonetization is the act of stripping a currency unit of its status as legal tender. It occurs whenever there is a change of national currency: The current form or forms of money is pulled from circulation and retired, often to be replaced with new notes or coins. Sometimes, a country completely replaces the old currency with new currency	http://www.investopedia.com/terms/d/demonetization.asp
NBFC (Non-Banking Financial Company)	A Non-Banking Financial Company (NBFC) is a company registered under the Companies Act, 1956 engaged in the business of loans and advances, acquisition of shares/stocks/bonds/debentures/securities issued by Government or local authority or other marketable securities of a like nature, leasing, hire-purchase, insurance business, chit business but does not include any institution whose principal business is that of agriculture activity, industrial activity, purchase or sale of any goods (other than securities) or providing any services, and sale/purchase/construction of immovable property	https://www.rbi.org.in/Scripts/FAQView.aspx?Id=92

Teaching Note

Background and Synopsis

This case is a story of a large financial services firm which offers a portfolio of products and services under different legal entities. Firms in financial services business have existed in this format across the globe partly driven by the regulatory requirement; however, it can often lead to a non-unified experience for the customer. The firm is now contemplating the decision in looking at the pros and cons associated with selling all services under one umbrella, continue operating under different entities, or adapt something in between (a Hybrid model if possible) to make it convenient for the customer. Each decision has a trade-off and requires careful analysis of all aspects before coming to the conclusion (e.g., regulatory barriers, training sales force for cross selling, compensation issues, etc.).

The case presents to the reader an overview of the Indian Financial services landscape which is currently undergoing a sea change. With the advent of technology and changing regulations, a growing younger population which is underserved in their financial needs is creating opportunities to go forth and capture the customer's additional share of the wallet for firms in this space. However, the point of differentiation is becoming more and more difficult with huge commoditization happening, which are making both the product life cycle and innovation life cycles shorter. Added to this, a growing organization creates its own challenges of collaborating, which becomes increasingly difficult with size, scale, and different cultures and sub cultures that exist under a firm. In these conditions, how leader takes decision becomes the key differentiating factor.

While there is a lot of material on the topic of Decision Making and the importance and relevance of how key decisions are taken, much of this focuses on the classical approach to decision making: i.e., using decision trees, looking at probabilities, and arriving to a conclusion. This reliance on data has worked well in the past decades; however, given the rapid pace of change and uncertainty business face today, of what is often called the VUCA impact, this approach alone is not enough. In the recent years, a lot of work has been done on behavioral biases which also impact the decision making process and how the success or methods of past cannot guarantee same results in future.

The case has been written to bring forward the decision making process of senior executives who often fall prey to their own biases of past when making decisions. The focus of the case is to make students and participants apply a process rather than the accuracy or pros and cons of a particular solution. Readers are expected to apply a decision making process to break free of their own biases avoiding gut-based decisions to arrive more conclusively and consciously to a decision.

Teaching Purpose and Objectives

- The Case is designed to provide a standardized decision-making framework to improve quality and expediency of decisions for working executives.
- To explore the role that bias can play in derailing the decision-making process.
- To discuss the leadership opportunities and challenges associated with making rapid-fire collective decisions.
- To identify what leaders must do more, better, and differently to improve decision-making outcomes at their firms.
- Lead and influence to get consensus buy-in in decisions taken.

Additional Readings Suggested

There is a lot of good material on the subject of Decision Making. The instructor can customize the content based on the need and fit for their respective audience. In addition to the blocks below, the instructor can also consider using a self-assessment instrument on predominant Decision Making styles. The DMSI instrument by Johnson and Coscarelli is widely used. It gives user an accurate view of his or own style and how to manage effectively with others of similar and different styles. Once the user learns them, the user can begin to understand himself or herself, adjust their own style, and manage personal and professional relationships effectively.

1. Sibony, O., & Lovallo D. (2010). "The Case for Behavioral Strategy", *McKinsey Quarterly*.
2. Hammond, J., Kenney, R., & Raiffa, H. (1998, September–October). "The Hidden Traps in Decision Making", *Harvard Business Review*.

3. Morse, G. (2013, April). What Ron Johnson Got Right, *Harvard Business Review*.
4. Snowden, D., & Boone, M.E. (2007, November). A Leaders Framework for Decision Making, *Harvard Business Review*.

Discussion Questions and Analysis:
The key questions for the instructor in the facilitation are as follows:

1. What are the different choices that one can take in this situation? What are the pros and cons of each of these choices?

Answer: There are effectively three options the firm can pursue. Each has its advantages and disadvantages. Each choice and their pro/cons are explained below:

Decision Choice 1: Take the "House of Brands" Route

ABFSG has created separate entities for the 11 different lines of business and offering it makes. Each entity has grown and positioned itself as a unique brand in the market. Continuing to offer services in the current set up means customers deal with a familiar product, brand, and service structure. Internally, ABFSG sales forces and advisors serving these customers would be clear about the product knowledge, compliance, and their target audience. They would also know the commission structure associated with the products they sell and the clear KPIs laid by the firm to achieve their targets.

The down side of this set up is multiple (ABFSG) brands are etched in the minds of one common customer. The company misses out on the opportunity to cross sell and there is no holistic advice given to the client. Each company would work in isolation and resulting in potential "conflict of interest" as multiple channels sell a product.

Decision Choice 2: Take the "Branded House" Approach

ABFSG takes a branded house approach with focus and emphasis on cross selling. Cross selling will allow the firm the following:

- A great opportunity to increase the revenue.
- Benefits of efficiency in serving one account over many.
- With more services, the customers are less likely to be displaced by competitors.
- The more a customer stays with ABFSG, the higher the switching cost.

Benefits of Cross Selling to Customers

- Efficiency and Leverage by using a single provider for multiple products.
- Finger pointing is eliminated. One firm reduces the finger pointing which is often a common problem which can often straddle between two firms.

Downside and Barriers to Cross Selling

- Ineffective control and monitoring of cross-sell activities affects every stage of value chain: enrollment, benefit fulfillment, servicing, and billing.
- Lack of process will lead to a feeling of deceptive marketing practice and miserable customer experience.
- Lack of internal communication and product knowledge.
- Different purchasing points within an account, which reduce the ability to treat the customer like a single account.
- The fear of the incumbent business unit that its colleagues would botch their work at the client, resulting with the loss of the account for all units of the firm.

Decision Choice 3: Take a "House Blend" Option

ABFSG creates a separate entity in which key customer segments are created which can give "bundled products". This would be a hybrid of option 1 and 2. The bundled product gives customer the choice of key products under one offering which saves the time of dealing with multiple agents and advisors. The cost of transaction would become smaller and the servicing to be easier.

The downside of this approach would be the regulatory hurdle of creating and managing another entity and ensuring all compliance rules of different products are intact and adhered to. This would also throw the question of consolidating some entities. This approach also calls for cross product training and advisors willing to sacrifice their own targets to do what is right for the customer.

2. Please share the process on how you arrived at the decision? (Individually first) and then as a group?
Answer: The facilitator must assess if the student applied the framework thoroughly (shared in Appendix 1). Question any part of the process in which they skipped or rushed the framework. The objective here is to point that decisions are made using the process and not through intuition or gut.

3. Where the solutions sets different in doing this exercise individual vs. as a group?
Answer: If the solutions to the problem have brought forward different answers, doing this individually vis-à-vis as a group, it is likely person from different domain areas have their own rationale of why it would work or not work. The instructor should hear the pros and cons and the strength of each of these arguments. Also, see in the process that if the group overcame each other's biases to come to a collective decision.

4. Were you able to uncover the biases as part of this activity?
Answer: Facilitate any biases the class is able to acknowledge or how students have become self-aware in the process. Ask how they would ensure they would continue practicing this method going forward.

REFERENCES

Insurance-at-Digital 20x by 2020 BCG & Google by Alpesh Shah & Burjor Dadachanji.

The (PFRDA) Pension Fund Regulatory and Development Authority Act, 2013 No. 23 of 2013. Published by Gazette of India (Ministry of Law and Justice, Legislative Department, September 19, 2013).

Journal of Financial Services Marketing, ISSN: 1363-0539 (print), 1479-1846 (electronic) Journal no. 41264.

Leading Change in the Social Sector: A Bottom-up Revival of Two Weaving Clusters in India

Savitha Suri and Payyazhi Jayashree

INTRODUCTION

Savitha Suri, had just engaged in another debate with saree enthusiasts on social media, with regard to the Goods and Services Tax (GST) in India, (introduced on July 1st, 2017), and what this implied for an already struggling Handloom sector. The handloom products which were earlier exempted from the GST would now have a tax imposition set in the range of 5% to up to 28%, with increasing concerns raised by handloom enthusiasts and revivalists and those committed to the sector, that rising costs would negatively impact the livelihood of those who were already struggling with the domination of the power loom sector and thus the lack of demand for the more expensive handlooms. Many were still grappling with questions as to how this would play out in the

S. Suri (✉)
Pravaaha Communications LLP, Mumbai, India

P. Jayashree
University of Wollongong, Dubai, UAE
e-mail: payyazhijayashree@uowdubai.ac.ae

long run for the weavers, and the weaving industry, with several activists for handmade products, even demanding the tax to be removed.

HANDLOOM SECTOR IN INDIA

India's tryst with hand woven textiles dated back thousands of years, to the Indus Valley Civilization. Evidence of tie and dye techniques and printing techniques, such as the traditional block-printed Ajrakh from this period abound, as do those of textile exports to far off lands. The weavers of Bengal, India, for example, had for centuries produced fabric so fine that it was called "woven air" and was fancied by the European markets. Even in the late eighteenth century, Bengal exported fabric along well-established trade routes to Asia and Europe with estimated revenue of nearly 20 million rupees a year. It is said that Bengal's textile production rose by 33% on demand from Europe alone, in the mid-eighteenth century. At this stage, India accounted for nearly 25% of the world's textile exports.

The advent of industrialization, however, saw the shift of the country's economy from an agrarian one to an industrial one. This shift was neither conceptualized, nor executed by the Indians. Much of it was executed without their consent, and Indians found themselves unwilling participants in a process that they neither fully understood nor controlled.

The setting up of textile mills in India, to counter British imports of cheaper cloth, proved to be a decisive factor in the rapid decline of the handloom industry. The farmers and weavers had always constituted the backbone of the country's economy and the thriving power loom industry with its mostly cheaper products, as compared to the handlooms, led them to struggle for survival. Industrialization, post-industrialization and the setting up of textile mills, and the domination of much cheaper mass-produced power looms, led to the erosion of "local produce, local consumption models," and thus ambiguity regarding predictability of supply and demand considerations for the weaving clusters, and the near death for the local weavers. The subsequent migration of the weavers from rural to urban areas in search of a livelihood, led not only to many weaving clusters dying down, but also to loss of the weaving traditions and heritage, and the weaver skill-base, with the younger generations of weavers and artisans, unwilling to be engaged with a sector that did not generate any income. The textile mills paved the way for urban centres in India, like Mumbai and Surat, to come up, and create thousands of jobs for migrants from rural India. The trend of former weavers moving to textile mills for jobs, prevalent even today, further lead to a declining pool of skilled weavers in rural areas.

In recent times, decisions such as repealing the National Handloom Act and more recently the implementation of GST, by the Government of India, which imposed a 5% tax on handlooms going up to 24%, to an already beleaguered sector, had not only received widespread criticism, but also discussions among the saree enthusiasts, revivalists, and those working within the Handloom sector, to come up with sustainable solutions.

ECOSYSTEM—THE THREE LAYERS

The sustainability of weaving clusters was further complicated because of the varied nature of the end user and the three different layers which they occupied. At the top of the pyramid were the experts, the Textile elite, a minority, who came with a strong foundational knowledge of weaves, besides awareness of the ground level understanding of the weavers and the weaves, often having had worked with them. The consumption pattern of this band was dictated by sound design and technique of the textile under consideration. Price was rarely a deterrent and the textiles were usually sourced directly from the producers/weavers/artisans themselves.

The largest component (occupying nearly 90% of the pyramid) was occupied by the enthusiasts, neo-converts (thanks to saree pacts and pacters and online saree forums), and the indifferent populace. This latter cohort, also the most populated layer, consisted of the budget conscious buyer, who was also the weakest in terms of textile know-how. This layer bought based on what was easily accessible and available, given their budget. Provenance, authenticity, and preserving the craft were NOT the key deciding factors for this segment. And thus, this largest layer was increasingly drawn to power loom versions, which were cheaper than handlooms and thus threatened the survival of the Handloom industry.

The space between the two extremes was occupied by connoisseurs. This middle band had a reasonable amount of knowledge that came out of interaction and reading/traveling extensively. Purchases were based on a certain exclusivity that came from either the textile itself or the manner of purchase. Budgets tended to be higher than average and textiles were usually sourced from the largest (and most authentic possible) reseller.

THE MIDDLEMEN

Another layer in this process value chain that further increased the complexity of the ecosystem was the role often played by the middlemen. Initially, the "middleman" was a do-gooder who connected the rural producer with his urban customer. In most cases, the middlemen were naïve and unaware, without much understanding of the market realities, or pricing structures, and the net worth of the art or weave and thus not informed enough to negotiate terms. Over time, this middleman began dictating the terms and conditions of sale and began taking his share of the income. Often, the middleman came from within the community, and as per power structures within the social hierarchy, the wealthier person often donned this role. The middleman was also the money lender to weaver in most cases, and hence, the control of the produce was often with him. This practice was still the case in several weaving clusters. Savitha was aware that the lack of organized financing, distribution, and marketing channels for independent weavers, was one of the biggest roadblocks in their progress toward a sustainable livelihood.

Over time, the original middleman became a "wholesaler" who sold to an assorted bunch of "retailers" who in turn peddled to various customers. As time went, more layers of middlemen and agents were created, with each additional layer resulting in decreased (or constant) income for the weaver, although the price paid by the customer would go up exponentially, with each additional layer. Thus, a power structure was created, such that the weaver was essentially at the bottom of the structure and the middlemen and agents at the top.

Regardless of whether weavers had more power or could negotiate better deals, what clearly existed was an almost patriarchal hold of the middleman, over "his" weavers. He often ran the cluster as an extension of his own home, and the weavers became an extension of his family. This arrangement offered a certain sense of familiarity and stability to the weavers, who rarely showed the courage or initiative to move away, to form an independent business establishment. The patriarchal hold of the middlemen also meant that, the fortunes of the cluster depended on the decisions made by the "head." Should these favor the steady and growing business, it spelt comfort and stability to all under his care. If decisions were unfavourable, then everyone had to pay the price. The dependencies were so ingrained that introduction of newer systems whether through design intervention, infrastructure infusion, or different business modules were all dependent on how welcoming the "head" was of these decisions. Weaving was a hereditary profession and largely worked on tacit knowledge and ran on a traditional business model. Breaking from this mould would require new skill-sets, and hence, while middlemen might have their benefits to weavers, it was increasingly evident that alternative models had to be examined, such that weavers had more autonomy and were informed and empowered enough, to exercise more agency in decisions that affected them.

SPANDANA—Where It All Began

Udupi is a small town in the state of Karnataka. A predominantly pilgrimage town, it is surrounded by weaving clusters that specialized in simple cotton sarees for daily use of the local population. As with many other weaving clusters across India (with a steady drop in local demand and almost negligible visibility beyond a narrow geography), the weaving clusters had started shutting down, with younger weavers migrating in search of jobs, leaving the older ones to eke a meagre living. The system there was a simple one. The weavers congregated to the Co-operative every Tuesday, with whatever they had woven, and subjected to their products passing scrutiny, with each weaver earning a little less than INR 100 per saree. These sarees were then either put up for sale at the Co-operative or sent to the government emporium for sale. Declining demand for what were increasingly seen as "ajji seere" or "grandmother's saree" meant that stocks languished on the shelves, or worse, in the godowns where they were prone to damage (poor storage, rodents etc.). In early October 2016, a saree pacter from an online group of saree enthusiasts, chanced upon these sarees being sold for as little as INR 100–400, against a normal price of INR 750–1200, which is what the sarees were worth. The weavers had been left with no other alternative but to dump stock that had been lying around for months on the shelves owing to a near absence of demand. This dismal scenario distressed her enough, to post about their plight on one of the online groups, KAITHARI[1] that she was a member of.

Savitha remembers that there were two trigger points for Spandana—or the Udupi cotton saree revival project. The story as shared in the KAITHARI group, shook her up and she thought, 'here we were in a saree group, discussing the authenticity of weaves and how we must nurture the sale of handlooms, with so much talk, and so little was being done to support the weavers'. She felt compelled to share the story with her mother, primarily because, she and her mother did an annual donation program of sarees—where they picked up about 50–60 sarees, to give away to women who could not afford them. The story regarding the plight of the weaver had sparked something within Savitha. She told herself that 135 sarees were not a big number and that she could buy them all and give it away as part of their annual sharing of sarees. Soon after making this decision, she called up a familial friend who ran a commercial establishment and said this was essentially for Amma (her mother) and her, and she would appreciate it very much if he could please pick them up. The friend in turn responded that if altruistic motivations were what was driving her, then he would also get involved and see if he could create some demand for the sarees, and he would try and either sell them or do something with it. She instructed him to pick up all the 135 sarees from the cooperative, and shared that they could figure out what do with it later. Meanwhile, more than 20–50 women in the KAITHARI group said they were also interested in buying this saree, as the story had touched a chord amongst many.

Savitha knew one of her strengths was that she had a very organized way of working, and even though at that point of time, Savitha was not thinking of a large initiative, she created an order form to make things easy for herself, and such that people who were interested in buying the saree, could place an order through the form. She called the project "SPANDANA" (or 'a mindful, nourishing touch') to give it an identifying tag, aligned with the project intent itself, and thus started her journey. The entire project was initiated and managed by Savitha, with

[1] "KAITHARI" is a Facebook group that is an online platform to share knowledge and experiences on handlooms and handcrafted textiles. The group celebrates the hand-woven textile and its creators. Started in 2015 with just a handful of members, the group now has over 10,000 members from across the globe.

a clear purpose, aimed at helping the weavers clear an existing stock of 135 sarees at a fair price. And because this commercial establishment was willing to support her at no cost, they were able to sell those 135 sarees. When eventually she looked back, she realized that her mother and she did not end up picking up anything because every single saree got sold out within KAITHARI itself. Savitha was also very keen to make sure that, if they were going to charge INR 775, per saree, which was the price for the saree, then INR 600 should go to the weaver. When the money reached the weavers, the weavers called up Savitha, and said that they were weaving more sarees, and if she would like to pick up an order, they would be happy to supply. Savitha again utilized the online plat-form, KAITHARI to announce that more UDUPI sarees were available for sale. As the order had started flowing in, she told herself at that point of time, "let's run this a bit longer"—maybe 250 sarees or 500 sarees and then see where it went. Today as Savitha sat at home reminiscing about the year gone by, she felt so proud that as of today, the sale of the UDUPI had reached 3400 sarees, and she realized how this entire pro-ject had grown organically, with just a gentle push from her, leading to a self-sustaining Business model.

Savitha was only too conscious that the project had its moments of sluggishness, no doubt, but what reinforced or created the weaver's trust for her was that the weavers noted that 135 sarees were picked up by a complete stranger (this being Savitha) for the original cost price, and she gave the money upfront to the weavers. The weavers were particularly enthused that Savitha didn't take any money, and she gave them INR 600, per saree. These formed the foundation for trust and when the weavers created their new design after 10 years of no work, with new colours, it was evident that the initial push and the inflow of money had indeed made a difference to their self-confidence which acted as a conduit for increased innovativeness. And when they reached sale of a 1000 sarees, Savitha started thinking in terms of put-ting together Business continuity plans, because she felt that some-where she had a moral responsibility to do so. She realized that the weavers were subconsciously looking at her for support, trusting that she was going to help them. After preparing the Business Continuity plan, she then approached and presented her plans to a large num-ber of corporates. While there was some interest, her efforts toward Corporate sponsorship, did not lead to any positive outcome, because she had gone through a Facebook group—which was firstly not a registered commercial entity, and second, it did not have any staff on its rolls and was, therefore, in no position to manage payments and logistics. A tie-up with a Bangalore-based commercial establishment for handlooms eventually took care of logistics and payment procedures. These early challenges became an impetus for Savitha to launch Anvaya, her own registered company, which she hoped would lead to a wider sponsorship (from entities that were in a position to invest), by putting in place, a strong Business plan for revival of these non-operational clusters. Savitha also created a price structure that was aligned with the Fair price principles, such that the total price was split into 3 components—75% going to the Weaver Co-operative, 15% for packing and shipping charges, and 10% to the store handling the initiative's execution.

Looking back, Savitha knew how far she had come, but it was not all smooth sailing. There were many challenges that she faced during execution of the project. Specifically,

- The weavers were senior citizens with little support from their next generation.
- Health and infrastructure issues were, and continued to remain, niggling worries. For example, Savitha and her team found production had dropped drastically at a cluster a certain month. Investigating the cause led them to a startling fact. Located in one of the hottest regions of the state, the cluster had no electric fans. Weavers were unable to start weaving before 4 pm and could weave only for a couple of hours. Even if they did start in the morning, they needed to take frequent breaks, leading to a fall in production. Savitha then ran an appeal for funds, and collected INR 10,000, that was used to install 8 fans at the cluster. It was increasingly evident to Savitha and her team that across clusters, health and wellbeing initiatives were urgently needed.
- Considering the voluntary nature of work that was being done by Savitha and her team, it was difficult to approach any Corporate funding allocated for Corporate Social Responsibility activities, or even draft a business continuity plan in a formal manner.
- The absence of a formal organization to supervise the initiative meant that control over sales, design, payments was difficult to exercise in a sustainable manner.

The Outcome
Despite the emergent nature of the challenges experienced, the success of the initiative was multi-fold. Specifically,

- **Sales**: Against the original intention of clearing dead stock of 135 sarees, Savitha and her team sold nearly 2000 sarees in a period of just 9 months.
- **Increased Weaver Earning**: Weavers were now receiving an average of 75% of sale proceeds per saree.
- **Improved Quality**: With renewed interest and cash in hand, weavers were experimenting with better quality yarns, dyes, and designs. There was a tremendous improvement in quality of the products, further reflecting the weavers' renewed enthusiasm and commitment.
- **Expansion and Awareness**: From the 5 clusters that were engaged in weaving in October, Savitha now had nearly 25 clusters that had restarted weaving.
- **Renewed Interest**: Looking at the progress in the weaving clusters, younger weavers were now beginning to come back to the looms.
- **Community Initiatives**: Taking this beyond simply buying their products, a Community Initiative saw Savitha and her team collect funds to install electric fans in one of the clusters. This simple act saw production go up at that cluster within weeks.
- **Product Diversification**: there had been requests for other products such as yardage and dupattas, to be made for which there was a need for fund and design infusion (Table 1 and Fig. 1).

Table 1 The impact

	Then	*Now*
No. of looms	8–10	40
No. of days to weave 1 sari	3	1–1.5
Earnings in INR (average) per sari	200	450
Activity	Individual	Family
Sales	135 (dead stock)	2600 (Spandana alone)
Product category	Sarees	Sarees, yardage

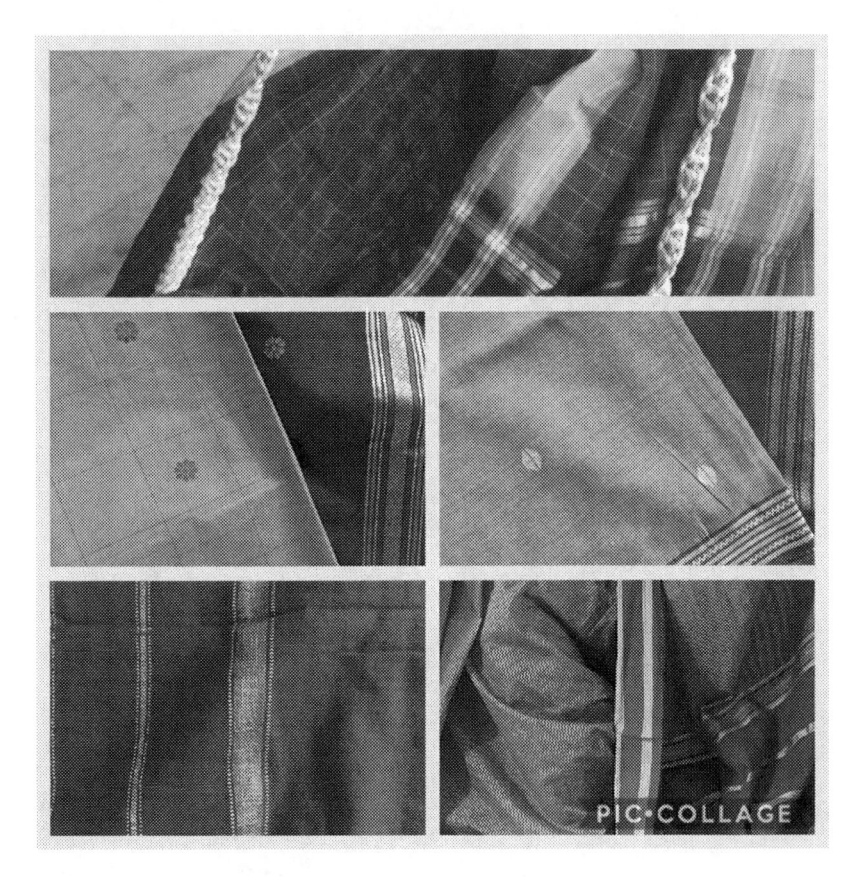

Fig. 1 Evolution of Udupi cottons through Spandana

CURRENT STATUS

- Efforts were now underway to put in place strong and ethical Business Continuity Plans for these clusters to ensure that the momentum was not lost.
- Product innovation remained a challenge owing to lack of funds and technical knowledge and expertise. This had led to a slump in demand and they were now seeing a stagnation in production (as of September 2017).

- The challenges remained in terms of giving a more sustainable selling platform for the weavers. The absence of digital literacy necessitated a dependence on middlemen and the danger of going back into the loop was, therefore, real.
- The lack of human resources to work on the ground with the weavers had led to a vacuum being created in that area.

Sustaining Momentum

Savitha realized that sustaining the momentum for change required resource investments and she was looking at how she could get buy-in from the Corporates to invest money into the cluster and take it up. That was currently her focus also because she didn't work through a government body or any state funded mechanism, but was working as an independent individual on the ground, who had no support in terms of formal systems that took care of all of that. She was also confident that the likelihood of getting Corporate support was much more now, since she also had established credibility at both ends of the spectrum—the consumer end and the supply end, through the SPANDANA project.

Primary Motivations

Savitha reflected on her own motivations and she knew that one of the reasons she had joined a saree group such as KAITHARI was because of the unlimited potential that such a collective online forum could have, for awareness building, and for creating a sense of urgency for change. More importantly, she truly believed in an individual's capability and potential to create change. She remembered having a conversation recently, in another heated debate in an online forum, related to apathy for weavers, where she said "If we could revolutionise wearing of the saree through a 100 saree pact,[2] I couldn't see why we could not extend it further to making a real difference on the ground, where it matters the most". Somewhere Savitha had always been looking for an opportunity to initiate that little bit of change to make a direct benefit on the ground. She also believed in the power of collectives and she believed that online groups formed by those with a common passion

---

[2] 100 saree pact.

for a product or an ideology could be a constructive force for positive change. In the online forum that she had first heard the weaver story, the members were always talking about buying and wearing sarees, and at the other end, the weavers were looking for a sustainable livelihood, and the space offered by the online forum was seen by Savitha as a perfect opportunity to bring both ends of the value-chain together, in a manner that added value to both.

In the SPANDANA project, Savitha did not face any resistance, because there was a gap and her efforts filled the gap. She had only acted as a catalyst and had facilitated change at a time when no one was even interested in buying a weave which was, therefore, dying a natural death. The SPANDANA project in fact had created a chain of middlemen, for whom one more weave was opened up, and a new customer base, and thus another opportunity to sell, which led to an automatic desire for change all across the value-chain. However, Savitha's subsequent revival project, turned out to be a much more complex exercise, despite all the learning that she had had.

SPOORTHI—The Journey of the KUNBI Revival

SPOORTHI was an attempt to revive the KUNBI. The mention of Goa evokes images of beaches, shacks, casinos and a laid-back idyllic life. Handlooms are nowhere in the reckoning. The Goans, however, have an iconic weave called the Kunbi (kaapod). Traditionally worn by the women of the Kunbi community (farm labourers), the red fabric was a short, coarse garment draped at knee length and looped across the shoulders (with or without a blouse depending on the religious affiliation of the wearer).

The Portuguese rule in Goa saw a ban on ethnic clothing in favor of European dresses and the weaving went underground. A thriving underground weaving industry saw the "kaapod" emerge as a symbol of resistance. Strangely though, the entire industry went silent once Goa became independent. The last weaving activity of note is believed to have ended in 1984.

SPOORTHI (meaning inspiration) was launched in November 2016 by Savitha Suri to draw attention to, and make accessible, the iconic Kunbi to a larger and more discerning group of handloom enthusiasts. The Goan "kaapod" (KUNBI) had captured the imagination of several textile enthusiasts and when the Goa-based fashion designer Wendell Rodericks created a Kunbi inspired collection in 2010, it was hailed as a landmark moment in textile history. This, however, did not gain further traction and remained confined to being a designer's interpretation of an iconic weave. This also led to a few people searching for the original Kunbi with its original design palette of red and white. This attempt at revival of the KUNBI was where the negative power play came in and the actual market disruption brought forth by the project Kunbi led to resistance.

MARKET DISRUPTION

The Kunbi revival project had completely disrupted the market. Savitha had been at the receiving end of severe backlash from multiple quarters. The reactions were not a surprise. Savitha—an upstart, who was not even a qualified designer or a style expert, was being perceived as having the audacity to place an order for over 250 Kunbi sarees in the first round of production, and that too pricing it at a rate which was very affordable. While the SPANDANA project had made the middle-men happy, the attempt to revive the Kunbi created disruption for the connoisseurs and revivalists. The reason for the backlash was primarily because Savitha had taken away the elitism associated with the product, which a designer version had brought in, making the KUNBI something that common women could afford. What had helped Savitha through this difficult period was that she had immense faith in the people who she was working with, combined with tremendous confidence in the authenticity of the product. Savitha chose to maintain a stoic silence in the face of criticism, although she did remember standing up to clear her name once—as a lot of things were being said, including that she was making a lot of money through this project. She chose to speak up at this point, more for her family, as throughout this journey, her family's support was unconditional and she didn't want them to be at the receiving end of all the negativity. But throughout this journey, she also had immense faith that once the product was out in its finished form, everyone would acknowledge that, this was worth the wait and worth the money, they had paid.

THE ORIGINS OF THE KUNBI REVIVAL STORY

Savitha reflected back on what had prompted her to venture into this unknown journey of reviving the Kunbi. Her son's favourite holiday destination was Goa, with every Christmas being spent as a family in Goa.

It was during one of those journeys, as she prepared for another endless day on the beach, that she decided that, she would get away for a bit to explore the city, particularly driven by her love for art and history and architecture, which Goa was a haven for. And it was then, as she set out on her own, to explore the city, that Savitha stumbled upon the Kunbi. Being a textile enthusiast, Savitha had always wanted her hands on the Kunbi, as although she had seen pictures of it, she was unable to find the Kunbi anywhere. Her passion for the Kunbi had her searching for it for five years in vain, and finally, just last year In August, she had relented and bought Wendell Rodrick's designer adaptation of the Kunbi launched in 2010, as part of the "Kunbi tribe" (Gulf Heritage 2015)—a more contemporary version of the Kunbi to suit modern tastes—the first designer saree that she had ever picked up—as she conceded that, perhaps, she would never find the authentic red and white chequered Kunbi, the robust weave, as worn by the Kunbi tribal women in Goa in the twentieth century. When she got the designer adaptation of the KUNBI, and felt the weave, Savitha contemplated that if this adapted designer version (which had retained some of the original features of the Kunbi weave) was so beautiful and could be recreated, then why wasn't anyone attempting to revive the original authentic Kunbi weave in its authentic form. It was then that Savitha and her family decided that they would go in search of the original Kunbi, one final time. In the next fifteen days during Diwali break, Savitha and her family went to every village in Goa, carrying a visiting card, with the Kunbi on the front of the card and Savitha's number on the back, which she then handed to three-quarter of rural Goa, approaching everyone with the same question, that is, if they had seen an original Kunbi. As luck would have it, it was during this last visit that Savitha stumbled upon this researcher from the Goa Home Science College who had worked on a government approved and funded project in 2012 to revive the original Kunbi (Figs. 2 and 3).

Savitha looked at the government approved samples for the authentic Kunbi and she realized that her search had come to an end. A personal search that consumed nearly four years of Savita's time had finally found fruition in November 2016. In 2012, the Goa Home Science College had applied and got government approval for a Kunbi Revival Project. The project was funded by the State government and three designs had been approved to be part of the project. Further, this government-funded project had been completed as per Goa Government

Fig. 2 Authentic
Kunbi

Fig. 3 Wendell's
interpretation

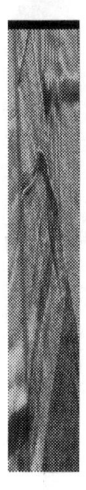

approved designs, with the research team having been successful in creating the original Kunbi with the help of weavers, who they had trained as per the Kunbi specifications. This project had received no publicity and the head of the project was visibly excited when Savitha spoke to her about reviving the Kunbi in a manner that could lead to sustainable livelihoods, while making alive a part of Goa's history and culture. She remembered being told—"no one has ever asked me to, but I would love to do this." Savitha then looked at the government-approved samples for the Kunbi and she was confident that a lot of research had gone into the project and hence, one could trust the authenticity. When asked about the timelines, she was informed that fifty sarees would take three months. Savitha had replied that her minimum order would be 150 sarees, to which the project head said with some visible doubt, "you first get the orders, and then we will see" as she was confident that the numbers would not reach more than fifty. She didn't believe anyone was interested in the Goan Kunbi anymore. When Savitha rolled out the order forms again in the KAITHARI group comprising fiercely passionate saree enthusiasts, and closed it three days later, Savitha ended up with two hundred and forty-five orders. It was then that the magnitude of the project hit the project team and Savitha, as they then started identifying how to get adequate number of trained weavers to complete the project as per specifications and on time. Her main challenge initially was that she had no money to invest. She had some management skills though, and deep commitment to the project, combined with unlimited enthusiasm.

THE JOURNEY

In November 2016, an online order form was created, which included contact details and design preference indicators. Orders were restricted to not more than four pieces per individual. Dupattas and stoles were added to the product range. The order form was kept open for three days at the end of which 245 orders were received. This was 5 times more than the expected number and proved all calculations wrong. Meanwhile, estimates provided by the College showed that 50 sarees would take three months and would cost approximately INR 1600–1800 each. To this, they had to add packaging and shipping costs which were set at 10% of total bill (per order).

The original intention of using the same commercial establishment (as for Spandana) was done away with, after members felt it would give the establishment undue access to customer database and also defeat the purpose of a Weaver Initiative. This created issues for receiving payments and final dispatches. With no other alternative available to them for funding, they went with the College's suggestion that they take an advance amount of INR 1000 per saree through crowd-funding and then take final amounts before delivery.

The mammoth task of collecting money began with the decision to use a personal account for this. It was Savitha's personal bank account being used with tax implications and associated challenges. With estimated timelines of 3–4 months, the wait for the sarees began.

It was in March 2017 that the first set of 2 sample sarees were received—4 months after the order was placed. The sarees were showcased at a meeting of the Mumbai chapter of the KAITHARI group and received good reviews. But it was not until May end that Savitha and her team received the first lot of sarees for dispatch. 180/245 sarees were received, 2 out 3 designs ordered were woven in a period of 6 months.

The Authenticity of the KUNBI

Savitha cried like a child when she held that first sample of the revived and authentic Kunbi saree in her hand. A dream had taken shape for her. Two hundred more orders followed. By May, there were queries and in some cases, impatience from those who had placed the order for the sarees. Finally, in May 2017, the first batch of sarees had been delivered to the customers, except for one design which was yet to be completed. It was also at this stage that a setback was experienced, when one of the designs—the big checks Kunbi—had not quite turned out as per specifications for the saree, which meant that the entire lot had to be woven from start. All of this meant further delays and explanations to all the customers who had placed an order for that particular design.

The costing itself had been done as per fair price principles, with the cost of labour and yarn having been worked out, besides dyes and logistics. As per standard industry practice for total order value, ten percent was allocated to packaging and shipping, as per standard industry practice for total order value, with 90% going to the weaver (in the case of Kunbi) (and 80% in the case of Udupi). Today, when they had reached 600 Kunbi sarees and people were unequivocally stating that this was a very fine product and this was value for money, it felt good. But more than that, Savitha got her validation when she went and met the last surviving Kunbi weaver in Goa and he looked at her and said—"today if I die then I die with the knowledge that the weave has not died with me, as it has come back to Goa". Savita remembers her eyes tearing up when she heard the master weaver authenticating the revived Kunbi. This validation that she had got when the master weaver said "The Kunbi was waiting for you" and gifted her a few vintage samples of his work. This was a reward for all the work and struggles that had gone into the revival. That for her was more important than any other outcome, as this project for her, was not about money. It was a zero-profit initiative. But more than that, it was the pride that she felt in the revived Kunbi, because she believed that market disruption was very important if change had to be brought from the ground up, much like an earthquake—a break from the past. The Kunbi revival project needed that disruption—a wake-up call. Later, the experts came in and further endorsed the authenticity of the Kunbi, which further strengthened what she had believed all along—the worth of the product. She thought to herself—"Being a disruptor sometimes is a very good thing. It shakes up the status quo for people to sit up and take notice and feel compelled to do something about it." Savitha had started with a purpose, driven by her commitment to the weavers, which was to facilitate the process of demand creation for the weaves, such that the weavers had a sustainable source of livelihood and she was happy that this purpose was now served.

Execution Challenges

Kunbi revival had, however, been particularly challenging. Spandana had a third party helping with the logistics and all that Savitha had to do was creating content for Marketing and creating awareness and a desire to generate the need for the product. The third party had come in purely because of a personal connection, but as the supply and demand considerations started becoming more sustainable, a model was developed and an 85–15 split was introduced to the proceeds of the sales. But more importantly, the third party got access to a customer database because of the order forms which was valuable for him in the long run, for his continued business, and he was quite happy. The spin-off that Spandana did for him as a middleman with opportunities for his Business to grow exponentially was more than what he had expected.

The challenges associated with Spoorthi (the Kunbi project) were more complex though as this was completely done single handedly, only with support from her family—right from placing the order to creating the content to despatch to coordinating to funding (the project was fully crowd-funded)—everything was done alone—with no team to work with.

Today, when they looked at the six hundred sarees being woven, she could hear the unspoken expectation from these weavers not to take this source of livelihood away from them. The KUNBI was a story of

India's first crowd-funded, private textile revival, with no governmental intervention, and with no big corporate names or designers. Without intending to, Savitha had created a silent revolution in textile revival. Yet again, this for Savitha was a non-profit, venture with 85% of the proceeds going to the weaver, 15% to the project team who was managing the weaving team, with the remaining miscellaneous charges for courier of the finished products going to Savitha as she was individually leading this process. Her purpose was to create sustainable livelihoods while playing a role in reviving a lost legacy. Savitha felt vindicated in her belief that, change could begin from the bottom-up and one does not always require the government to step in for change to happen, even in a large country like India with its complex and multilayered ecosystem.

Steps Forward

Savitha was still coming to terms with how all of this had taken shape in such a short span of time. She was incredibly grateful for the journey. Her success with Spandana had led Savitha to have a meeting with the government of Karnataka, the day before, to revive the Gajendragad cluster. Savitha's success with the Udupi and the Kunbi had given her substantial credibility to be able to lead revival projects in the future, with the government of Karnataka equally enthused—even telling her that these were the kind of ground level change agents, that the country needed to revive a beleaguered sector, with a request, if Savitha and her team could support with reviving the cluster by working with the government on this project.

Both the Spandana and Spoorthi revival projects had led the weavers to be able to have a sustainable livelihood, with the income now coming in more regularly, not only because the demand was being created through awareness building, but also because of the technical finesse and quality of the weaves, which Savitha had focussed all her attention on, and which she knew was fundamental for the orders to keep coming in. Even with some delays at the supply end (such as when the entire first lot of Kunbi with big checks had to be discarded because of not passing quality control), a majority of the buyers believed in her intent and commitment to the project. Second, her efforts were driven not by extrinsic concerns such as a return on investment as this was not a Business venture for her which she could personally profit from, but driven more by her own intrinsic desire to create value where it mattered the most, in ways that were driven with a long-term focus. The robust demand creation processes had ensured that three months' worth of efforts in weaving had got sold in three days. The weaver's rising morale reflected in their enthusiasm for weaving new designs and experimenting with more colours. It was evident to Savitha that one didn't need organisational machinery or lots of money. The biggest learning for Savitha was her realization that all you needed was intent and to create a chain of enablers and it would all work out at the end, because enabling did not have a Business intent. Savita saw her role as someone who had enabled the process and even during difficult times her belief in the integrity of her purpose and the quality of the product had helped her stay on track.

In fact, in 2012, when the government funded project had revived the Kunbi saree, these were confined to being displayed for Home Science Textile classes. For four years, the sarees were languishing on mannequins and cupboards with no other means of visibility. Despite having a clear four-year head start on the weaving process, not much was done beyond, as it was not a priority. The college was not allowed to sell anything commercially and did not have the money for investment to scale it up. This is where Savitha came in as a catalyst, a change-maker. The partnership was significant for Savitha too as she knew that she was getting an authentic product, with evidence that this was approved by the government. It was just her being at the right place at the right time. When Savitha came in, the KUNBI project got some momentum with a weaving cluster exclusively trained to weave the KUNBI, and the demand generated through crowd-funding.

As she reflected on all that she had learnt and continued to learn through working with the grassroots, Savitha felt grateful. She knew what an incredible opportunity this was, as there were many weavers in Goa who would go through the vocational training, and then they would go back to being construction workers or relocate to the city to take up small jobs. Savitha saw this as a fantastic opportunity for playing a key role in generating employment at the grassroots level for Goa, while reviving the lost heritage. Savitha was conscious of the vital role played by revivalists in the life cycle of a textile. In her role as a "market revivalist," she had created visibility for a weave thus drawing it out of obscurity. Further, she was aware that different stages of the life cycle of a weave/cluster required different interventions. For example, Sally Holkar's revival of the iconic Maheshwari saree of Madhya Pradesh, not only led to the exponential rise in the fortunes of the textile and those associated with it, but also the product itself was now at a stage in its life cycle, which made design intervention and adaptability, a key factor in its survival. Similarly, Judy Frater's revival of the Kala Raksha and Bhujodi was an excellent example of how mindful design intervention along with empowerment of the weavers could create an environment conducive to sustainable growth.

However, Savitha was also aware that, for long term sustainability, a holistic approach would be required. There were many players in the market, with a mushrooming of online retailers, not all of them were conducting business in an ethical or informed manner, often selling weaves that were neither authentic nor handloom, at a price, either at the low end of the spectrum or at the very high end of the spectrum, thus being discrepant with principles of fair pricing. Buyers themselves were not always informed or discerning about the authenticity of the weaves that they were buying, which again eroded the investments being made for reviving authentic weaves with the intention of giving a new lease of life to these weaving clusters. The tendency for experts to speak in unfamiliar vocabulary and to niche segments further added to the lack of awareness. At the other end of the spectrum were weavers themselves who were not competent enough to calculate the price value of the efforts, varied levels of skills required, and the resources that went into weaving a particular style. Furthermore, many of them were not entrepreneurial enough, either to connect directly with the customer, in the absence of specific technical, marketing or branding skills, often depending upon middle men and agents, to market and sell their products, without any opportunity or understanding of how to exercise agency regarding pricing of their product. The complexity of the ecosystem made Savitha reflect on the challenges ahead. She knew that a collective effort, involving multiple stakeholders, was the only way forward for sustainable solutions.

For example, governmental initiatives such as Paramparik Karigar, an association of craftsmen and artisans found by Kamaladevi Chattopadhyay, in 1996, and Dastkar, a non-profit organization, started in 1981, were excellent platforms to nurture not only the capacity building of weavers and craftsmen and artisans, but also providing them with a sustained means of livelihood, by providing opportunities to market and sell their products, through direct engagement with the customers, without being exploited by middlemen. All these efforts and interventions were focussed on increasing one's pride in the indigenous art and craft and weaves of India, and had resulted out of acknowledgement for the challenges facing a sector that employed the maximum number of people, after the agriculture sector. Recently in an interview, the Minister of Textiles, Smriti Irani had shared that, her Ministry was making proactive efforts towards involving weavers in policy-making decisions, besides supporting weavers to buy new looms—with 90% funding being provided to those weavers who were applying their knowledge, gained at government centres, to design and market their products. These efforts were based on the belief that entrepreneurship was necessary for the economic growth of a country (First Post, June 9, 2017).

Savitha reminisced that if SPANDANA had created the base for mindful buyers, SPOORTHI had created sustainable livelihoods. Her efforts toward revival of these two weaving clusters had begun to provide a steady income for scores of families for over a year. However, she knew that the interest the project had created needed to be exponentially multiplied, to make it a sustainable model. The success of SPOORTHI had a lot to do with the buyer's own desire to own a rare weave and be part of textile history. The unmistakable pride in being a part of probably the country's first crowd-funded textile revival initiative (done solely by women and without any government support) coupled with a high-quality product had laid the foundation for long term plans. Savitha looked out from her balcony, at the wide expanse of the Mumbai skyline, grateful and with a sense of purpose, as if to acknowledge that a new chapter, full of many unknowns, was just about to begin, and there was so much more to do.

TEACHING NOTE

Synopsis of the Case

Although the Handloom sector's contribution to employment is second only to Agriculture in India, and is estimated to be about 45%, the setting up of textile mills as an outcome of industrialization and post-industrialization, and the subsequent power loom domination lead to a steady decline of weaving clusters and the livelihoods associated with the same, besides the demise of the weaving heritage and erosion of the skill-base. The case study is an illustration of how amidst these challenges to the Handloom Industry, Savitha Suri mobilizes bottom-up change and creates customer engagement at both ends of the value stream (weaver and consumer). Specifically, the revival journey of two weaving clusters are discussed, these being, a: SPANDANA or the healing touch—a social change initiative that led to impactful outcomes, including the number of looms increasing from ten in 2016 to forty by the end of 2017; from each weaver earning INR 200 per saree as labour, to INR 450 in 2017, an year after the SPANDANA journey started; and from 135 sarees at the beginning of the SPANDANA initiative to nearly 3000 sarees being woven, just an year after the project began, with innovations in design and colour, as further evidence of growing confidence and empowerment of the weavers. The case also illustrates a second revival journey, the SPOORTHI project—which was one of the first ever crowd-funded initiative in the Handloom sector in India, that led to the revival of another long-forgotten weave—the Goan Kunbi, with this bottom-up change creating some market disruption. The case offers insights on how a value-based approach, driven by ethical intent and a chain of enablers, is the biggest driver for social change.

Teaching Purpose and Objectives

The case is suitable for both undergraduate and postgraduate classes and can be used to provoke class discussions on: entrepreneurial leadership, change management, and ethical dimensions of entrepreneurial action.

Teaching Purpose

To discuss enablers of sustainable business models in the Social Sector, in an emerging market context, with a specific focus on how value-based and purpose-driven approaches are fundamental to successful social entrepreneurship ventures.

Key objectives include the following:

- To critically evaluate the qualities of entrepreneurial leadership.
- To discuss the change dynamics associated with bottom-up reorientation efforts.
- To appraise and evaluate the role of ethics and trust in social entrepreneurship.

Additional Readings Suggested

Students are required to refer to relevant scholarly articles in change management, social entrepreneurship, and entrepreneurial leadership. Two key readings are recommended, as follows:

- Hayes, J. (2014). *The Theory and Practice of Change Management.* 4th Edition, Palgrave Macmillan.
- Kuratko, D.F. & Morris, M.H. (2013). *Entrepreneurship and Leadership*, Edward Elgar Publishing Limited.

Discussion Questions and Analysis
Theme 1: Entrepreneurial Leadership
Question 1

Discuss facts of the case and evaluate the key features of Savita's entrepreneurial leadership efforts with reference to relevant theoretical models of entrepreneurial leadership.

Analyses

Drawing from entrepreneurial leadership literature, the discussion may focus on key features of entrepreneurial leadership, including authentic leadership, entrepreneurial action in the face of uncertainty, the drivers for converting third person opportunity to first person opportunity, and the establishment of operational control mechanisms for effective and efficient utilization of the limited resources available to entrepreneurs.

Theme 2: Change Management
Question 2

Discuss the key features of the change dynamics that enabled the revival process (as illustrated in the case) to succeed, with reference to relevant process models of change.

Analyses

Drawing on relevant process models of change, the discussion may focus on, forces for and against change, how Savitha Suri converted the need for change into a desire for change, dynamics of stakeholder management, and the key issues that could be considered to make the change sustainable.

Theme 3: Ethics of Entrepreneurial Action
Question 3
Evaluate Savita's ethical stance with regard to her revival of the two weaving clusters What are the key features of the customer engagement process that helped her to succeed?

What advice would you give to Savitha for institutionalizing her values, especially at later stages of her venture development?

Analyses
Drawing on relevant ethical frameworks, the discussion may focus on the relationship between key entrepreneurial characteristics such as, internal locus of control, need for achievement and tolerance for ambiguity, and implications for Savitha Suri's ethical stance. The discussion may focus on how Savitha used ethics and trust as her key value proposition, to create a chain of enablers, and thus achieve customer engagement at both ends of the value stream—consumers and weavers. Further, the analyses can focus on the mechanics of institutionalizing Savitha's core values as her social entrepreneurship venture scales up, with a focus on articulating a clear vision, mission, policies and procedures, and the setting up of other implicit and explicit structure and processes.

References

Dastkar. Available at http://dastkar.org/. Accessed 14 Sept 2017.
First Post. June 9, 2017. Smriti Irani to Firstpost: Involving Weavers in Policy Implementation the Way Forward for Indian Textiles. http://www.firstpost.com/politics/smriti-irani-to-firstpost-involving-weavers-in-policy-implementation-the-way-forward-for-indian-textiles-3536057.html. Accessed 15 Sept 2017.
Gulf Heritage. November 18, 2015, Goa's Traditional Kunbi Fabric Sees a Revival. Available at http://gulfnews.com/culture/heritage/goa-s-traditional-kunbi-fabric-sees-a-revival-1.1622088. Accessed 19 Sept 2017.
Paramparik Karigar. Available at http://www.paramparikkarigar.com/. Accessed 16 Sept 2017.

Internationalization of Bangladesh Banking Sector: Lessons from an Emerging Economy

Suborna Barua and Bipasha Barua

BACKGROUND

The dynamics of banking business worldwide is changing every day, and people, corporations, and markets are becoming increasingly interconnected due to technological progress. As a result, the movement of funds from one country to another has become easier over time. Since finance is the lifeblood of corporations, access to and the availability of adequate financing is essential for smooth running of economic activities. Banks are known as the engine of economic growth as they play the dominant role in doing this. While globalization is creating a single global marketplace for commodities and businesses around the world, banks appear to be one step ahead through more efficient and effective cross-border delivery of banking products and services with the help of advanced technology.

S. Barua (✉)
Department of International Business, University of Dhaka,
Dhaka, Bangladesh
e-mail: sbarua@du.ac.bd

B. Barua
Department of Banking and Insurance, University of Dhaka,
Dhaka, Bangladesh

© The Author(s) 2019   75
A. Sikdar and V. Pereira (eds.), *Business and Management Practices in South Asia*, https://doi.org/10.1007/978-981-13-1399-8_4

Bangladesh is considered one of the future economic global leaders as identified by several agencies; it is one of the fastest growing economies in the world (IMF 2016), and one of the Next-11 highly potential emerging economies (Goldman Sachs 2007). PricewaterhouseCoopers identify it as one of the countries to lead the world economy by 2050 with greater economic power than Australia, the Netherlands, Spain, South Africa, Malaysia, Thailand, and others (Hawksworth and Chan 2015). In Bangladesh, the banking sector is the backbone of the financial market, as it mobilizes the largest amount of funds in the economy. However, Bangladesh's banking sector is currently experiencing its fourth-generation wave with seemingly limited growth opportunities in the domestic market. Many practitioners believe that too many banks are chasing too few customers in the sector resulting in unhealthy competition. This observation appears valid as many banks, especially the relatively newer ones, are struggling to survive while many others are experiencing slowdown in profitability and business growth. As a result, exploring foreign markets for greater growth and business opportunities appears to be a promising alternative for Bangladeshi banks. A greater exposure to international markets may help bring continuous innovation in products, services, and operations to deliver entrepreneurs and corporations with global quality solutions. Of course, the appropriate risk-return trade-off has to be ensured. Going international looks promising as international business and personal transactions relevant to Bangladesh has been increasing considerably; domestic entrepreneurs are increasing their geographical portfolio of international business, multinationals are setting operations in the country, and international migration and trade is increasing at a faster rate. Realizing these expansions, many banks are already providing international banking products and services from home or moving abroad, and this trend appears positive. Certainly, this motivation has been augmented by the opportunity of easy, fast, and cost effective cross-border banking solutions, thanks to globalization and technological progress. In this circumstance, several issues come up. For example, understanding on the state of bank internationalization is very limited and, therefore, policy makers or regulators apparently have little idea as to how the sector is exposing itself to international markets and its follow-up impacts on performance of the banks. Again, in a fast growing economy like Bangladesh, bank internationalization should complement this growth. As knowledge is limited, there seems to be a need for an urgent evaluation on the preparedness of the sector to go international at a full force, and how ready it is to complement the fast growth of the overall economy. The few studies available suggest that many challenges are obstructing the internationalization process in the banking sector, even leading to adverse impacts on the overall financial performance of the sector. There also needs to be a more comprehensive understanding as to how banks respond to those challenges and how regulators and policy-makers can help facilitate a smoother internationalization process for the banks. Understanding these issues will not only benefit Bangladesh, but also it would essentially work as an effective reference for other emerging countries in the world.

AN OVERVIEW OF THE BANKING SECTOR IN BANGLADESH

According to Bangladesh Bank, the central bank of Bangladesh, the country has 57 scheduled banks and 6 non-scheduled banks in Bangladesh under the full control of the Bangladesh Bank Order, 1972 and Bank Company Act, 1991. The non-scheduled banks operate under their own separate laws although they are overseen by the government. Table 1 shows the portfolio of the banking sector. There are also 33 Non-bank Financial Institutions, which are direct competitors to the commercial banks, mainly in the credit market.

Most banks have started branching out toward the rural population in recent times. With too many banks chasing too few customers in a small economy, the banking sector as a whole is recently expecting few mergers. Especially, the fourth-generation banks are struggling in terms of market positioning and generating enough business.

Table 1   Composition of banking sector in Bangladesh

Bank type	No.
State Owned Commercial Banks (SOCBs)	6
Specialized Development Banks (SDBs-State Owned)	2
Private Commercial Banks (PCBs)	40
Conventional PCBs	32
Conventional PCBs	8
Foreign Commercial Banks (FCBs)	9

Source Bangladesh Bank

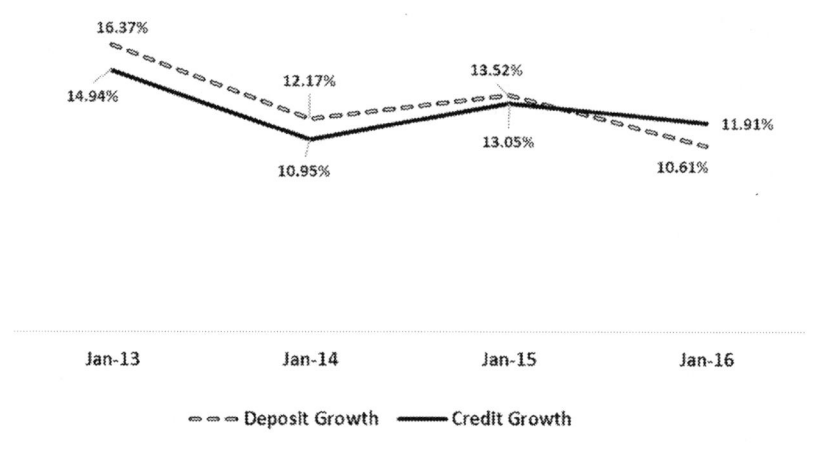

Growth of Bank Deposit and Credit

16.37%
14.94%
12.17%
10.95%
13.52%
13.05%
10.61%
11.91%

Jan-13   Jan-14   Jan-15   Jan-16

⚬ ⚬ ⚬ Deposit Growth   ▬▬ Credit Growth

Fig. 1 Growth of deposit and credit

As Fig. 1 suggests, the sector as a whole is facing slowdown in both the savings and credit markets. The decline in the growth of deposits might be attributed to the increasing cost of living, higher interest rates offered by government investment schemes, and so on. On the other hand, credit growth has slightly recovered from its trough in the past few years, although it has not yet exhibited a rising trend. Several structural problems in economy, for example, lack of infrastructure and governance, corruption etc. may have contributed to a reduction in real sector expansion, leading to reduced demand for credit. In addition, there are signs of substitution effects of higher levels of Foreign Direct Investment (FDI) and foreign loans coming into the market.

The slowdown in the business volume is reflected in the overall profitability of the sector.

Table 2 provides the comparative profitability situation of the overall banking sector over time. Profitability, as reflected in the return on assets (ROA) and return on equity (ROE) measures, decreased by more than half from 2011 to 2012 and remained at this level over subsequent years, albeit with a very high level of volatility. While state-owned banks contributed to much of this slowdown and volatility, the profitability of private commercial banks (PCBs) was also stagnant over the past three years.

Table 2 Profitability of the banking sector

Bank type	Year	SCBs	DFIs	PCBs	FCBs	Total
Return on Assets	2008	0.7	−0.6	1.4	2.9	1.2
(ROA)	2009	1.0	0.4	1.6	3.2	1.4
	2010	1.1	0.2	2.1	2.9	1.8
	2011	1.3	0.1	1.6	3.2	1.5
	2012	−0.6	0.1	0.9	3.3	0.6
	2013	0.6	−0.4	1.0	3.0	0.9
	2014	−0.6	−0.7	1.0	3.4	0.6
	2015	0.0	−1.2	1.0	2.9	0.8
	2016 (June)	−0.2	−2.0	0.7	2.7	0.4
Return on Equity	2008	22.5	−6.9	16.4	17.8	15.6
(ROE)	2009	26.2	−171.7	21.0	22.4	21.7
	2010	18.4	−3.2	20.9	17.0	21.0
	2011	19.7	−0.9	15.7	16.6	17.0
	2012	−11.9	−1.1	10.2	17.3	8.2
	2013	10.9	−5.8	9.8	16.9	11.0
	2014	−13.6	−6.0	10.3	17.7	8.1
	2015	−1.5	−5.8	10.8	14.6	10.5
	2016 (June)	−9.5	−9.5	9.4	13.2	7.1

Source Bangladesh Bank Annual Report 2016

BANK INTERNATIONALIZATION: TRENDS AND PATTERNS

The patterns of bank internationalization have not been of academic and policy focus lately in Bangladesh. In addition, the central bank publishes little official information. As a result, understanding of the internationalization of Bangladeshi banks appears limited. Figure 2a, b presents the data published by the central bank on Net Foreign Assets (NFA) held by the deposit money banks in Bangladesh. NFA are the sum of foreign assets held by the banks, less their foreign liabilities (which are mainly credit and deposits).

NFA shows a volatile pattern in terms of volume while its ratio with respect to domestic assets held shows a declining pattern. The volatility of NFA over time is reflected in its growth presented in Fig. 2b.

Apart from the above data published by central bank, there is no information on how the banking sector in Bangladesh has been embracing internationalization. A survey study conducted by Barua (May 2015) reveals the trends and patterns of bank internationalization in Bangladesh. Among the 41 banks studied in the survey, 34 are PCBs, 6 are State-owned Commercial Banks (SCBs) and 1 is a Specialized Bank

Net Foreign Assset of Deposit Money Banks in Bangladesh

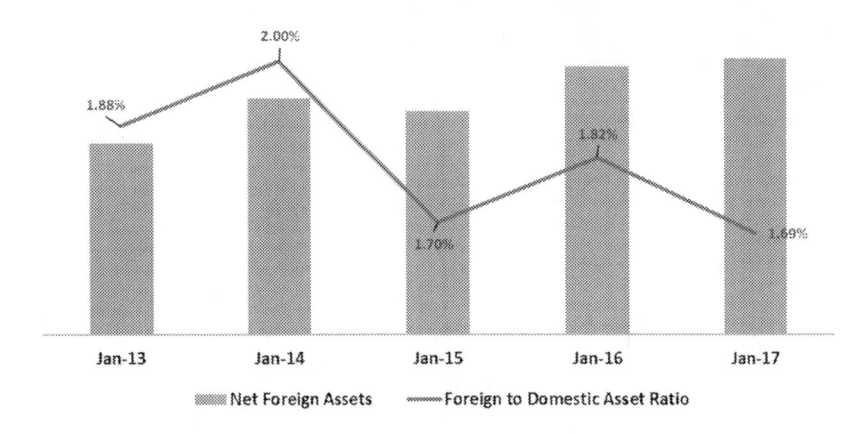

Foreign Asset Growth

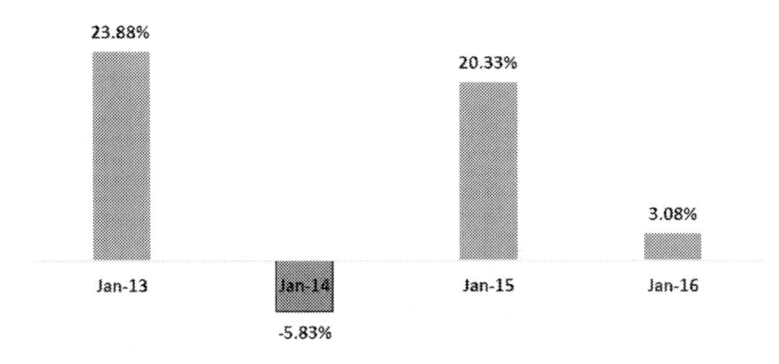

Fig. 2 **a** Net Foreign Assets in million USD and as ratio of domestic assets (*Source* Authors calculation based on Bangladesh Bank Economic Data). **b** Annual growth of Net Foreign Assets (*Source* Authors calculation based on Bangladesh Bank Economic Data)

(SB). The survey results show that around 90% of the banks surveyed (37 banks) had some forms of international operation. The forms of international operation largely range from merely having foreign trade products to investment or lending in other countries to establishing subsidiaries. A detailed discussion the overall internationalization follows based on the findings from the survey.

Outreach and Forms

Figure 3 shows that most of the banks have international banking activities with the United Kingdom and the United States. This may be attributed to the large and growing Bangladeshi communities in those two countries. A majority of the banks also have a presence in nearby economies and neighbors, for example, India, Malaysia, and Saudi Arabia. The reason is that India is a large trading partner of Bangladesh, and Malaysia and Saudi Arabia are top destinations for migrants and labor exports.

The role of the large migrant communities is clear, as three-quarters (76%) of the banks reported offering currency exchange services abroad. About 60% offer wholesale banking products and services such as export–import facilitation, trade financing etc. while 51% offer retail services also such as regular deposit and lending. A mere 11% deliver capital market services such as securities investment intermediation internationally (Fig. 4a).

Interestingly, as Fig. 4b indicates, more than 90% of the banks reported that they had established subsidiary operations, which is the most cost-intensive option to go international relative to others. About 72% provide services through bilateral arrangements with foreign banks, e.g., Correspondent, Agent Banking. About 59% deliver international trade-related products such as trade financing, LC arrangement, etc. from offices inside Bangladesh (33% with and 26% without offshore banking divisions and services).

Degree of Internationalization

Khan and Barua (2016) and Barua et al. (2017) have measured internationalization of Bangladeshi banks using seven "progressive" layers based on greater coverage, collaborations, and physical existence outside Bangladesh (higher layer indicates higher degree of internationalization). The results are shown in Fig. 5.

While Bangladesh has a growing economy, the banking sector is in its early stages of internationalization, being a very insignificant international player. As a result, the number of banks doing business internationally at higher layers (e.g., subsidiaries, joint ventures, or branch networks) should be lower and vice versa due to large capital investment requirements, up-skilled management ability, and preparedness to compete at the global level and greater risk taking ability.

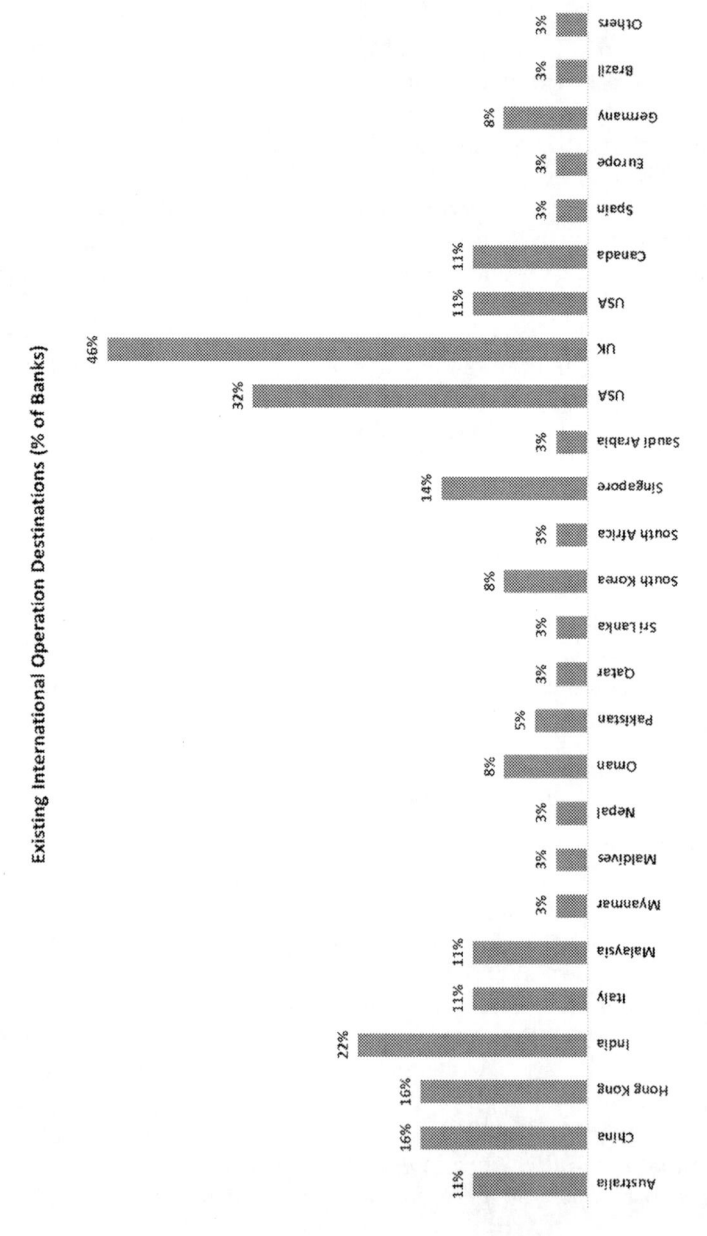

Fig. 3 International engagements of Bangladeshi banks (*Source* Khan and Barua 2016; Survey by Barua 2015)

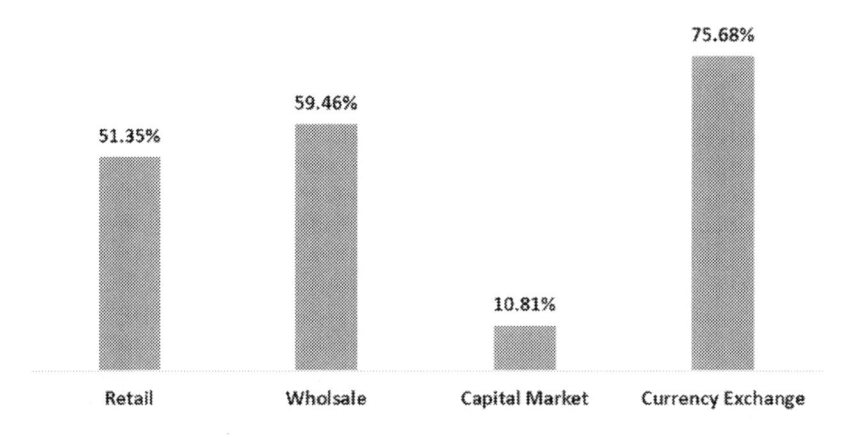

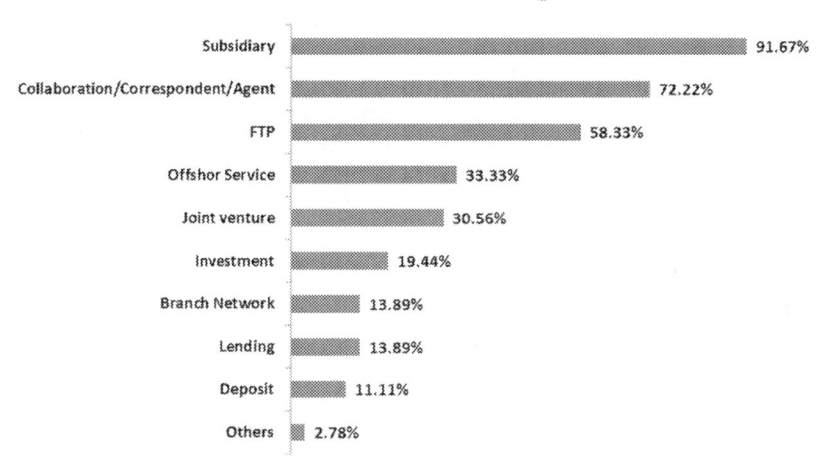

Fig. 4 **a** Products and services. **b** Forms of presence (*Source* Khan and Barua 2016; Survey by Barua 2015)

However, Fig. 5 presents a contrasting view. About 97% of the banks have already achieved the highest level of internationalization (i.e., subsidiary set-up) and 32% have joint venture investments internationally. In contrast, 62% banks offer foreign trade products and 35% have offshore

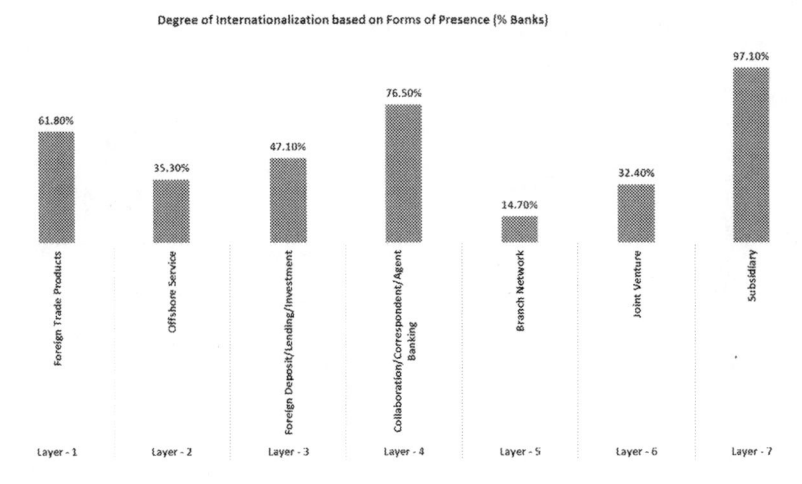

Degree of Internationalization based on Forms of Presence (% Banks)

Fig. 5 Degree of internationalization of Bangladeshi banks (*Source* Khan and Barua 2016; Survey by Barua 2015)

services based in home, which seem to be surprising as these two are considered as the basic forms of bank internationalization. The response rate for foreign investment/lending/deposit (47%) is quite high at this stage of bank internationalization in Bangladesh. However, 77% of the banks reach international markets through collaborations such as agent banking and correspondent banking that are popular modes among those who want to avoid large capital investments and greater risks.

About 30% of the banks have experience of 15 years or less, while around 27% have experience of 25 years or more. The period before 1990s is generally considered as the first generation, the period between 1990 and 2000 as second generation, and 2000–2010 as "Third Generation" with respect to banking sector development in Bangladesh. Hence, it is perceived that the fourth generation is currently underway.

MANAGERIAL ASPECTS IN INTERNATIONALIZATION

Incentives and Motivation

The study reveals that the management of almost all banks (97%) were motivated by the potential of increasing the customer pool and hence

Table 3 Motivation/ incentives to go international

Incentives/motivations	Degree of importance (Figures in % banks)
Increasing customer pool	97.22
Business and profit opportunity	97.22
Risk diversification	91.67
Existence of NRBs	83.33
Product diversification	80.56
Mature domestic market	72.22
Increasing brand image	19.44
Others	19.44

Source Khan and Barua (2016) and Survey by Barua (2015)

the business volume and profitability, as the results in Table 3 indicate. However, 92 and 81% also reported the motivation to diversify their business risk and product portfolio, respectively, although most of them reported these two factors as moderate motivators. While Non-Resident Bangladeshis (NRBs) provide significant level of incentive to 83% of the banks, about 72% regarded the maturity of the domestic market as a key concern.

It appears that there is a serious basis for these motivations. The survey revealed that about 70% of banks expressed their interest to expand their current international operations, while 80% of the banks having no current operation would like to introduce. Consistent with earlier survey outcomes, it is interesting to find that about 62% of the banks (as shown in Fig. 6) would like to start or expand their subsidiary operations, although it involves a larger amount of investment commitment and greater risk. It means these banks would like to overtake the less-costly layers of internationalization.

A modest 46% of the banks are interested in introducing or expanding on-going offshore services, which generally is the expected mode. A fair number of banks (45%) are interested to go for cross-border lending and deposit activities, while 20% prefer collaborations and branch networks.

Managerial Independence

The survey reveals interesting insights on the degree of independence of their international operations with physical existence (e.g., subsidiary, branch) from their head offices at home (in Bangladesh).

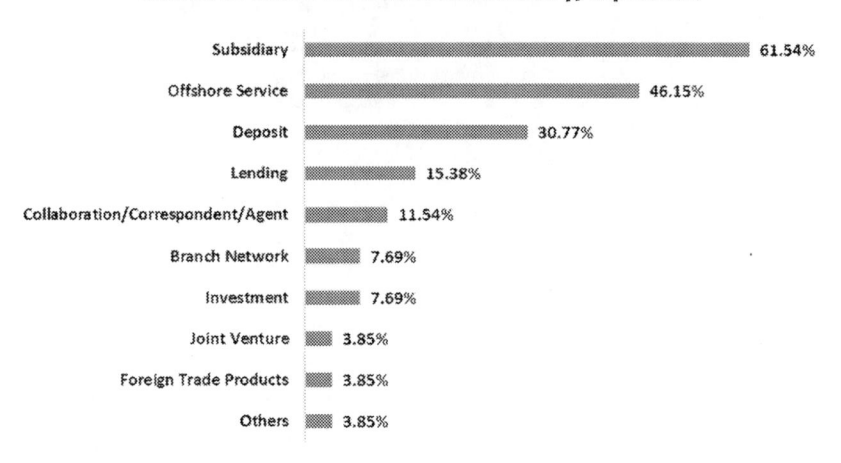

Fig. 6 International entry/expansion modes (*Source* Khan and Barua 2016; Survey by Barua 2015)

Table 4 Independence of foreign operation

Independence for	Degree of independence (Figures in % banks)
Decision making	16.67
Command and control	16.67
Communication	19.44
Human resources	16.67
Product and service delivery	11.11
Increasing scope of operation	16.67
Use of fund abroad	5.56
Others	2.78

Source Khan and Barua (2016) and Survey by Barua (2015)

The results in Table 4 indicate the level of independence exercised by international operations of the banks with respect to decision-making, chain of command and control, communication, and product and service delivery. However, human resources activities (e.g., recruitment) and utilization decisions of funds remain relatively more centralized.

Table 5 Training human resources on international banking

Training type	Figure in % banks
Externally arranged in Bangladesh	43.24
In-house arranged in Bangladesh	83.78
Foreign training arranged in-house	24.32
Foreign training arranged externally	13.51

Source Khan and Barua (2016) and Survey by Barua (2015)

Managing Human Resources

In international banking, having skilled human resources at the international level is paramount. The competiveness of the banks in the international market requires human resources of superior quality and with adequate global banking knowledge and skills. However, only 11 banks report of having international banking-oriented training. Table 5 reports the training types offered to the employees of these 11 banks. Less than half of these banks had some form of training schemes; among them, 84% had in-house training, and about 43% sent their employees to training programs organized by external parties within Bangladesh. The proportion of these banks arranging international training in-house and sending employees abroad is significantly lower, at 24 and 14%, respectively.

Policy Orientation of the Management

Embracing the international market is fundamentally a management policy-level matter within a bank. Therefore, it is important to understand the policy perspective of the banks' top management level regarding internationalization (reported in Fig. 7). The top management of about 41% of the banks view bank internationalization positively as it would contribute to Bangladesh's economic development. However, of the banks, only 14% believe it would bring sustainable growth for the overall banking sector. Regardless of whether it is "sustainable" or not, about 27% of the banks perceive that higher growth can be achieved through enhanced capability and expertise.

The survey revealed that more than three-quarters of the banks were strong advocates that the overall sector should go for international market aggressively by designing internationally competitive business strategies, equipping with necessary preparations (as shown in Fig. 8).

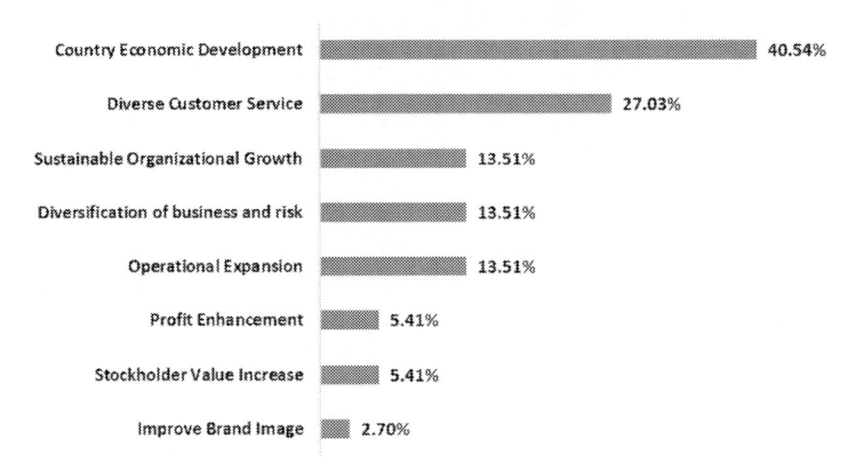

Fig. 7 Policy orientation of bank management (*Source* Khan and Barua 2016; Survey by Barua 2015)

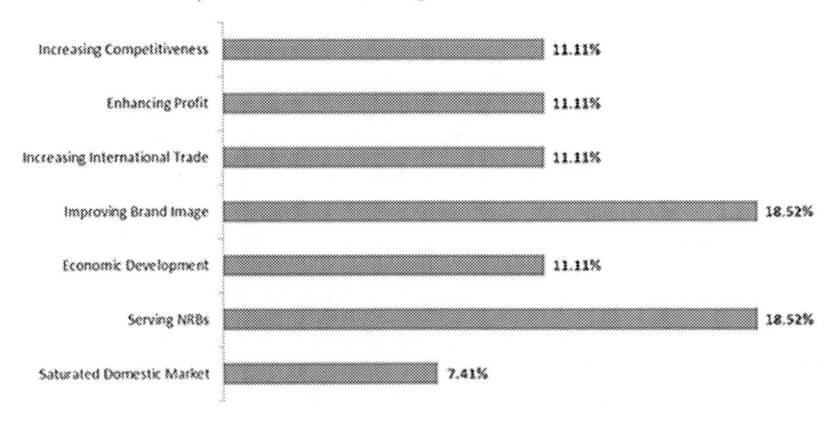

Fig. 8 Banks' perception on overall internationalization (*Source* Khan and Barua 2016; Survey by Barua 2015)

This perception, of course, has some strong basis as reported by the banks, for example, building global brand image, the opportunity to serve fast increasing NRB base improvement in trade and competitiveness, etc.

MANAGERIAL CHALLENGES OF INTERNATIONALIZATION

The are several managerial challenges faced by bank internationalization in Bangladesh, which makes the introduction and delivery of international banking services difficult, risky, and costly as reported by the banks having international activities (shown in Table 6). Majority of the banks consider lack of experience and differences in regulatory and compliance requirements between the home and the host as the major challenge faced. Importantly, Bangladesh's domestic regulations regarding international banking is not adequate, so far. On the other hand, banks often face high-level, complex host country regulations that effectively bar them from entering, expanding, or generating adequate profits. Learning through experience is always an important factor in competing in the highly competitive international markets. Again, to be able to do that, banks must have highly skilled and internationally qualified human resources. About half of the Bangladeshi banks reported that they lack both international experience and quality human resources, which make it difficult to enter or expand in international markets. As a reflection of the management theories on culture, about half of the banks reported social and management cultural differences as critical factors, among others. The other "moderate to high-level" major challenges include tougher competition and operational complexity. Interestingly,

Table 6 Challenges faced by banks in internationalization

Challenges	Figures in % banks
Lack of experience	32.43
Regulatory complexity	40.54
Higher degree competition	5.41
Cultural difference	10.81
Operational complexity	18.92
Domestic linkage	10.81
Wining marketing strategy	10.81
Lack of human resources	24.32
Different managerial culture	13.51
Increased riskiness	2.70

Source Khan and Barua (2016) and Survey by Barua (2015)

banks appear to have very high-risk aptitude, as less than 3% considered increased risk as a challenge in the internationalization process.

Banks, having no international operation or no interest in expanding their current ones, provided more insights that are aligned with earlier findings presented in Table 6. Lack of experience and resources, regulatory barriers and complexity, and tough competition in foreign market are considered the major challenges. However, some new aspects, for example, lack of liquidity, higher operating cost, and poor country image of Bangladesh, are discovered.

INTERNATIONALIZATION IMPACTS ON FINANCIAL PERFORMANCE

Perceived Impacts

In line with the positive policy perspective toward internationalization, banks largely believe that their current international banking activities have significant positive impacts on their domestic performance (as shown in Table 7). About 90% of the banks perceive that there is a large positive improvement in their domestic banking practices arising out of learning from the international operations. A similar proportion of the banks also believe that it will improve their brand image and overall profitability.

The potential improvements in operation and business volume, coupled with risk optimization, would necessarily have a positive impact on financial performance. Figure 9 shows that more than three-quarters of the banks believe that they are already experiencing significant positive impacts on their profitability arising out of whatever internationalization they have achieved.

Table 7 Areas of improvements from international banking

Sources improvement by IB	Degree of improvement (Figures in % banks)
Operational excellence	90.24
Profitability	92.68
Brand image	92.68
Employment generation	2.44
Increase foreign trade	4.88
Global presence	4.88
Diversification	4.88

Source Khan and Barua (2016) and Survey by Barua (2015)

Quantitative Evidence

Based on the survey data of Barua et al. (2017), six financial performance measures are used: ROE, ROA, Earnings before Provision and Tax Margin (EBPTM), Net Profit Margin (NPM), Operating Cash Flow to Equity (OCFEQ), and Cash Flow to Asset (CFASS), to estimate the quantitative impacts of internationalization on the financial performance of the banks. As internationalization indicators, five measures are constructed using the survey data: Level (Layer) of Internationalization (LOI), Number of modes a bank is internationally exposed (FEtypes), Number of countries with physical presence (FCpresnence), Number of countries banks are linked with (FClink), and Age of international exposure (IEage). Impacts are assessed using three separate groups: (i) all 35 Banks, (ii) 29 PCBs, and (iii) 6 State-owned Banks (SOBs) using panel data from 2005 to 2014.

Based on the analysis, it appears that the overall net impact among all banks is negative, as the combined effect of all significant

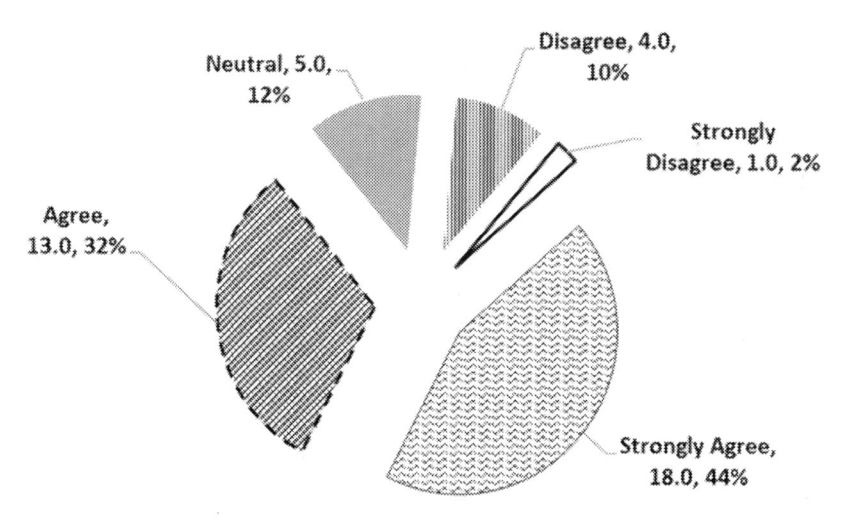

Internationalization Signficantly Impacts Profitability

Neutral, 5.0, 12%

Disagree, 4.0, 10%

Strongly Disagree, 1.0, 2%

Agree, 13.0, 32%

Strongly Agree, 18.0, 44%

Fig. 9 Perceived impacts of internationalization on profitability (*Source* Khan and Barua 2016; Survey by Barua 2015)

internationalization variables have a negative coefficient value for three major financial performance measures: ROA, EBPTM, and NPM. A marginally positive impact is reflected on OCFEQ. The estimations provide further evidence that the overall negative impact on profitability of the banking sector is arising mainly from SOBs. PCBs are, on average, performing significantly better in terms of improvement in profitability by internationalization of their banking business. This finding appears meaningful, as PCBs are fully profit-driven, while SOBs are not. In the advent of tougher competition, PCBs tend to be dynamic in finding new markets with considerable profit opportunity. Contrastingly, SOBs are generally short of dynamism, poorly managed, crippled with very high default rates, and driven with political agenda by the governments, which prevent them to function efficiently and effectively with whatever international outreach they have. This would necessarily result in the loss of business and hence profit. However, it is also true that SOBs in Bangladesh are the largest in terms of asset size and coverage, have greater access to international markets with the greatest age of international experience and carry greater risk-taking ability with government guarantees. The overall result is summarized in Table 8.

Table 8   Internationalization variables and their summarized impact

	Fclink	FCpresence	FEtypes	LOI	IEage
All Banks	1 EBPTM (−)	2 EBPTM (−), OCFEQ (+)	1 NPM (−)	1 EBPTM (+)	3 ROA (−), EBPTM (−), NPM (+)
PCBs	1 ROE (−)	2 ROA (+), OCFEQ (+)	1 ROA (+)	3 ROA (−), EBPTM (+), NPM (+)	2 ROA (−), ROE (−)
SOBs	1 ROE (+)	1 ROA (+)	2 ROA (−), NPM (−)	3 ROA (+), NPM (+), OCFEQ (−)	4 ROA (+), ROE (−), EBPTM (−), NPM (+)

Notes Sign in the parenthesis indicate direction of impact. Number in cells indicates number of performance variables significantly affected by a particular internationalization variable and sign in parenthesis shows the direction of the effect
Source Barua et al. (2017)

Internationalization indicators show greater sensitivity toward income-based performance measures than on cash flow-based ones (shown in Table 8). The age of international banking, layer of internationalization, and foreign country physical presence are the main factors for both PCBs and SOBs. ROA appears to be the most sensitive to internationalization indicators for PCBs, while ROA and NPM show greater sensitivity for SOBs. While the overall impact of physical presence is negative, separate results for PCBs and SOBs provide information that is more particular. The FC link shows a negative impact on profitability for all banks and PCBs, while it is positive for SOBs. Bank age or experience in foreign operations display a greater linkage with SOBs, perhaps, because they are old and vastly experienced when compared to PCBs.

CONCLUSION

Bangladesh is a growing economy, and so is its banking sector. Although Bangladesh has been identified as a future potential economic leader, its banking sector has no significant place or rank yet in the international market. It is true that the internationalization wave in Bangladesh's banking sector does not have a long history, and hence, can be considered as being in the take-off stage. However, the banking sector has a critical role to play in the process of Bangladesh achieving significant economic power. Since banks are the major capital mobilizer within the domestic market of Bangladesh, greater levels of internationalization may bring greater opportunities to bring in more finance and investments from international markets and of course, with greater degree of risk. As international sources report, Bangladesh's economy is booming with huge real sector investment opportunities, and international investors are trying to grasp the opportunities instead of low returns generated in lower-growth economies. Hence, Bangladesh's banking sector has an enormous potential to attract investors and low-cost financing from the international markets. On the other hand, internationalization may help enhance the sector's capability, skill, and service quality and product innovation. It would also help improve sectoral and country image and generate greater bargaining power for the economy in the international market. However, as found from the survey, there are several critical challenges to overcome, which require careful review and policy implementation. While internationalization would bring opportunities, it presents greater risks as well for the sector as a whole. For example, it may be questionable as to why Bangladeshi banks are significantly biased toward cost-intensive approaches (e.g., subsidiary, branch), and do not perceive increased risk as a challenge toward internationalization. It is also notable that so far, the net impact of internationalization is negative on the financial performance of the overall sector. In the backdrop of the scenario, it is important for Bangladesh Bank, the central bank of Bangladesh, to oversee and consider appropriate actions, especially because current regulation is not enough to deal internationalization comprehensively. As a result, a deeper investigation to determine the possible role of the regulators and policy-makers appears necessary.

Teaching Note

Case Synopsis

This case aims to provide an overall state of internationalization of Bangladeshi banks, as a reference to the emerging economies. Since Bangladesh is one of the fastest growing economies of the world and is expected to be one of the leading economies by 2050 in terms of economic power, it is important that the banking sector grows sustainably and, therefore, bank internationalization wave complements this growth. As the "engine of economic growth," banks are the dominant players in Bangladesh's financial market. Due to quick market saturation and a highly competitive domestic market and the need for innovation, banks in Bangladesh are tending to move toward international markets.

This case, with respect to Bangladeshi banks, provides information on the nature and extent of international banking activities, their impacts on performance, and tries to explore the related challenges and policy perspectives. Bangladeshi banks do not follow the usual internationalization path, tend to be biased toward cost-intensive modes and allow significant independence to the international operations, however, face several challenges and deficiencies. Internationalization, achieved so far, has a general negative impact on the performance of the banks although the banks believe it is beneficial for them. As a result, banks tend to expand their international activities more. Based on the findings and discussions available, several questions come forward that must be addressed by the policy-makers and academics to ensure that bank internationalization in Bangladesh can be a perfect complement to the nation's high rate of economic growth.

Teaching Objectives and Academic Positioning

The case provides information for analysis that is very critical for both the managers, academics and policy-makers. As a result, the learners (or students) of the case should be able to get a comprehensive understanding on how bank internationalization has taking off in emerging economies. The learners will be able to realize lessons on at least the following particular areas:

- Degree and nature of internationalization of Bangladeshi Banks
- Diverse measures of internationalization that can be utilized to examine banks
- Managerial challenges in advancing bank internationalization in a fast-growing economy
- The nature of financial and operational impacts of internationalization on the overall sector

Suggested Teaching Method

While relevant information and data are available in the case, it is recommended to advise the learners to look for additional data, information, and reading in studying the case and addressing the discussion questions. A list of such additional sources is outlined at the end of this teaching plan.

While discussion will require utilizing the information given in the case, a background understanding on Bangladesh's economy may be effective in case the audience lacks enough information on the country. Prior to beginning with the case discussion, spending 10–15 minutes on the overall economic indicators of Bangladesh would be useful in such instances. This will complement the general introduction to Bangladesh and the performance of the country's banking sector provided in sections "Background" and "An Overview of the Banking Sector in Bangladesh" of the case. The discussion should also reflect the generalized focus of this case on bank internationalization in developing countries, considering Bangladesh as an example.

Section "Bank Internationalization: Trends and Patterns" of the case delivers the main discussion on the nature and patterns of the ongoing internationalization process in the sector. As there are limited external materials on the discussion presented in this section, the mentor would have to rely on mainly the data and information presented within the case. For additional reading on Bangladeshi banks' internationalization, the two root articles by Barua et al. (2017) and Khan and Barua (2016) can be used as further references. The mentor has to explain to the leaners that this case discussion is an outcome of a survey-based study. In this section, further references on the concepts, measurements, and theories of internationalization may also be discussed in case the learners are less oriented to these concepts (please see additional readings).

Section "Managerial Aspects in Internationalization" highlights the key managerial issues with respect to the internationalization of the banks, i.e., motivation, policy orientation, independence, and developing human resources. The mentor should highlight that these four areas are critical for top management in any bank that wants to enter or expand in the international market. The mentor can provide a general overview on the role of the four key areas in managerial decision making before beginning the chapter.

Section "Managerial Challenges of Internationalization" discusses the managerial challenges faced by the banks in Bangladesh in their internationalization process. As a result, this section is very critical with respect to the objective of the case. Understanding the challenges and their role in obstructing the internationalization process would provide perspectives to the learners on generic difficulties faced by banks in an emerging economy. The world's most international banks are from developed countries. Hence, given the challenges in this section, the mentor should provoke the discussion as to what makes the real differentiation in becoming more internationalized financial institutions between developed and emerging economies.

Section "Internationalization Impacts on Financial Performance" provides two dimensions of the impacts of internationalization. The mentor should first discuss the "perceived impacts" carried by the top management of the banks. Then turning to the quantitative evidence, the mentor should highlight the how much the perceived impacts are true and what contradictory perceptions the top management carry. This section is a key section of the case where the mentor would be able to evidence that whatever "perception" or "feeling" top management of banks have may not be entirely true, and therefore, looking at the quantitative evidence is necessary for a bank management to understand the real impact. It is important to note that Bangladeshi banks do not keep much record of their international operations separately and hence, they are highly likely to hold perception contradictory to the quantitative evidence.

The final section closes the case, explaining the policy matters from regulatory aspects and provoking the complementary role of internationalization in a fast growing economy. The mentor should engage the learners into discussion as to how lack of regulation may deter a sustainable internationalization process and how a smooth and sustainable internationalization of the banking sector may truly complement the economic growth of a country.

Suggested Discussion Questions and Analysis Keys
Three critical discussion questions are suggested below. However, the mentor should exercise the description to generate more relevant discussion questions additionally, as deemed necessary based on the teaching/training/workshop requirements. In addressing the discussion questions, learners should be allowed or advised to utilize data and information from additional reading and other external sources in addition to the case detail in order to make the learning highly vibrant, resourceful, and impactful.

1. *From a managerial perspective, summarize your understanding of the overall internationalization of Bangladeshi banks. Based on your understanding, do you think the sector is progressing on the right track?*
   The question relates to mainly section "Bank Internationalization: Trends and Patterns." The question should be answered by pointing out the general trends and patterns, for example, number of banks engaged in international banking, analyze their product and country portfolio, incentives and motivations for internationalization, and so on. In addition, the learners would evaluate how sustainable the current internationalization wave is given the current sectoral situation and country's economic environment, for example, is it too aggressive or too defensive? Are the modes of international entry/expansion appropriate? Is it the right time to adopt internationalization? Can the current internationalization trend complement the fast economic growth? Therefore, the learners will generally evaluate the entire internationalization wave going on.

2. *What are the major motivations and challenges that bank managers face in Bangladesh? Rate the challenges in terms of the immediate attention needed. How would you recommend that these challenges be dealt with?*

The question is mainly relevant to sections "Managerial Aspects in Internationalization" and "Managerial Challenges of Internationalization." The learners should discuss each and every incentive and challenges reported. The challenges should be discussed in terms of how many ways and to what degree each of them can impact the current and future internationalization progress. Then the learners would have to make a rating based on their own justification and reasoning. The learners then would be required to devise appropriate policy and regulatory recommendations from the perspective of top management of banks to mitigate each of the challenges. The learners would also have to identify how applying their recommendations will help improve the sustainability and potential benefit of internationalization, from the perspective of top management of the banks.

3. *Internationalization impacts financial performance negatively; however, management of many banks believe it is bringing good to them and the sector should go ahead. Evaluate the situation and discuss on the role of central bank to facilitate internationalization that could generate positive returns.*

This question is mainly relevant to section "Internationalization Impacts on Financial Performance." The learners will carefully study the section and then try to justify the differences between the perceived impact and the quantitative evidence. The learner should try to evaluate the correctness of the perception of the bank managers, given the whole case context. In addition, the learners should look at the quantitative evidence and try to explain the potential reasons behind the impacts of each internationalization variables on different performance measures. In the context of this understanding, the learners should again try to evaluate the risks and benefits of the current internationalization wave in Bangladeshi banking sector and suggest future directions with specific discussion on possible regulatory efforts for Bangladesh Bank, the central bank of Bangladesh, to monitor, facilitate, and regulate the overall internationalization process. Such regulatory efforts may include, but not limited to, monitoring the cost-intensive international expansion of the banks, preventing banks to expose to high-risk international markets, ensure greater data security, preventing banks from unhealthy expansion, avoiding systemic risk, i.e., sectoral vulnerability to external economic shocks.

Additional Reading

Bangladesh Bank. (2017). https://www.bb.org.bd/. Accessed 15 Aug 2017.

Barua, S. (2015). "Survey on Internationalization of Bangladeshi Banks", Research Project at the Department of International Business, University of Dhaka.

Barua, S., Khan, T., & Barua, B. (2017). "Internationalization and Performance: Evidence from Bangladeshi Banks", *The Journal of Developing Areas*, vol. 51, no. 2, pp. 105–118.

Buch, C.M., Koch, C.T., & Koetter, M. (2013). "Do Banks Benefit from Internationalization? Revisiting the Market Power-Risk Nexus", *Review of Finance, European Finance Association*, vol. 17, no. 4, pp. 1401–1435.

de Wit, H., Gacel-Ávila, J., Jones, E., & Jooste, N. (eds.). (2017). *The Globalization of Internationalization: Emerging Voices and Perspectives*, Routledge.

Khan, T. & Barua, B. (2016). "Internationalization of Bangladeshi Banks: What Can We Learn?" *American Journal of Trade and Policy*, vol. 3, no. 3, pp. 109–117.

Rybczynski, T.M. (1986). "The Internationalization of the Financial System and the Developing Countries: The Evolving Relationship", Staff Working Paper no. SWP 788. Series on International Capital and Economic Development; no. 4. Washington, DC: The World Bank. http://documents.worldbank.org/curated/en/429611468782145960/The-internationalization-of-the-financial-system-and-the-developing-countries-the-evolving-relationship. Accessed 17 Aug 2017.

Slager, A. (2006). *The Internationalization of Banks Patterns, Strategies and Performance*. Palgrave Macmillan.

Wheeler, C., McDonald, F., & Greaves, I. (eds.). (2003). *Internationalization Firm Strategies and Management*. Palgrave Macmillan.

REFERENCES

Barua, S. (2015). "Survey on Internationalization of Bangladeshi Banks", Research Project at the Department of International Business, University of Dhaka.

Barua, S., Khan, T., & Barua, B. (2017). "Internationalization And Performance: Evidence From Bangladeshi Banks", *The Journal of Developing Areas*, vol. 51, no. 2, pp. 105–118.

Goldman Sachs. (2007). *Beyond the BRICS: A Outlook at the Next 11, Chapter 13 in BRICS and Beyond*, Goldman Sachs Research Global Economics Group. Available online at: http://www.goldmansachs.com/our-thinking/archive/archive-pdfs/brics-book/brics-full-book.pdf.

Hawksworth, J., & Chan, D. (2015). *The World in 2050: Will the Shift in Global Economic Power Continue?* PricewaterhouseCoopers. Available online at: https://www.pwc.com/gx/en/issues/the-economy/assets/world-in-2050-february-2015.pdf.

IMF (International Monetary Fund). (2016, April). *World Economic Outlook: Too Slow for Too Long.* Washington, DC.

Khan, T., & Barua, B. (2016). "Internationalization of Bangladeshi Banks: What Can We Learn?" *American Journal of Trade and Policy*, vol. 3, no. 3, pp. 109–117.

Bangladeshi Banking Innovations: A Case Study on Mobile Banking

Sadia Noor Khan, Maimuna Akter and Fahad Zeya

INTRODUCTION

> Mobile banking is an alternative to the traditional banking through which banking service can be reached at the doorsteps of the deprived section of the society.
>
> —Atiur Rahman, Ex-Governor of Bangladesh Bank

In the launching ceremony (April 2011) of Dutch Bangla Bank Mobile Banking service, these words from Atiur Rahman shaped a new road for the underprivileged group of the society. Along with this, the challenges of mobile banking service providers in the local market have been to shoulder how maximum customers can be attracted and retained with the contented adoption rate. The platform clearly gave access to the customers to the alternative ways of banking but it was then vague where the value and strategy of the very new concept resided.

There are currently 1.75 billion smart phone users in the world and the total number of mobile phone subscriptions has

S. N. Khan (✉) · M. Akter · F. Zeya
Department of Banking and Insurance, University of Dhaka,
Dhaka, Bangladesh

A. Sikdar and V. Pereira (eds.), *Business and Management Practices in South Asia*, https://doi.org/10.1007/978-981-13-1399-8_5

reached 121.860 million at the end of January 2015 in Bangladesh.[1] Bangladesh is, in many ways, a country in advance of its time in terms of mobile access. Even though being ranked as a low income country, over 50% of the population subscribes to mobile services and has outpaced all its peers in terms of network coverage. The amalgamation of limited disposable income and further mature mobile usage means the customers of Bangladesh are more perceptive toward mobile banking services in their daily lives.

Mobile banking also known as M-Banking, SMS Banking can be used for account transactions, payments, checking balance, credit applications, and other banking transactions. Through mobile messaging, banks offer value added services to the customer at marginal costs.

Many banks of Bangladesh are gradually realizing that customers are to be given substantial opportunities to be trapped with the mobile banking. Mobile banking in Bangladesh is very young. In 2012, Dutch-Bangla Bank Limited (DBBL) has for the first time introduced its mobile banking service growing the banking service from cities to remote areas in Bangladesh.

The concept of Mobile Banking has come to ensure some promises. A mobile is more or less always with the customer. Users can use it over a gigantic geographical area. Anywhere and anytime, features of mobile services trigger the point of mobile banking. People do not need to go to banks or ATM booths to avail banking services. They have their banking services in hand. Mobile Banking serves the customers with convenience, privacy, cost and time effectiveness, and overall savings. With more passing days, more people are availing mobile banking services. In Mobile Banking, Bangladesh is working as a role model for other developing countries. Since the inception, the growth rate of mobile banking has touched a remarkable level. The spectacular statistics of nearly 264% mobile banking growth rate over the last four years (2012–2015) is an indicator that mobile banking has enabled almost everyone with any handset to transact, regardless of the distance across the country.

---

[1] Adapted from Sadia Noor Khan et al. 2017. Factors Influencing Adoption and Usage of Mobile Banking: Bangladesh Experience. *International Journal of Finance and Banking Research* 3(1), pp. 1–12.

HISTORY AND DEVELOPMENT OF M-BANKING IDEA

People are familiar with the traditional banking in which they have to go to banks physically and do their transactions. With the rapid pace of growth of the banking sector, the number of customers is on the rise. The excessive load of customers makes the bank branches jam-packed and it kills much time. Not only it is time consuming, but also it needs more paperwork, signing of checks for withdrawal, filling up the deposit slip for deposits. For traditional banking transactions, there are fixed banking hour between 10 am and 4 pm (except public holiday).

To cover some problems regarding traditional banking services, most of the banks establish their Automated Teller Machine (ATM) booths in many areas. From ATM booths, people can withdraw their money by using plastic money (Debit Card). But this mechanism also has some problems. Carrying Debit Card is sometimes risky as some recent hijacking incidents have been reported in Bangladesh while transacting in the ATM booths.

Here, mobile can play a great role which may lessen the extra hassle borne by customers. In Bangladesh, more than 60% of the total population has their personal phone. Among them, many have more than one. People here can avail the mobile banking services regardless of their age, education, gender, and occupation. People do not need to do extra paper work or uneducated persons do not need to sign in any documents for transactions. The only thing they have to deal with is keeping a Personal Identification Number (PIN) in memory. For every transaction, anywhere and anytime they have to use the PIN number. They do not need to maintain any banking hour for their transaction as well. There is also no need to carry any plastic money with them for mobile banking. People may transact anytime with the help of mobile banking agent shop which is quite common in every area of Bangladesh. Mobile Banking is far less risky than ATM booth transactions. For transferring of money, they do not need to go to agents. They can transfer money by themselves to anybody and they only have to go to agents to do Cash-in or Cash-out. Thus a single device can be used for multifunctional options.

Mobile banking in Bangladesh is very young. In 2012, DBBL has for the first time introduced its mobile banking service expanding the banking service from cities to remote areas in Bangladesh. This service was inaugurated by the Bangladesh Bank Ex-Governor Atiur Rahman by depositing Tk 2000 and withdrawing Tk 1500 through Banglalink and Citycell mobile networks. Mobile banking service started its full fledge

Exhibit 1   Mobile banking growth

	MFS accounts		Transactions		Agents	
	Number (million)	Growth (%)	Number (USD million)	Growth (%)	Number	Growth (%)
2011	0.44		26.67		9093	
2012	2	355	256.7	863	59,559	555
2013	13	550	847.2	230	82,000	38
2014	25.25	94	1345.6	59	54,0948	560
Average growth		264		227		227

Source Adapted from Sadia Noor Khan et al. 2017. Factors Influencing Adoption and Usage of Mobile Banking: Bangladesh Experience. *International Journal of Finance and Banking Research* 3(1), pp. 1–12

operation from 2014. Right now, 28 banks have the license for doing mobile banking by their branches and many banks are waiting for authorization. Even though 28 banks have license but 19 banks are providing mobile banking services. Moreover, the number of agent is 538,170 around the country whereas the total registered client is 28.646 million and active account is 12.234 million with total transaction Tk 129695.1 million. The average daily transaction is about Tk 4323.1 million which is huge for a country like Bangladesh.

Mobile Banking Service in Bangladesh Since Its Inception: The stunning statistics of nearly 264% mobile banking growth rate over the last four year bears testimony to the fact that mobile banking has enabled almost everyone with any handset to transact, regardless of the distance across the country. Exhibit 1 shows that in 2011, mobile banking service in Bangladesh started its journey with a slow pace. At that time, the mobile banking accounts were 0.44 million in numbers, only 26.67 million US dollar transactions held and overall operation was conducted through only 9093 agents. The next year, the growth rate became 355, 863, and 555% consecutively which shows outstanding response from the customers. No financial inclusion in the history of Bangladesh showed such reaction ever. The growth of mobile banking did not stop but rather broke all the records in the next two years. In 2015, the familiarity of mobile banking reached door to door. People become more reliant on the mobile banking service for their daily transaction. Bangladesh as a developing country has created a replicable model for mobile

Exhibit 2 Present scenario of agents and clients in leading mobile banking provider

Service Provider	Number of agents	Number of clients
bKash	80,000	80.1 million
DBBL MB	62,572	2,010,283
mCash	61,000	150,000
TBMM	20,000	100,000
uCash	10,000	90,000
mPay	8000	51,000
Primecash	3000	100,000

Source Adapted from Sadia Noor Khan et al. 2017. Factors Influencing Adoption and Usage of Mobile Banking: Bangladesh Experience. *International Journal of Finance and Banking Research* 3(1), pp. 1–12

banking service. Compared to the neighboring countries like India and Pakistan, Bangladesh has set an outstanding example for any developing country. Right now, 19 service providers are offering mobile banking services in Bangladesh. Most of them have started their journey after 2012. Some pioneer banks are getting competitive advantages.

Exhibit 2 shows that DBBL and bKash mobile banking have brought a huge number of people under banking services within a very short period of time. bKash of BRAC bank beats DBBL on a large scale though it has started its operation one year later. The branding of the service name and intense marketing effort has helped them to achieve huge market share within a very short period. The number of agent of bKash is around 20% higher than DBBL and number of client is almost four times greater than that of DBBL. There are at least 10 mobile banking service providers in Bangladesh. bKash has almost half of the market share followed by Dutch-Bangla mobile banking and rest of the providers have almost a quarter of total market share. According to Mahindra Comviva, a mobile financial solutions provider, Bangladesh is in the leading position in the Southeast Asian nations in terms of Mobile Finance Services.

WHY PEOPLE ADOPT MOBILE BANKING SERVICE?

People in Bangladesh use mobile banking services for various purposes. Exhibit 3 shows that maximum respondents out of 400 users of mobile banking services are for *Airtime Recharge* (loading balance into mobile to make call or message) and *Fund Transfer* (57.1%), *Bill Payment* (Gas, electricity, or water bill) (32.1%), *Balance Inquiry* (43.8%), and

You use mobile banking services for:

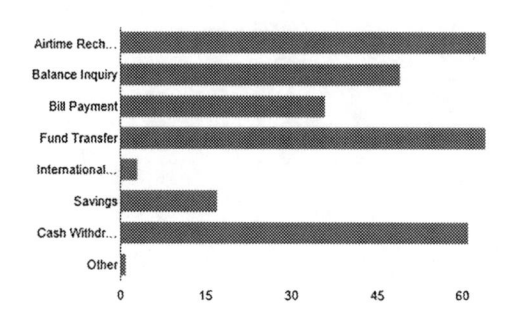

Airtime Recharge	64	57.1%
Balance Inquiry	49	43.8%
Bill Payment	36	32.1%
Fund Transfer	64	57.1%
International Remittance	3	2.7%
Savings	17	15.2%
Cash Withdrawal	61	54.5%
Other	1	0.9%

Exhibit 3 Usage of mobile banking services (*Source* Adapted from Sadia Noor Khan et al. 2017. Factors Influencing Adoption and Usage of Mobile Banking: Bangladesh Experience. *International Journal of Finance and Banking Research* 3(1), pp. 1–12)

Cash Withdrawals (54.5%). Some of the mobile banking service provider (e.g., bKash) used to provide some interest on remaining balance in the account. But from the mid 2016, they have stopped this service which may demotivate the customers who prefer small saving in their mobile banking account. Above all, using mobile banking service sometimes has been proven superior to traditional banking services.

Mobile Banking Service—A Panacea in Emergency

Fawaz, a student of BBA Program from University of Dhaka, residing in Surjasen Hall (Boys hostel) inside campus area, enlightened an interesting scenario how mobile banking service helped him during an emergency. One night, he had an emergency and needed some money. But then all banks were closed and so he went out with his Debit Card of a bank. He roamed around three nearby ATM booths in search of money but all three ATM booths either had no cash or had technical problems. He got dejected and was in a dilemma what to do next as he had an emergency. Suddenly, he recalled that he had a bKash account (Brac Bank Mobile Banking Service) his mobile. He checked the balance and went to a nearby bKash agent which is only 300 m away from the university campus. He instantly cashed-out the money and met up his emergency need. He was very grateful to the mobile banking service.

GRAY AREAS OF MOBILE BANKING

To conceptualize the gray area, few studies have been conducted on mobile banking services, its utility, prospects, and problems and adoptability of mobile banking. The few researches reveal some important factors which are useful for clearing out the vague areas.

- It is revealed that the adoption rate of mobile banking is far behind than the pace of technology advancement. Complications in functionality and on privacy related issues grounds customers feel doubtful about the convenience and security of using mobile banking service (Sharma and Kansal 2012).[2]
- Mobile banking is preferred by low or middle income group compared to rich people. The study revealed that the safety of savings using mobile banking services has been increased more than before. People now prefer to do mobile banking for small saving instead of keeping cash at home, under the mattress or with the person.
- Some study revealed that mobile banking is user friendly and a person of every age may use it without having technical aptitude. It ensures time and cost effectiveness. People of low or middle income no longer have to open the account from bank branches. They carry their account in their cellular phones.

Mobile banking has its viability among the people of developing countries like Bangladesh, India, and Pakistan. User friendly banking services, savings facility, time and cost effectiveness during transactions, up to

---

[2]Sharma, A. and kansal, V. 2012. Mobile Banking as Technology Adoption and Challenges: A Case of M-Banking in India. *International Journal of Scientific and Research Publications* 2(2).

date checking balance facility—all these attributes have recently created a revolution in the banking and financial services. The thing regarding which concerns should be expressed is the privacy issues. For privacy issue, mobile banking services of any bank provide a secured PIN code. This PIN code is working like a password and it is different for every customer. Customers themselves can alter the PIN code as many times as they want if needed. Recently, some forgery cases have been reported while doing mobile banking service. Nevertheless, more emphasis should be given on privacy issues.

> **Fraud Call Story—Using Mobile Banking Service:**
>
> Rahela, a mobile banking service (bKash) user said, "Once I got a call from an unknown number. The speaker over there in a crying voice was telling that he mistakenly deposited TK 500 in my bKash number. He was constantly requesting to return the money into his number as he needed the money for his mother's treatment. He said that he would be on hold while I was transferring the money. Initially, I got confused and emotional as well but then I disconnected his call and checked my balance and found no Tk 500 extra amount in my bKash balance. The issue became clear to me that it was nothing but a fake call. The person called me again and asked me for money in the same tone. Then I yelled at him and threatened him that I will take action against him if he calls me again. Hearing this, he put his phone down and never called me again."

Mobile Banking Ideas and Influence on People (Bangladesh Perspective)

The usage of mobile banking services for the people depend on some qualitative factors show.

Influence of M Banking Ideas on People

The influences of Demographic Profiles and Users' Perceptions have been discussed below (Exhibit 4).

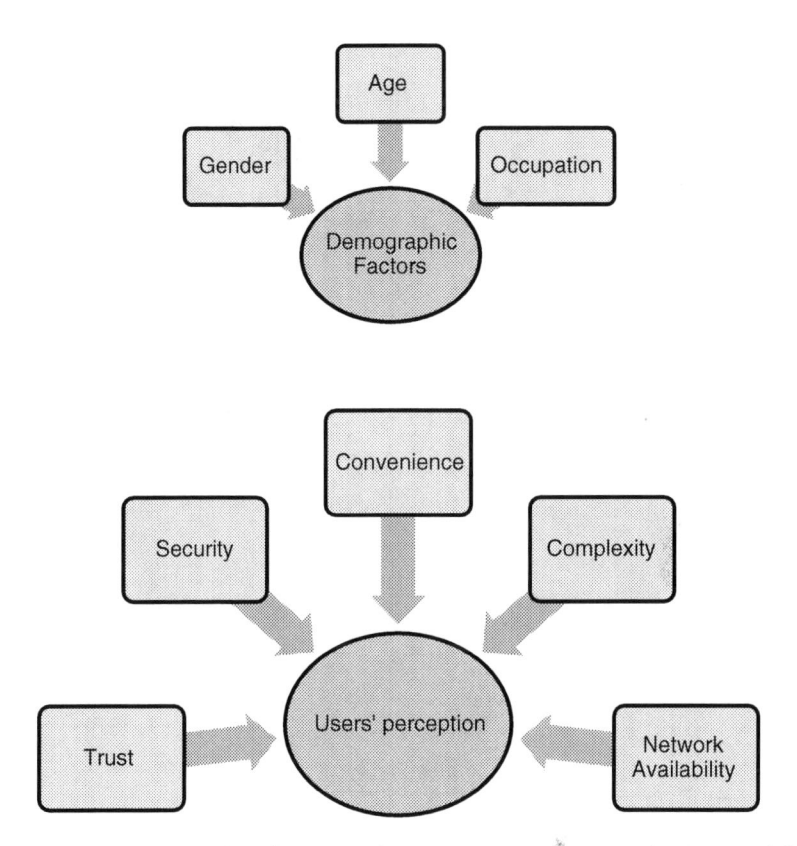

Exhibit 4 Demographic factors and users' perception on adopting mobile banking (*Source* Adapted from Sadia Noor Khan et al. 2017. Factors Influencing Adoption and Usage of Mobile Banking: Bangladesh Experience. *International Journal of Finance and Banking Research* 3(1), pp. 1–12)

(a) ***Demographic Factors***: Demographic factors are related to *gender*, *age*, and *occupation* of the people enjoying mobile banking.

 I. Gender: Mobile banking users in Bangladesh belongs to both male and female group. Exhibit 5 shows that male users occupy almost 80% of total market. In Bangladesh, as male seems to be more engaged in different jobs, educational institutions, and business than female, there is dominance of the specific gender over mobile banking usage. Though the mobile banking users from male group are greater than those of female group, it does not indicate that gender has influence over the mobile banking usage.

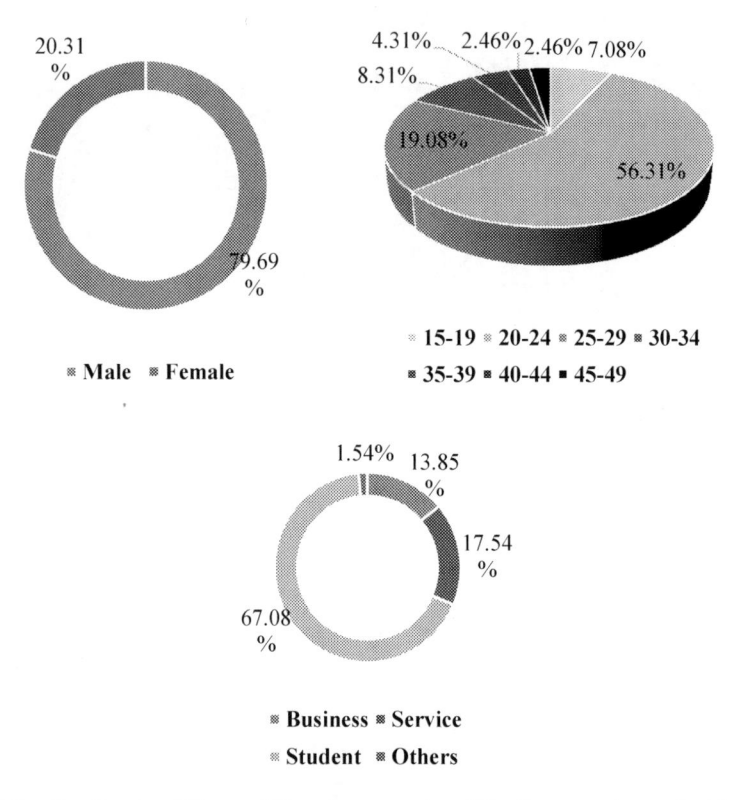

Exhibit 5   Gender (%), age (%) and occupation (%) of surveyed sample (*Source* Adapted from Sadia Noor Khan et al. 2017. Factors Influencing Adoption and Usage of Mobile Banking: Bangladesh Experience. *International Journal of Finance and Banking Research* 3(1), pp. 1–12)

II. Age: From young to old aged, people should be brought into this study. The dependability of the society people may have some influence on using mobile banking activities. Exhibit 5 shows that among the total number of mobile banking users, users of age 20–24 occupy a major portion. In Bangladesh, from 20 to 24 ages people are students and some are service holders. They are inclined to use mobile banking service compared to other groups. The average age of people using mobile banking is 24–25. The results depicted in the Exhibit 6 developed with the result of regression show that though the age limit 20–24 occupies a major proportion of the total mobile

Exhibit 6   Influence of age limit on rate of mobile banking adoption

	15–19	20–24	25–29	30–34	35–39	40–44	45–49
Rate of mobile banking adoption	b=4.395 R^2=.292 (P=.460)	b=−.813 R^2=.641 (P=.199)	b=.660 R^2=.062 (P=.751)	b=2.958 R^2=.529 (P=.272)	b=3.798 R^2=.800 (P=.106)	b=5.781 R^2=.421 (P=.351)	b=3.262 R^2=.664 (P=.185)

Source Adapted from Sadia Noor Khan et al. 2017. Factors Influencing Adoption and Usage of Mobile Banking: Bangladesh Experience. *International Journal of Finance and Banking Research* 3(1), pp. 1–12

banking users in Bangladesh, none of the age limits have particular influence to the total increase of mobile banking adoption rate in Bangladesh.

III. Occupation: From students to housewives and from business men to service holders, all are to be brought into this mobile banking service. Exhibit 5 shows that students hold a major portion of total customers in market with a rate of 67%. Service holders also occupy a huge percentage of almost 18%. Most of the students who study far away from their home are dependent to their parents for expenses. Hence, their proportion to total user is higher than that of other users.

Exhibit 7 regression run to show influence of different occupations on mobile banking adoption rate conclude that though most of the users of mobile banking service are service holders and students, none of the occupations used here have significant impact on mobile banking adoption rate in Bangladesh. Students are more inclined to use mobile banking service for their small and daily transaction. The major portion of service holders or business men is to be included in the same pace. The housewives are also in the group of small saving but the concern is that they are not engaged up to the mark in mobile banking services.

(b) **Users' Perception**: People using mobile banking service are very much concerned about some qualitative factors. Some independent variables such as *trust, security, convenience, complexity* and *network availability* were used in measuring customers' adoption regarding mobile banking services.

I. Trust: Trust means a consumer's belief that his/her privacy regarding personal and transaction information (which are accessible to the Bank and the Operator) will not be harmed, and the technology is reliable enough to protect his/her private information from unauthorized parties (e.g., hackers). A consumer will adopt the M Banking services, only when s/he will have trust in the bank, operator, and the technical system.

Trust: In response to the statement—"*There is no chance of leakage of my personal and transactional information*", majority (47.8%) of the respondents showed their agreement or strong agreement. As there are very few cases regarding such malfunction and mobile banking seems to be easy to use, majority of the users see mobile banking as trustworthy (Exhibit 8).

Exhibit 7   Influence of occupation on rate of mobile banking adoption

	Businessman	Service holder	Student	Doctor	Garment workers	Housewife	Unemployed
Rate of mobile banking adoption	b=3.862 R^2=.639 (P=.201)	b=.519 R^2=.218 (P=.533)	b=−.619 R^2=.390 (P=.375)	b=20.103 R^2=.764 (P=.126)	b=20.103 R^2=.764 (P=.126)	b=1.885 R^2=.027 (P=.836)	b=−.915 R^2=.006 (P=.924)

Source Adapted from Sadia Noor Khan et al. 2017. Factors Influencing Adoption and Usage of Mobile Banking: Bangladesh Experience. *International Journal of Finance and Banking Research* 3(1), pp. 1–12

Exhibit 8   Perception of trust

Responses	Frequency	Percent		
Strongly disagree = 1	21	10.2	Mean	3.1512
Disagree = 2	48	23.4	Median	3
Neutral = 3	38	18.5	Mode	4
Agree = 4	75	36.6	Std. deviation	1.20113
Strongly agree = 5	23	11.2		
Total	205	100.0		

Source Adapted from Sadia Noor Khan et al. 2017. Factors Influencing Adoption and Usage of Mobile Banking: Bangladesh Experience. *International Journal of Finance and Banking Research* 3(1), pp. 1–12

II. Security: Security means a consumer's belief that his/her money can be securely saved and transferred using M Banking. A consumer will adopt and use M Banking, only when s/he is convinced that the money to be saved or transferred will be safe from theft.

In response to the statement—"*Hackers can transfer my money to their accounts, without making the bank and operator security systems aware*", almost 50% respondents agreed or strongly agreed with the statement. As people of Bangladesh are very much conscious about security and moral hazard, majority of them think it to be less secured due to lack of knowledge over mobile banking (Exhibit 9).

III. Convenience: Convenience means the consumers find using M Banking more beneficial than traditional banking or cash-in-hand practices in terms of time saving, transportation cost saving, facilitating of small fund transfer, and ease of saving. A consumer will adopt M Banking when s/he will find it saves time, money, make transaction, and saving easier.

In response to the statement—"*It is better to pay some service charge in M Banking than spending on conveyance to make a payment, or transfer a fund to someone*", majority (almost 60%) concluded mobile banking to be cost effective and convenient as it causes very little cost and inconvenience to users (Exhibit 10).

IV. Complexity: Complexity means the degrees to which a consumer finds the processes of depositing and transferring fund difficult to understand, and hassle-some to execute. A consumer won't use a technology that s/he can't understand or doesn't find it user-friendly.

In response to the statement—"*I find the operation processes (depositing and withdrawing money, transferring fund) too*

Exhibit 9   Perception of security

Responses	Frequency	Percent		
Strongly disagree = 1	7	3.4	Mean	3.3951
Disagree = 2	36	17.6	Median	4
Neutral = 3	58	28.3	Mode	4
Agree = 4	77	37.6	Std. deviation	1.03136
Strongly agree = 5	27	13.2		
Total	205	100.0		

Source Adapted from Sadia Noor Khan et al. 2017. Factors Influencing Adoption and Usage of Mobile Banking: Bangladesh Experience. *International Journal of Finance and Banking Research* 3(1), pp. 1–12

Exhibit 10   Perception of cost and convenience

	Frequency	Percent		
Strongly disagree = 1	9	4.4	Mean	3.5512
Disagree = 2	23	11.2	Median	4
Neutral = 3	47	22.9	Mode	4
Agree = 4	98	47.8	Std. deviation	1.00553
Strongly agree = 5	28	13.7		
Total	205	100.0		

Source Adapted from Sadia Noor Khan et al. 2017. Factors Influencing Adoption and Usage of Mobile Banking: Bangladesh Experience. *International Journal of Finance and Banking Research* 3(1), pp. 1–12

complex to understand", majority (almost 43%) respondents disagreed. Though convenient to use, mobile banking seems still complex to some of people in Bangladesh as they are technologically less advanced and are habituated to paper work (Exhibit 11).

V. Network Availability: Network availability is solely dependent on the telecommunication companies operating in Bangladesh. In Bangladesh, at present Grameen Phone, Banglalink, Robi, Airtel, and Teletalk are providing these services.

In response to statement—"*Operating an M bank a/c often becomes tougher because of unavailability of mobile operator network*", majority (almost 49%) showed their agreement or strong agreement. Though telecom companies are now covering major portion of Bangladesh, network problem is still remaining in pick hours. Therefore, mobile banking transactions often get hampered (Exhibit 12).

Exhibit 11   Perception to complexity

	Frequency	Percent		
Strongly disagree = 1	16	7.8	Mean	2.8244
Disagree = 2	73	35.6	Median	3
Neutral = 3	61	29.8	Mode	2
Agree = 4	41	20.0	Std. deviation	1.05644
Strongly agree = 5	14	6.8		
Total	205	100.0		

Source Adapted from Sadia Noor Khan et al. 2017. Factors Influencing Adoption and Usage of Mobile Banking: Bangladesh Experience. *International Journal of Finance and Banking Research* 3(1), pp. 1–12

Exhibit 12   Perception to ambiguous network availability

	Frequency	Percent		
Strongly disagree = 1	14	6.8	Mean	3.2341
Disagree = 2	43	21.0	Median	3
Neutral = 3	48	23.4	Mode	4
Agree = 4	81	39.5	Std. deviation	1.09536
Strongly agree = 5	19	9.3		
Total	205	100.0		

Source Adapted from Sadia Noor Khan et al. 2017. Factors Influencing Adoption and Usage of Mobile Banking: Bangladesh Experience. *International Journal of Finance and Banking Research* 3(1), pp. 1–12

Though the model doesn't take into account the actual technological and policy changes in the industry which also influences adoption and usage of M Banking, in developing country like Bangladesh the above mentioned *demographic* as well as *users' perception* variables play a vital role. Aligned with this, the growth and sustainability of mobile banking service in Bangladesh are also reliant on these factors.

The results depicted into Exhibit 13 conclude that security, cost and convenience, and complexity have significant influence over adoption rate of mobile banking in Bangladesh. Whereas trust and network problem seem to have no influence over the adoption rate of mobile banking.

Bangladesh is a developing country. People here are very much concerned about their security, cost and convenience, and complexity or flexibility issue in using mobile banking service. The earning level of major portion is low and so they need assurance for their small amount of saving. Working hours for any sector in Bangladesh is not that much flexible.

Exhibit 13   Influence of perception on rate of mobile banking adoption

	Trust	Security	Cost convenience	Complexity	Network
Mobile banking adoption	$b=28.453$ $R^2=.673$ $(P=.1791)$	$b=-83.974$ $R^2=.844$ $(P=.081)$	$b=179.050$ $R^2=.808$ $(P=.101)$	$b=-32.585$ $R^2=.823$ $(P=.093)$	$b=37.695$ $R^2=.394$ $(P=.372)$

Source Adapted from Sadia Noor Khan et al. 2017. Factors Influencing Adoption and Usage of Mobile Banking: Bangladesh Experience. *International Journal of Finance and Banking Research* 3(1), pp. 1–12

Along with this, they have to kill their most of the time sitting idle in the traffic jam. So, going to bank branches and doing banking activities many a time adds hassle to their daily life. In terms of complexity, most of the people are still uneducated about mobile banking service. So they are averse to have this service. They need such service which is completely user friendly. Hence security, cost, and convenience and complexity can contribute significantly to the variability of rate of mobile banking adoption rate.

Trust is obviously a personal issue but the growth (264%) of mobile banking in the previous four year shows much trust. Network availability is reliant solely on the telecommunication market. Sometimes the network gets down and hampers the activity but it has no major negative influence on transaction and mobile banking adoption rate on the people.

INTERNATIONAL COMPETITIVENESS OF MOBILE BANKING (FINANCIAL INCLUSION VS. MOBILE BANKING)

Financial inclusion means the delivery of financial resources at an affordable price to the less-advantaged and low-income group regardless of the income stratum. Mobile banking is an example of financial inclusion. In developing countries like India, Pakistan, and Bangladesh, the need of inclusive financing is boundless.

All of the three countries are doing well in their inclusive financing targets. But India and Pakistan is lagging behind from Bangladesh in the growth of mobile banking. Exhibit 14 shows the comparison of financial inclusion and mobile banking data of Bangladesh, India, and Pakistan. The data suggest that the financial inclusion percentage of these countries stand close. But mobile banking is the area India is lagging substantially, compared to her neighbors.

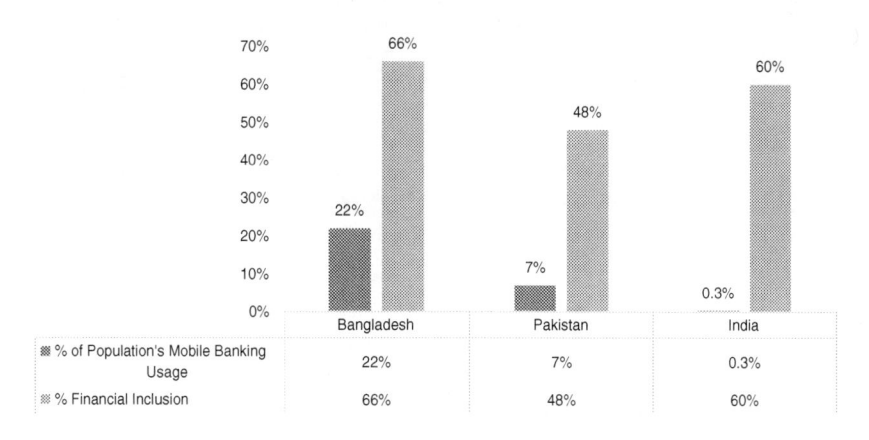

Mobile Banking and Financial Inclusion

	Bangladesh	Pakistan	India
% of Population's Mobile Banking Usage	22%	7%	0.3%
% Financial Inclusion	66%	48%	60%

% of Population's Mobile Banking Usage   % Financial Inclusion

Exhibit 14   Neighboring country comparison on M banking (*Source* Adapted from Sadia Noor Khan et al. 2017. Factors Influencing Adoption and Usage of Mobile Banking: Bangladesh Experience. *International Journal of Finance and Banking Research* 3(1), pp. 1–12)

The silent revolution of Bangladesh's experience of mobile banking's phenomenal growth can be a replicable model which demands further scrutiny of the underlying driving factors contributing to an unconventional financial inclusion and payment mechanism, with a minimal and affordable cost. This paves the way for people of every income stratum to avail financial services and enables them to transact through a profitable model for all the stakeholders involved.

GROWTH AND CONCERNS OF MOBILE BANKING IDEAS

Since its inception in 2011, mobile banking sector in Bangladesh has been experiencing exponential growth. This is the only example of financial exclusion which creates a revolutionary effect on the customers. Bangladesh is among the biggest mobile banking market in the world and grabs almost 8% total registered global mobile banking user. The industry has seen a remarkable height in mobile banking market from 2013 to 2015. The number of registered accounts increased five times within this two year and it has become 25 million from 5 million. The transaction has also risen surprisingly from 10 million in January 2013 to 77 million in February 2015. The idea was initiated only with the transaction basis. Gradually, the concept got bigger and expanded. A lot more new features have been added to attract the new market which seems successful. Airtime recharge, bill payments are some features that created a radical effect on the people. Interest given on keeping some minimum balance into account is the idea of bKash. People got keener to save their small amount with mobile banking service. Fund transfer anywhere/anytime motivated people to open mobile banking service.

Mobile banking service in Bangladesh has been a hit financial service project so far. The growth of the service is outstanding. Seeing the future, concerns regarding mobile banking issues like safety, trust, network availability should be focused. Though the upward growth is still prevalent, time will come when the service is saturated. Then the proper work on concerns regarding mobile banking service will decide whether the concept holds on in the market or not and if it does then how long it will sustain. Kamaljeet Rastogi, global head of business development of Mahindra Comviva, said that, "Mobile money is growing at the rate of 30% per year and this rate of growth is expected to continue for the next two years and then it should become stable."

As the target market of Mobile Financial Services (MFS) are limited to or no access to banking services, the possibility of mobile banking in Bangladesh is illimitable. At this time, some open questions come regarding mobile banking sector. Can mobile banking service meet up the demand of less advantaged group of people? Will it be able to grow at the same pace in the future years? Can mobile banking in Bangladesh work as a role model for the rest of the developing country like herself? All its existence will depend upon the present and future policy to be taken to maintain the future development of this notable illustration of financial inclusion.

TEACHING NOTE

Synopsis

The main objective of the case study is to explore the factors, demographic variables, and users' perception that influence the adoption of mobile banking in Bangladesh. The case also discusses the status of mobile banking usage using age, gender, and occupation as demographic variables, and the perception of users toward mobile banking in terms of trustworthiness, security, cost and convenience, complexity, and network availability. It includes specific reference to how these demographic variables and users' perception influence mobile banking usage.

A survey has been conducted by Sadia Noor Khan et al. on a sample of 400 mobile banking users for a period of 4 years, i.e., 2012–2015. Analysis has revealed that majority of the users are male and students of age 20–24 years. They perceive mobile banking to be trustworthy, secured and cost effective, though complex and vulnerable to network problem. The study has also revealed that differences in demographic characteristics have no influence over mobile banking adoption. It has come out that perception to security, cost and convenience, and complexity in using mobile banking service influences variations in mobile banking adoption. Demographic profile is shown to have no influence on increase in mobile banking adoption rate of Bangladesh. Though male occupy a major portion of total customers in market, gender proves to have no dominance over mobile banking adoption, because in Bangladesh, both male and female are now getting engaged with study and work equally, and they are using mobile banking service irrespective of their gender. Hence, a particular gender has no dominance over adopting mobile banking service. In addition, people from all age limits are now using mobile banking for their education, study, occupation, business etc. Therefore, people of a particular age limit do not necessarily have influence over the overall mobile banking adoption rate. On the other hand, users' perception over mobile banking is used to show its influence on mobile banking adoption rate. A single conclusion is tough to be drawn as perception regarding different factors has different influence on mobile banking. As people of Bangladesh are more conscious about their security and cost, these two factors seem to have significant influence on mobile banking. People of Bangladesh are educationally and technologically less advanced. Complexity in usage may cause decrease in mobile banking usage which indicate that higher complexity may cause huge decrease in mobile banking usage.

Learning Objectives

As the case is related to adoption and usage of mobile banking service, I suggest that the students could learn some of the ideas as below:

- The students could learn how factors are influencing in adopting mobile banking service
- The students can relate and compare other financial inclusion services with the mobile banking which is an example of financial inclusion
- The students could also learn about the two sides (good-mobile banking and bad-fraudulent activities) of the technology
- The students can identify other factors which stimulated the fastest growth ever in the field of inclusive financing

Position in Course
The case can be used in both undergraduate and post graduate program. As the case is related to mobile banking, both business and technical courses (e.g., Economics of Money and Banking, E-Commerce, etc.) can be related to this.

Suggested Readings
Michael Porter's Five Forces Model can be related to this case. Mobile Banking market though is in the upward trend, the day will come when it will saturate.

Product Life Cycle can be related to this mobile banking concept. Development, Growth, Maturity, and Decline will be the best analysis factor in this case.

Assignment Questions

1. Why low or middle income group of people tend to do more mobile banking?
2. In what way can mobile banking in Bangladesh work as a role model for the developing countries?
3. What factors stimulate and influence the adoption and usage of mobile banking in Bangladesh?
4. What are the proposed success factors that would help mobile banking concept to sustain for the longer term in the market?

Analysis

1. **Why low or middle income group of people tend to do more mobile banking?**
   In Bangladesh, majority of the population are connected to farming directly. Their income is very low and they hardly have left over to save. So, they think that they have no use in opening accounts with the bank. But it is true that people from any income group need some transaction either daily or occasionally. Low or middle income group of people prefer not having account into the bank and also they avoid go.ing bank branches for extra hassle. Their saving is very small and transaction of daily basis is not so big. So, they prefer mobile banking over the traditional banking service provided in the banks of Bangladesh.

2. **In what way can mobile banking in Bangladesh work as a role model for the developing countries?**
   The concept of Mobile Banking has come to ensure some promises. A mobile is more or less always with the customer. Users can use it over a gigantic geographical area. Anywhere and anytime, features of mobile services trigger the point of mobile banking. People do not need to go to banks or ATM booths to avail banking services. They have their banking services in hand. Mobile Banking serves the customers with convenience, privacy, cost and time effectiveness, and overall savings. The more days are passing by, the more people are availing mobile banking services. In Mobile Banking, Bangladesh is working as a role model for any developing countries. Since the inception, the growth rate of mobile banking has touched a remarkable level. The spectacular statistics of nearly 264% mobile banking growth rate over the last four year (2012–2015) is indicating that mobile banking has enabled almost everyone with any handset to transact, regardless of the distance across the country.
   Financial inclusion means the delivery of financial resources at an affordable price to the less-advantaged and low-income group regardless of the income stratum. Mobile banking is an example of financial inclusion. In developing countries like India, Pakistan, and Bangladesh, the need of inclusive financing is boundless. All of the three countries are doing well in their inclusive financing targets.

But India and Pakistan is lagging behind from Bangladesh in the growth of mobile banking. Exhibit 14 shows the comparison of financial inclusion and mobile banking data of Bangladesh, India, and Pakistan. The data suggest that the financial inclusion percentage of these countries stand close. But mobile banking is the area India is lagging substantially, compared to her neighbors.

The silent revolution of Bangladesh's experience of mobile banking's phenomenal growth can be a replicable model which demands further scrutinizing of the underlying driving factors contributing to an unconventional financial inclusion and payment mechanism, with a minimal and affordable cost. This paves the way for people of every income stratum to avail financial services and enables them to transact through a profitable model for all the stakeholders involved. For example, in Bangladesh, the use of mobile banking has spread out in the insurance sector (MetLife, Bangladesh is using bKash for transaction which is unfamiliar in the neighboring countries).

3. **What factors stimulate and influence the adoption and usage of mobile banking in Bangladesh?**
   (a) Demographic factors: No influence in adopting mobile banking service
   (b) Users' perception on some variables discussed below:
   - Security, Cost and Convenience, and Complexity—Having influence (people are low income group and many of them have little knowledge about technology, so they don't want to compromise with the security, cost and complexity issues)
   - Trust and Network Availability—Having no influence (network problem doesn't have such impact on the transaction process and for trust issue, no such major issues have been found so these factors don't have major impact)

4. **What are the proposed success factors that help mobile banking concept sustain for the longer term in the market?**
   Mobile banking service in Bangladesh has been a hit financial service project so far. The growth of the service is outstanding. Seeing the future, concerns regarding mobile banking issues like safety, trust, network availability should be focused. Though the upward growth is still prevalent, time will come when the service is saturated. To be very specific, a lot more new features (e.g., more

savings facilities, insurance coverages) should be added to mobile banking service to ensure diverse banking. Then the proper work on concerns regarding mobile banking service will decide whether the concept holds on into the market or not and if it does then how long it will sustain.

Teaching Suggestions

1.	Financial inclusion and mobile banking
2.	Development of Mobile Banking
3.	Factors helped in adopting mobile banking service
4.	Reason behind the fastest growth for the new concept
5.	Market Acceptance for the newly arrival service
6.	Prospects of Mobile Banking service in the developing country
7.	Undiscovered factors that may stimulate in adopting mobile banking service
8.	Strategies to be taken to sustain in the longer term

Epilogue

Financial institutions are now rearranging the banking industry of Bangladesh and as such Mobile Banking has come to be established in the market. This is mostly the practice of banking and financial services with the help of mobile devices. This platform is updating to offer highly interactive mobile applications that meet the needs of customers. Through the case the authors found out that the adoption and usage of mobile banking in Bangladesh is dependent on various variables like—convenience, network availability, complexity, security, and trust. So the mobile banking service providers need to ensure offering this service at cheap cost with high security so that customers feel convenient to use it and can rely on and trust this new dimension of financial inclusion in Bangladesh.

bKash: Revolutionizing Mobile Financial Services in Bangladesh?

Shamima Yesmin, Tonmoy Ananda Paul and Md. Mohshin Uddin

INTRODUCTION

In the recent past, Bangladesh has seen the development of one of the world's fastest growing mobile money ecosystems. bKash came into the mobile financial service provider market targeting the low-income masses of the country and emerged as a mobile banking giant capturing almost 75% of market share, to become the second largest mobile money provider in the world, behind Kenya's mPesa (Kaniz Fatema Nourin Choudhury 2016). bKash serves mainly as a subsidiary of BRAC bank. It started operating in July 22, 2011 as a joint venture of BRAC Bank Limited, Bangladesh and Money in Motion LLC, USA. By the end of 2013, bKash was being used by 22% of the adult population, a fast start in country of 170 million inhabitants. Unlike large mobile money businesses in other countries which added mobile financial services to its existing customer base, bKash acquired each client by its own efforts as it was not a mobile network operator (MNO) and thus did not have an existing consumer base. bKash relies on the existing MNOs on

S. Yesmin (✉) · T. A. Paul · M. Mohshin Uddin
Institute of Business Administration, University of Dhaka, Dhaka, Bangladesh

© The Author(s) 2019 125
A. Sikdar and V. Pereira (eds.), *Business and Management Practices in South Asia*, https://doi.org/10.1007/978-981-13-1399-8_6

Bangladesh to provide its services. bKash aims to serve the bottom of the economic pyramid (BOP) (lower income category demographic) by providing a broad range of financial inclusion services.

SERVICES BKASH PROVIDE

The bKash service is delivered using USSD interface accessible via a basic handset, charging zero cashing-in fee and low cashing-out and person-to-person transfer fees. These elements of bKash help BOP users can send money in a fast, secure, and affordable manner. According to the "Guidelines on Mobile Financial Services (MFS) for the Banks" issued by Bangladesh Bank in 2011, mobile financial services are required to be provided by a bank or a company that is classified as a bank subsidiary by the central bank. So bKash is a joint venture between BRAC Bank (51%) and a U.S.-based company, Money in Motion LLC (49%). BRAC Bank is responsible for regulatory compliance, while bKash manages nearly all facets of the mobile financial service operations and must deposit the full value of its mobile account balances with a prudentially regulated commercial bank (Chen and Rasmussen 2014). Later, The International Finance Corporation (IFC) and the Bill & Melinda Gates Foundation joined as minority investors in 2013 and 2014, respectively.

Primary Values that bKash claims to offer are as follows:

- **Fast**—Money travels within seconds
- **Affordable**—Lowest in cost, especially for lower tokens
- **Secure**—Under regulation and compliance
- **Convenient**—Few easy steps, supported by any handset in USSD format
- **Nationwide**—available within walking distance

bKash services at a glance includes Cash In, Send Money, Cash Out, Salary Disbursement, Interest against saving, Loan Repayments, ATM withdrawal, Merchant Payments, Mobile Airtime Recharge, and Foreign remittance. Western Union, MasterCard, and bKash have partnered to launch a service for Bangladeshis to receive international remittance in the most convenient manner. Thus people staying abroad can use Western Union to send money to their loved ones living in Bangladesh, and anyone with an active bKash account can avail this service and receive the money directly into their bKash account, 24/7. As the money is transferred through MasterCard's secured network, the efficacy of this new service is highly ensured.

CURRENT SCENARIO OF ʙKASH

bKash is neither a MNO nor a bank, but a separate company that built its business on its own and managed to become the market leader within two years of operation. It started as a subsidiary of BRAC bank which already had the advantage of strong rural presence and involvement with micro finance institutions. The business model of bKash is unconventional in the way it drives transactions and earns revenue through fees. Many banks focus only on credit, savings, and building balance sheet and only targets urban region customer segments. bKash has differentiated itself by including the workforces that drive revenue from Ready Made Garments (RMG) sector and small-medium entrepreneurs. bKash has established a nationwide reach from the beginning and aims to serve everyone. bKash owes its fast success to a specialized business structure built to deliver mobile financial services.

bKash enjoyed an enabling and flexible regulatory environment from the central bank of Bangladesh, Bangladesh Bank. Bangladesh Bank provided license to 28 financial institutions for providing mobile financial service to avoid monopolization in the MFS market. Though first debated in 2008, Bangladesh Bank was not comfortable to the idea of allowing nonbanks and particularly MNOs like Grameen phone to launch their own services. However, Bangladesh Bank was comfortable with issuing a license to a well-managed commercial bank, and the 2011 regulation included a clause that allowed banks to set up subsidiaries specifically to offer mobile financial services. This allowed conventional banks to join in partnership with funders with relevant experience to establish separate mobile financial services company. Thus, this nuanced light-touch regulation provided the opportunity for BRAC Bank to set up bKash to offer mobile financial services while still being regulated under the umbrella of banking norms (Chen and Rasmussen 2014).

bKash's annual report shows a cash heavy company of revenues earning from various sources like cash out through agents (Tk. 11,156,986,894), person to person (P2P) money transfer (Tk. 508,239,161), Cash out through ATM (Tk. 1,655,831), collection by merchant accounts (Tk. 63,534,444), disbursement to merchant accounts (Tk. 1,263,329), remittance collection from western union (Tk. 152,216), and commissions on airtime purchase (Tk. 356,856,233). The amount totals to 12,088,678,108 takas for the year 2016. Primary sources of revenue are cash-out at 1.85%, Taka 5 per wallet to wallet transaction, and interest on float accounts (Appendix B). While, the primary cost structure of bKash includes distributor and retailer commissions (80% of total revenue), fee to MNOs for USSD access (7% of revenue), and staffs and administrative expenses. Today, bKash is the market leader with around 75% market share in Bangladesh, while Bangladesh accounts for more than 8% of total global mobile money accounts.

INDUSTRY ANALYSIS

Evolution of MFS

MFS or mobile financial services have emerged as an inseparable part of our lives as mobile devices has become the heart of communication evolution. This indicates that service providers need to adapt digital payment strategies, as it is not a competitive advantage but a survival issue. In developed nations, banks provide mobile banking by using a smartphone app to securely perform bank transactions.

Mobile money is a stored value account that is accessed from the user's mobile phone. The account in the user's phone is managed by the MFS (bKash) in conjunction with the MNO. In developing nations where most people do not have regular bank accounts (the unbanked population), mobile money has gained popularity as it offers a form of "lite" banking as a replacement for formal bank accounts. The rising popularity of mobile money services could also be attributed to the ubiquity of mobile phone services in the developing nations, where areas may not have access to branch banking but do have reliable mobile coverage. This mobile money is an indication of the demand for financial services that were previously not available to the general population.

HOW MFS WORKS

Fast, secure, and user-friendly mobile telecommunication technologies are a crucial factor for the commercial success of Mobile Commerce. "Mobile payment" refers to use of mobile hand—held devices to make payments by the customer to the vendor for purchase of goods and services. Examples of Mobile Payment are "Mobile Wallet", by *T-Mobile* and "m-pay" by *Vodafone*. The consumer, mobile phone subscriber of the concerned network carrier, registers with the payment service and gets an individual PIN to authenticate itself via WAP or Short Message Service (SMS), in order to make payments. The subscriber does not need to get registered with each individual vendor, which is an advantage. The vendor also registers with payment service and thus could attract customers who would have liked to pay through Mobile Payment. The advantage for the vendor is that there is no need to worry about the credit-worthiness of individual customers (Tiwari and Buse 2007).

Mobile banking business model depends on banking agents, i.e., retail or postal outlets that process financial transactions on behalf of telecoms or banks. The banking agent deals with customer care, service quality, and cash management, which determines the success of the business model. These banking agents could be local airtime resellers of telecom providers or pharmacies, bakeries, etc. as used by banks in Colombia, Brazil, Peru, and other markets. Another difference lies in the nature of agency agreement between bank and the Non-Bank. The mobile banking business model can be classified as Bank-Focused, Bank-Led, or Nonbank-Led. In the bank-focused model, a traditional bank uses non-traditional low-cost delivery channels to provide banking services. The bank-led model offers an alternative to use retail agents (or through mobile phone) to conduct financial transactions instead of using bank branches. In the non-bank-led model, the financial transaction service is provided by a non-bank (e.g., telco) while the bank acts as a safe-keeper of surplus funds.

WORLD MFS SCENARIO

Mobile banking is used in many parts of the world, especially in remote and rural areas with little or no banking infrastructure. Thus mobile banking has gained popularity in African nations with Kenya ranking highly in SMS mobile banking. As of 2016, mobile banking applications have seen a tremendous growth in Kenyan banking sector. Equity Bank Kenya Limited's Eazzy banking application, The Co-operative Bank's Mco-op cash application, Safaricom's (part of the Vodafone Group) m-Pesa, and Zain's ZAP are popular mobile banking services in Kenya. Tangerine, MobiKash, and Funtrench Limited also have network-independent mobile money transfer in Kenya. Mobile banking service is also offered in Iran by banks (Parsian, Tejarat, Pasargad Bank, Mellat, Saderat, Sepah, Edbi, and Bankmelli); in Guatemala by Banco Industrial; in Mexico by Omnilife, Bancomer and MPower

Venture; and in Somalia by Hormuud Telecom's ZAAD service. In UK, Barclays offers a service called Barclays Pingit, allowing transfer of money from UK to many parts of the world using a mobile phone. Also in UK, Paym mobile payment system was launched by the UK Payments Council, allowing mobile payments between customers of several banks and building societies (Wambari 2009).

In the South Asian region, mobile banking service is also available. Telenor in coordination with Taameer Bank had launched a mobile banking solution called Easy Paisa in Pakistan. In India, Eko India Financial Services, the business correspondent of State Bank of India (SBI), and ICICI Bank, provides financial services (bank accounts, deposit, withdrawal, remittance, micro-insurance, and micro-finance facilities) to its customers (nearly 80% of whom are migrants or the unbanked section of the population) through mobile banking. In Nepal, Mobile Khata was the first mobile banking product launched by Laxmi Bank Limited in 2012. Mobile Khata currently runs on a third-party platform called Hello Paisa that is interoperable with all telecom providers and various banks of Nepal.

The very first mobile banking service in Bangladesh was launched by Dutch-Bangla Bank on 31 March 2011 with the "Agent" and "Network" support of mobile operators, Banglalink and Citycell. As 45% of the unbanked population in Bangladesh is mobile users, Dutch-Bangla Bank can now reach out to them. This service is available to any mobile handset that has subscription with any of the six existing mobile operators of Bangladesh. Under this mobile banking service, bank-nominated banking agent would perform banking activities, like opening mobile banking accounts, providing cash services (receipts and payments), and dealing with small credits. The service also allows cash withdrawal from an ATM validated by "mobile phone and PIN" instead of "card and PIN." Other services provided are transactions-related fund transfer, merchant payment, utility bill payment, salary/commission disbursement, and disbursement of government allowance.

KENYA AND M-PESA

M-Pesa (M for mobile, pesa is Swahili for money) is a mobile phone-based money transfer, financing, and micro-financing service launched in 2007 by Vodafone for Safaricom and Vodacom, the largest MNOs in Kenya and Tanzania. M-Pesa allows users to use their mobile phone

the reason for spread of their business. With the help of mobile accounts and ease of money transferring, even people of little or no knowledge were able to obtain financial services. The use of agents as middle-man was also proven advantageous as they could direct and help people with managing their money effectively.

MFS MARKET IN BANGLADESH

Since the launch of the first mobile financial service products in 2011, Bangladesh has seen a rapidly growing mobile financial services industry with 8% of the total registered mobile money accounts globally. At least 10 providers are already offering services in the market, namely, **bKash** (BRAC Bank), **Rocket** (DBBL), **mCash** (Islami Bank Bangladesh Limited), **MYCash** (Mercantile Bank Limited), **UCash** (UCBL), **IFIC Mobile Banking** (IFIC Bank Limited), **Trust Bank Mobile Money** (Trust Bank Limited), **OK Banking** (ONE Bank Limited), **FSIBL FirstPay Surecash** (FSIBL), and **Hello** (Bank Asia). An extensive survey done by USAID reflected that more than 80% of MFS users agreed that the services are safe, easy, and convenient, and 91% of MFS users and 88% of non-users agreed that "low transaction costs" is the most important priority for customers (Parvez et al. 2015).

Dutch-Bangla Bank was the pioneer of mobile banking in Bangladesh as it was the first bank to offer banking facilities through a wide range of mobile phones. Its service, named Rocket, is a banking process without bank branch that provided unbanked communities efficient and affordable financial services such as cash-in, cash out, merchant payment, utility payment, salary disbursement, foreign remittance, government allowance disbursement, ATM money withdrawal through mobile phone. Though the early players of MFS market in Bangladesh included bKash, DBBL Mobile Banking, and Trust Bank Mobile Money, bKash managed to soar in success in a very short span of time. The total MFS market of Bangladesh is being estimated as of amount 1500 crore BDT. bKash has captured 75% of the market share, followed by Rocket at 18% and the rest of the MFS providers are left with insignificant piece of the pie. mCash and UCash competes for the third position in market share. The growth of the market has largely benefited from domestic remittances covering transactions like cash-in (42% of total transactions), cash-out (37%), and person to person (P2P) transactions (19%). The comparisons between MFS providers (Appendix A) show us that the MFS providers charge about 1.5–1.85% for cash-out services and very nominal fee for Person to person (P2P) send money service. Almost all of the MFS providers allow their customer to open a mobile banking account for free, and some of them need to have an institutional banking account with the associated banks. The MFS providers use the MNOs to offer their services and share revenues with the MNOs. MFS providers also share their revenues with the distributors and agents. Prominent uses of MFS providers other than personal mobile banking service includes Transfer of foreign remittance in collaboration with Western Union Money Transfer by bKash; Surecash by Rupali Bank is used by education board to distribute government scholarship among primary, secondary students; DMP uses the service of UCash for their traffic rule violation payments etc. Many NGO's like Oxfam also employs the service of MFS providers in Bangladesh. MFS revolutionized the domestic remittance sending system and captured a big chunk of Bangladesh economy by penetrating the lower-income segment of Bangladesh (Fig. 1).

The ease, safety, and mobility of MFS are what make it more desirable than a conventional bank account. But the affordability and convenience of sending money is what played the major role in penetrating Bangladesh's market within very short time. bKash faces the threat of losing is majority share to Rocket (DBBL), but it is not an imminent

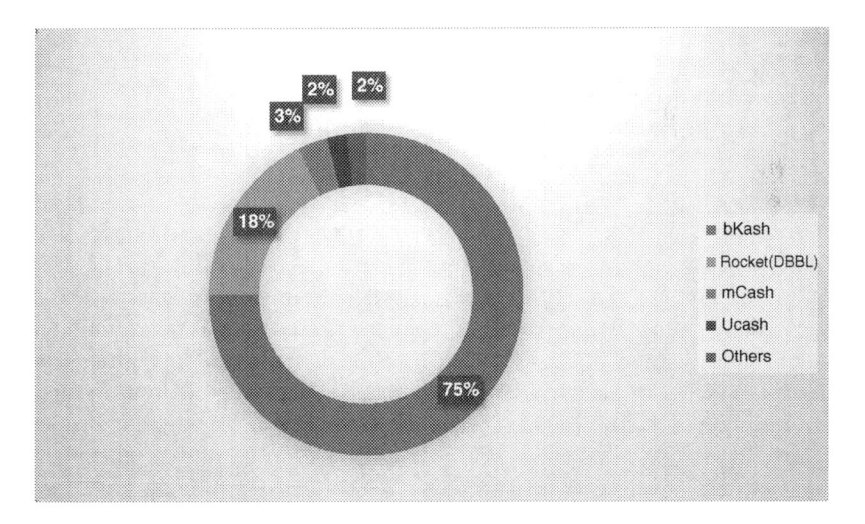

Fig. 1   Market share of MFS providers in Bangladesh

threat as bKash has already become a generic term in Bangladesh perspective. Regarding the cost advantage independent of scale, bKash has done successful marketing and set up touch-points all over the country to strengthen the distribution network. bKash achieved exemplary success in creating awareness and interest among its target segment and they also managed to deliver their service even in the remote areas of Bangladesh.

Attractiveness of MFS Market from bKash's Point of View

Since 2015, the competition in the mobile financing industry has become intense, not only due to launch of constant special offers and new value-added services, but also with the entry of newer and bigger entrants. The competitive environment in the industry and attractiveness of this segment can be explained using Michael Porter's five forces model.

There are a number of factors that determine the degree of difficulty in entering an industry. bKash required huge capital and sufficient amount of banking experience to enter in MFS providing industry. The characteristics of this industry include almost insignificant pricing variation and no switching cost. Due to network proximity and widespread distribution channels in form of agents, bKash became a domestic name for us within a very short span of time. BRAC bank, a well-known NGO owns 51% of bKash's equity providing it with initial investment and required banking experience. As bKash targeted the low-income category or the C level consumers in SEC classification, it received a grant of 1 million USD in its initial stage from Bill and Melinda Gates Foundation and later Gates foundation came on board as one of the investors. On the matter of bKash, Bill Gates lauded its services. He remarked that for a growing economy like Bangladesh where most of the workforces contributing in the country's economy are lower-income demographic, hassle free account opening and easily accessible interface is friendly to market. From Bangladesh Bank, bKash received favorable response in case of policy making and warded off the entry of MNOs in this industry. But bKash faced a huge blow recently when Bangladesh Bank formulated a policy of limiting the cash transactions without consulting the market leader bKash. It poses a threat of people opting for MFS accounts of more than one provider and making the market share of bKash's opponent grow.

In case of relationship with buyer, as the entrants grow in this industry, buyers gain more and more bargaining power. The buyers or service recipient, has all the suppliers or agents of MFS providers, also gain more bargaining power as Rocket, mCash etc. enters the segment. In an informative study collected from a random small-scale agent, bKash is the only MFS provider available throughout the country. bKash collects 1.85% of each cash-out transaction made OTC from agents whereas its nearest competitor Rocket charges 1.8%, but in cash of cash-out transactions from DBBL booths it charges 0.9% in each case. Again, in case of the revenue sharing with agents, agents receive 0.4 and 0.5% of the amount in each cash-out transaction from bKash and Rocket, respectively. The information shows how rocket strategizes to pose threat on bKash by increasing buyer and supplier bargaining power. The substitutes existing are credit cards or FIs that transfers foreign remittance. Due to lack of technological infrastructure like mobile apps, bKash is, therefore, more preferred than banking institutions.

MARKETING CONCEPT ADOPTED BY BKASH

A brand owns a category only when the brand name is used by people generically. The brand name and its associations give a product meaning in the consumer's mind, which bKash adopted successfully. "bKash" is a play on words—the word sounds like the term for progress when quickly said in the local language. The term "bKash" has become synonymous with mobile money payments and people uses phrases like "bKash me" instead of saying "send me money." Bangladesh is lauded for the amount and volume of foreign remittance inflow but the domestic inflow of remittance from urban working-class people to their family residing in rural areas is completely ignored. About 80% of the current workforce has family in rural areas, and the working members are sent to urban area in search of a better life. bKash does a lot for financial inclusions mainly in terms of reaching financial services to remote, rural areas which are difficult for other institutional financial service providers or banks to reach just because of the cost structure.

The line in the TV advertisements of bKash reflected the target population whom they are trying to reach, and they came out triumphant. With the help of bKash agents, available at every other block or so, even illiterate working-class people are being able to use financial services. The inclusion of agents created a pipeline for employment for many lower-skilled demographics. After achieving almost all of the market penetration in C class, bKash has also managed to reach the B category consumers. Small and medium entrepreneurs, housewives opening small

Facebook-based businesses, online marketers etc. bKash now targets the consumers at A category and is developing new product line for their target market. The collaborators of bKash include the financial institutions and the MNOs. The major cost drivers of bKash include commissions on cash-in and cash-out service for both agents and distributors and the service charge of MNOs. The revenue structure model shows (Appendix C) how bKash shares the revenue collected among MNOs, Distributors, and agents. To promote its service, bKash made significant investments in above-the-line marketing through television spots, radio, and billboards.

AIDA (attention, interest, desire, and action), is an acronym used in marketing and advertising, which helps marketing managers develop effective communication strategies to respond to customer needs and desires. As per the AIDA model, bKash has already created awareness, interest, and desire among its target group. Now approaching the maturity stage of product life cycle, bKash is concentrating on doing below-the-line (BTL) marketing with distributors. bKash also provides promotional offers, cash-back bonus, and serving as payment gateway in major trade fair, book fair, retailers etc. From income statement of bKash, it spends less than 10% of its revenue on promotional purposes focusing heavily on advertisements and incentives. On a daily basis, each agent observes transactions amounting up to 70–80 thousand takas and an active user purchase frequency can be summed up to at least 500 transactions per year.

In the competitive dynamics model, bKash is still in the growth stage but it is already showing signs of maturity as it rapidly approach the mature stage. The MFS industry is not matured yet as only about 30 million users avail the services among a population of 170 million. New entrants like Rocket is only in the awareness stage where they need to heavily invest on promotion with a view to creating interest among its target group. Although bKash penetrates 75% of the existing MFS market, the MFS market in Bangladesh is still a need-based segment. Therefore, until the mobile financial services become a behavior-based market segment, bKash will still be in the growth stage.

MOVING FORWARD

bKash is still growing at a quite phenomenal rate, even after six years of operating as market leader. Moving forward, they are starting to think about what additional services can be added on, what layers they can add to that, so bKash is actually allowing a lot more population to avail a lot more financial services at once. It allows them to manage their money better, manage their lives better so it actually has potential for longer term in a big economy like Bangladesh, particularly the rural economy. Diverging their focus from rural economy, bKash is targeting the urban class to convert their services from need-based to behavior-based service. bKash expects and welcome Rocket as a market challenger and they positively look forward to face more challenges in protecting their market share. Monopolizing the MFS industry will pose adverse effect on bKash in terms of socio cultural, political, and government policy levels. Upgrading and stabilizing its technology platform to handle more volume of transactions and maintaining its reputation as secure mode of handling financials are major challenges that bKash face. Another most important challenge is the handling of fraudulent activities and money laundering that occur through MFS. Customers of the country's largest mobile financial services provider like bKash are often becoming victims of fraud and harassment and are losing money to scammers, who are sending masked SMSs.

CONCLUSION

bKash didn't go for any conventional soft launch. bKash entered the market with huge investment and a solid marketing-mix strategy. bKash has become a generic name in mobile banking in a such a way that even their nearest competitor Rocket is referred as "bKash me in the rocket account". But the questions that need answered are to penetrate all the classes in SEC segmentation what more can be done by bKash and how is bKash planning to catch the attention of their potential target group? Recent trends have seen growing number of fraudulent activities surrounding bKash. Though individual bKash account safety is maintained by bKash itself, can bKash do more to avoid these fraudulent activities?

Corporate account pricing

	Opening corporate MM account	Bank account requirement	Business to person (B2P) payments	Collection (%)	Merchant settlement costs (%)
bKash(BRAC Bank)	Free	N/A	0.5%	1.50	1.30–1.80
Rocket (DBBL)	Free	N/A	Free	1.00	1.00
mCash (Islami Bank)	Free	N/A	Free	1.30	1.50
UCash (UCBL)	Free	Must have United Commercial Bank account	Free	0.35–0.080	1.00–2.00
SureCash (Rupali Bank)	Free	Must have account with Rupali Bank	1.00%	1.00	1.00–2.00
Mobile Money (Trust Bank)	Free	Must have Trust Bank Ltd. account	Negotiable	0.50	1.00
Ok banking (One Bank)	Free	N/A	0.5%	1.50	–
Mobile banking (IFIC Bank)	Free	N/A	Free	1.30–1.80	1.35–1.80

Source USAID

Individual account pricing

	Opening corporate account	Minimum deposit /other requirements	Cash in	Cash out from agent (%)	Cash out from bank	Cash out from ATM
bKash(BRAC Bank)	Free	N/A	Free	1.85	N/A	2%
Rocket (DBBL)	Free	Minimum balance of BDT 20 required	Free	1.80	0.9%	BDT 10Tk fee per transaction
mCash (Islami Bank)	Free	N/A	Free	1.80	1.50%	Free
UCash (UCBL)	Free	N/A	Free	1.00	1.00%	Free
SureCash (Rupali Bank)	Free	N/A	1.00%	1.00	N/A	N/A
Mobile Money (Trust Bank)	Free	Introduction by a TBMM account holder required	0.50%	1.00	0.925%	N/A
Ok banking (One Bank)	Free	GP or Robi SIM required	Free	1.50	N/A	N/A
Mobile banking (IFIC Bank)	Free	N/A	Free	1.80	1.85%	N/A

APPENDIX B: REVENUE OF BKASH (IN BILLIONS OF BDT)

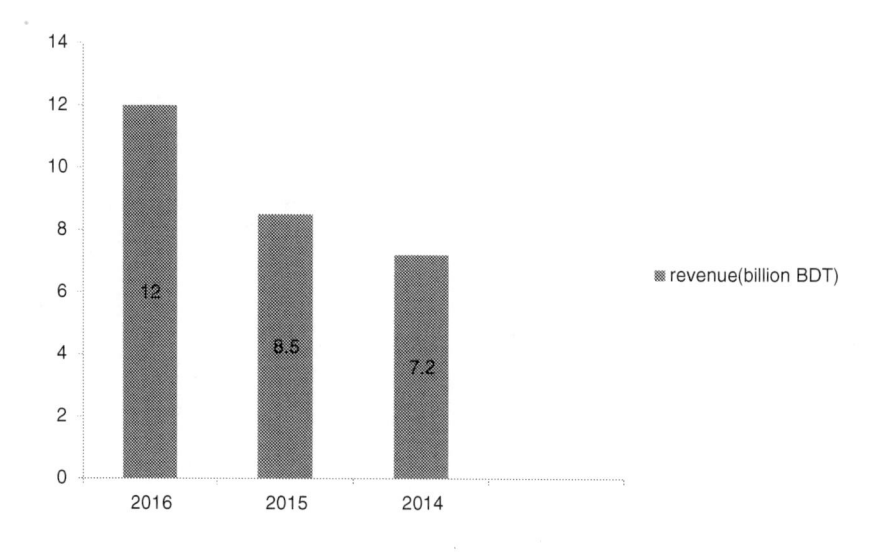

APPENDIX C: REVENUE SHARING MODEL OF BKASH

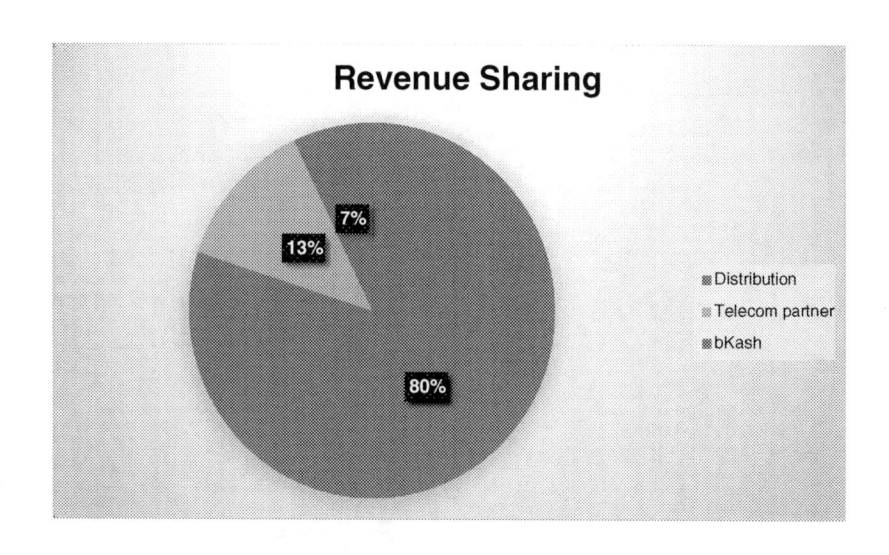

TEACHING NOTE

Synopsis

The case tells the compelling growth story of bKash Limited. Used by 22% adults of Bangladesh, a lower middle-income country with 170 million people, bKash services account for roughly 4.5 million transactions per day. Anatomy of bKash's success reveals three broad factors:

1. Targeting: On-point with the Pain Point
2. Specialized Business Model
3. Apposite Marketing Mix

The following discussion analyzes these three factors first, then moves forward with the present challenge the company is facing, and finally, analyzes on the discussion questions.

Targeting: On-point with the Pain Point

More than 70% of Bangladeshi population was living in rural areas in 2011, the year of bKash's inception, as reported by World Bank. The increasing urban migration rate has risen even more rapidly from sixty-seven (67) persons to ninety (90) persons per thousand during 2011–2015—according to Bangladesh Bureau of Statistics. This migrant population includes the working poor with strong ties with their families who are living in the village and depending on the migrant member's income. So, transferring money is a necessity to this low-income population.

Lack of financial literacy, fear toward formalized banking system, unavailability of nearby branches, and the complication of banking impose a barrier to this less educated working poor, who are unaccustomed to and uncomfortable with banking practice—and thus, often unbanked. They used to resort to the traditional alternatives, including courier services, personal contacts, post office, transport services, middlemen, etc. Security and trust issues from mishap of middleman or contacts, high costs of courier and postal services, and irregular and lengthy delivery period have prevailed in these alternatives—leaving this segment susceptible to fraud, inconvenience, lack of security, lack of financial stability, less control with their finances, and added transfer costs from third parties. This is the pain point bKash has catered to.

Specialized Business Model

bKash has developed a specialized business model in which the financial institutions provide the service, and take the compliance responsibility; MNO provide connectivity, while customers and agents use their own handsets. Ubiquitous mobile phones and favorable regulatory guidelines have been catalysts to this specialized model.

Ubiquitous Mobile Phone

Mobile phones are ubiquitous in Bangladesh. In March 2011, months before bKash's launching, the number of subscribers was almost 73 million which has doubled to 143 million in November 2017, as per Bangladesh Telecommunication Regulatory Commission data. The telecom operators had already established a nation-wide distribution channel of agents in almost every remote corner of the country—enabling the subscribers to recharge airtime at a walking distance. bKash capitalized on the already existing strong network of mobile-phone users and the agents.

Favorable Regulatory Guidelines

Government and regulatory support can be crucial factors in the highly regulated financial institution industry of a developing country where trust, security, and awareness issues are prevalent. The government's "Digital Bangladesh Vision" has aimed at the overall improvement of the daily lifestyle of general people through maximum use of technology, while "financial inclusion" initiatives target at expanding banking services to the population who are left out of formal banking and deprived of their financial services. The concept of mobile financial services industry seemed to dovetail with both the goals—paving the way for bKash and other early stage MFS companies.

Apposite Marketing Mix

bKash's marketing mix, comprised of the product, pricing, promotions, and placements, has been proven to be apposite for its targeted group.

1. *Product*: bKash's smart sequencing strategy initially focused on the simple and most needed services, like money transfer and gradually included more complex services to its offering. Well-targeted to it's less educated, tech-averse, and low-income customer, these services are affordable—with free account opening and deposit, compatible

with any economic handset with USSD, and easily usable allowing the user to transact only by typing numbers rather than typing anything in English. More importantly, it has developed trust through secure transaction, customer care, and helping agents.

2. *Price*: Free accounts with very low cost, that clearly outweighs the costs and hassle of alternative means, helped the bKash services' adoption and frequent usage.

3. *Place*: bKash utilized the already existing network of airtime recharge agents who are usually the small grocery store owners, thus, familiar faces to the community. Using this, existing network has helped bKash to be available in walking distances from almost every remote place of the country. In addition to commission from bKash transactions, these agents usually enjoy additional inflow of customers in their shop for these transactions.

4. Promotion: Attracting the less educated and low-income people who have skepticism and lack of confidence in technology—particularly with their finances—can be a daunting task in an environment where stories of fraudulent activities were abundant. This segment had the fear of losing money due to mistakes in transactions as well. bKash educated the customer through large scale awareness campaign plan which included mass advertising, street plays, short documentaries, and interactive games. The in-person usage guidance by the network of more than 120 thousand agents has further supplemented this effort.

bKash presently enjoys a dominant 75% market share. The brand name has become a generic name to Bangladeshi households who use "bKash" synonymously with mobile financial services. However, as bKash's targeted market approaches toward the urban households with middle to upper income level, amidst the rise of other MSF brands like Rocket, mCash, Ucash, etc., there is a new set of challenges for the MFS giant. Regulatory issues also make the game difficult. bKash needs to answer the following questions now:

1. How will bKash attract the urban middle-to-high income population? What can be the adoption and usage factors for this newly targeted group?

2. How can bKash better manage the fraudulent activities by scammers?

3. Can Rocket and the other competitors be a threat to bKash, especially with the competitive costs?
4. Government regulations have limited both the number and amount of transactions. How can bKash manage its impact?

Teaching Purpose and Objectives
The case provides the following lessons and insights.

- An in-depth analysis of the targeted group's pain-point can yield compelling business solutions to revolutionize their lifestyle.
- A customized and specialized business model can be innovated to serve the unique problem of the targeted group.
- It is possible for a heavily technological and complicated business process to thrive in a segment of less educated, tech-averse, unbanked population.
- Educating the customer, a seemingly costly and demanding task, can reap its benefits. Mass level campaigns with relatable stories and hand-holding were the ways in this case.
- Partnering with already existing entities, MNOs and agents in this case, can help to reach the targeted customer easily and closely through low-cost delivery channels.
- Technology needs to be adapted and usage process needs to be simplified—suiting to the customers.
- Sequencing and pricing strategy can play an important role in introducing a new concept.
- The marketing mix may need to be adjusted, even remodeled, when the company is expanding to a new market segment.

Additional Reading Suggested
The following materials are expected to help the reader better understand this case:

1. "Built for Change: Inclusive Business Solutions for the Base of the Pyramid" by International Finance Corporation, published in September 2016.
2. "Adopting mobile money: Lessons learned" by BRAC.
3. "Business Model of bKash"—a presentation by Mohammad Azmal Huda, Chief Technology Officer, bKash Limited.
4. "bKash Bangladesh: A Fast Start for Mobile Financial Services" by Gregory Chen and Stephen Rasmussen, CGAP, 2014.

Discussion Question and Analysis

Question 1: How will bKash attract the urban middle-to-high income population? What can be the adoption and usage factors for this newly targeted group?

Analysis: In the rural areas, the usage of bKash has been <u>need-based</u>. In the absence of access to finance, the working poor needed the services offered by bKash. Contrarily, with access to finance through many alternatives, the urban population is not in dire need of adopting bKash services. This banked population has a wide array of banking services, including credit and debit cards, internet banking facilities, ATMs, etc. Appealing to this urban segment to adopt <u>behavior-based</u> or lifestyle usage is the challenge.

A vital pain-point of this urban segment is the terrible traffic congestion. World Bank Analysis suggests that traffic jam in Dhaka eats up 3.2 million working hours per day. Moreover, they also need to stand in long inefficient queues for payments, deposits, and withdrawals for a variety of transactions in the densely populated Dhaka City. One area of bKash's proposition can be addressing these issues.

Probable bKash services relating the urban lifestyles

1. *Education*: Payment of tuition and other fees, admission test fees, semester fees, stipends, scholarships, etc. involving millions of students studying in thousands of urban educational institutions;
2. *Health and fitness*: Payment of fees for health services, including, doctor's appointment, medical check-ups, diagnosis, health insurance, clinic charges, hospital fees, fitness center charges, park membership fees, etc.;
3. *Utilities and other bills*: Payment of monthly bills on electricity, gas, water, internet, cable television, newspaper, etc.;
4. *Shopping and Restaurant*: Transaction with retail stores, supermarkets, shopping malls, clothing stores, groceries, stationery shops, restaurants, etc.;
5. *Entertainment*: Payment for tickets in movies, sports matches, music, dance, concerts, festivals, etc.;
6. *Transport*: Payment for tickets in bus, train, airplanes, taxi-cab services, ride-sharing services, on-demand vehicle services, etc.,

7. *Business:* Disbursement of salaries, collection of receivables, collection of revenue for small start-ups depending on distant deliveries of products and services, etc.; and
8. *Others:* Payments for citizen services like passport, trade-license, tax return, etc., remittance and cross-border transactions, etc.

Probable promotional activities to attract customers

1. *Cash-back offers* in transactions through bKash (occasion-based and promotional).
2. *Discount* from selected outlets, e.g., shopping mall, retail chain, restaurant, clothing stores, etc. when transacted through bKash (through partnership with them).
3. *Free or very low-cost installation* of bKash transaction and payroll systems in educational institutes, banks, businesses, hospitals, etc.
4. *Awareness campaigns.*
5. *Partnerships with events, festivals, contests,* etc. to manage their transactions through bKash.

The case solution is encouraged to include any other activities, innovations, and campaign plans to attract and retain the urban segment. Perception barriers of urban segments using MasterCard, Visa, or other prestigious payment platform to adopt a homegrown solution known for lower-income group can be one of the challenges bKash needs to deal with. Whether bKash can utilize the high smartphone penetration of this urban segment, without hampering the simplicity, security, and feasibility issues of this transaction process, can be another issue to work on. Appealing to the urban segments without losing the already existing rural client base needs to be strategic.

Question 2: How can bKash better manage the fraudulent activities by scammers?

Analysis: Since lack of financial and technological literacy exists in this growing stage industry, educating the people on these issues can reduce the fraudulent activities. Partnering with the regulators and other MFS providers to run awareness campaigns for the greater good of the MFS industry, collaborating with the law enforcement agencies with the detection and enforcement of the crimes, training sessions with the agents to better help the clients can be feasible ways.

bKash can also examine whether there is scope for improvement on its internal technology, monitoring layers, interface, and process to reduce the fraudulent activities—without causing much barrier or complication for the end-users.

Additional Questions and analysis:

Question 3: Can Rocket and the other competitors be a threat to bKash, specifically with the competitive costs?

Implications: The competition can indeed get tougher in the coming days. Some of the advantages bKash holds include—an already existing huge user-base, widespread network of agents, strong brand image, global recognition and reputation, strong visual presence through its banners and advertisements in every remote area of the country, etc. However, since there is no switching cost and almost uniform services with slightly lower costs seem to be rising, bKash needs to be watchful on its competitors' move. In the long run, if increased bargaining power of the end-users become inevitable, then, bKash may need to focus on the quality, costs, and differentiation points to retain its leadership.

Question 4: Government regulations have limited both the number and amount of transactions. How can bKash manage its impact?

Implications: The regulations, intended to curtail illegal activities, can affect bKash negatively. A by-product of these restrictions is likely to be the increase of its competitors' user base since the users requiring transacting higher amount than the permitted limit may resort to multiple MFS accounts. bKash can strategize to ensure that it becomes the first preference account of the MFS users. Provided bKash's dominant market position, impact, and relationship with government regulatory bodies, it can try to convince the government to further extend the limit to facilitate trade and commerce. Whether stringent monitoring measures can be effective in reducing illegal activities can be an important question to ask in this regard.

REFERENCES

Chen, G., & Rasmussen, S. (July 2014). bKash Bangladesh: A Fast Start for Mobile Financial Service. CGAP.

Ivatury, G., & Pickens, M. (2006). *Mobile Phone Banking and Low Income Customers*, s.l.: CGAP.

Kaniz Fatema Nourin Choudhury, D. U. A. (December 2016). *Overview of bKash*, s.l.: Academia.edu.

Parvez, J., Ariful, I., & Josh, W. (April 2015). *Mobile Financial Services in Bangladesh*, s.l.: United States Agency for International Development (USAID).

Tiwari, R., & Buse, S. (June 2007). *The Mobile Commerce Prospects: A Strategic Analysis of Opportunities in the Banking Sector*. Hamburg: Hamburg University Press.

Wambari, A. (2009). Mobile Banking in Developing Countries (a Case Study on Kenya). *Theseus.fi*. Issue. http://urn.fi/URN:NBN:fi:amk-200910094875.

Waverman, L., Meschi, M., & Fuss, M. (2005). *The Impact of Telecoms on Economic Growth in Developing Countries*, s.l.: Researchgate.

to deposit, withdraw, transfer money, and pay for goods and services. With the spurt in mobile phone subscription among Kenyan rural and urban populations, by 2010, M-Pesa had become the most successful mobile phone-based financial service in the developing world. M-Pesa has been lauded for providing unbanked people access to the formal financial system and for reducing crime in otherwise largely cash-based societies (Ivatury and Pickens 2006).

Studies have demonstrated the positive influence of mobile phone penetration in developing countries by playing a crucial role in boosting GDP growth. However, initial analysis of mobile banking systems suggest the need for better marketing and training to help consumers understand the capability of the system, as well as develop improved policy measures to ensure that the benefits of mobile banking are evenly distributed across all banking and consumer sectors (Waverman 2005).

How MFS Affected Bangladesh

Considering the scenario of Bangladesh where majority of the rural population is illiterate or has little academic knowledge, conventional banking system is neither useful nor user friendly for them. To open and maintain a bank account for personal purposes, one needs to be equipped with basic academic knowledge. Rural and remote areas of Bangladesh have provision of branches of government run banks, but those are rarely used for personal bank accounts. The boost in Readymade garments sector saw the rise of another issue. The population migrating from their hometowns in rural areas to work in cities like Dhaka and Chittagong started facing the difficulties of sending money home on a regular basis. Government postal service provides money order services, which is not cost effective for these customer bases. Sending small amount of money disguised as letters became popular and with came more cases of stolen/lost amounts. As it was an illegal process, therefore, no provisions or steps of safeguarding were offered. Also with the invent of newer technologies, both the postal system and quality of their service became obsolete. Another measure taken was to send money via people travelling to desired locations or help of bus services and other transportation modes. Sending money home became a troublesome and less secured process. MFS in Bangladesh owe a lot of their success to these small earners. The in-country remittance earners became the target market of MFS providers and a large customer base like this is

Pakwheels.com—A Period of Transition!

Farrah Arif and Sarah Suneel Sarfraz

INTRODUCTION

It was mid-July 2015 and with the monsoon rains in the background, Raza Saeed and Suneel Munj, the cofounders and managing partners of Pakwheels.com were thinking about the company's growth strategy for 2016 for the upcoming investor meeting, on the way to their office in Gulberg.[1] Finally, after ten years of starting the business, in December 2014, they had secured a funding of $3.5 million from Frontier Digital Ventures, which was a Malaysian venture capital fund focused on online platform businesses in the developing markets. Moreover, just when they thought that they were ready to develop an aggressive growth strategy, they received unsettling news. Their legal counsel informed them about a possibility of a discriminating cybercrime prevention bill called Prevention of Electronic Crimes Act (PECA) which was in the approval process by the national assembly of Pakistan. Moreover, there was a speculation about their main

---

[1] Gulberg is the Central Business District of Lahore, Pakistan.

F. Arif (✉) · S. S. Sarfraz
Lahore University of Management Sciences, Lahore, Pakistan
e-mail: Farrah@lums.edu.pk

S. S. Sarfraz
e-mail: sarah.sarfraz@lums.edu.pk

A. Sikdar and V. Pereira (eds.), *Business and Management Practices in South Asia*, https://doi.org/10.1007/978-981-13-1399-8_7

competitor, OLX[2] that it would be launching a huge and expensive three-week long media campaign of about $0.5 million to introduce its used car section in the local market.

Pakwheels.com was the market leader in the country's growing online classified automobile market. The website had been growing at an ideal trajectory and with the foreign investment Saeed and Munj were all set to make PakWheels a billion-dollar start-up in the next few years—a goal that had kept them from accepting acquisition offers from foreign companies so far. However, the threat of the PECA and OLX was looming in the background, while the PakWheels team was putting together a strategy to move forward for the Malaysian investor. "There was no doubt in anybody's mind that PakWheels success was based on the huge and diverse number of members and their freedom of speech at the discussion forums which generates immense consumer engagement and loyalty. They not only take pride in the website's achievements but also regularly contribute to the forums. We even have a founding members group in which a group of loyal members who have been with us for more than ten years are included, and they voluntarily represent the website at various forums," explained Saeed. Saeed feared that censoring, filtering, and controlling the forums could seriously hurt the community engagement at PakWheels. Apart from some splendid things like the good security controls, there were some ambiguous clauses in PECA 2015 that might adversely affect local technology businesses. If PECA 2015 was implemented in its strictest form, there was a strong possibility that the community rules would be made strict, and a certain percentage of loyal members would be lost. The bill's threatening elements included provisions that would allow the government to censor online content, criminalize internet user activity based on extremely broad criteria susceptible to abusive interpretation, and permit government access to the data of internet users without being approved by any form of judicial review process. These elements if implemented might be detrimental to technology-based businesses.

Similarly, OLX being a horizontal portal was not a direct competitor of PakWheels, but one of its sections was about buying and selling used automobiles, thus making it an indirect threat to the business. Munj explained, "Although we rely heavily on our loyal community members and their positive word of mouth, this will not be sustainable for long. For the first

---

[2]A horizontal online classifieds marketplace for used goods such as furniture, musical instruments, sporting goods, cars, youngster and baby items, motorcycles, cameras, mobile phones, property etc.

time in the history of Pakistan, we are seeing online brands deploying significant advertising budgets for mainstream media advertising. To compete with these deep-pocketed international giants, such as OLX, for a share of voice (SOV) was going to be a challenge for us".

Going forward, Saeed and Munj would have to decide the best way to scale up their business utilizing the investment fund in an efficient manner. However, before that might happen, they knew they needed to lay out a clear and compelling strategy which would create the most value for the business and its stakeholders by asking some tough questions. What should PakWheels team do to retain community engagement culture if PECA 2015 gets implemented in the country? Should they match OLX media budgets and respond with their ATL campaign? Alternatively, maybe just wait and strengthen their basic product and technology and see how the market changes in the future.

INITIAL YEARS

PakWheels was started on 18 July 2003 in Karachi, Pakistan by Hanif Bhatti, a businessman, and Jagdesh Pahuja, an IT professional. The reason for the start-up was to provide a platform to car enthusiasts to list their cars for sale and discuss about their shared interests in cars.

A modest amount of money was spent on domain and hosting. However, as the founders were interested in helping the small community of PakWheels members and thus treated them as a family. Soon this made people to start joining in by the numbers. In 2003, there was no social media available to advertise the launching of a website, so the only thing through which the website could be advertised was its content. PakWheels grew organically with people logging into the website, asking questions, getting helpful answers, posting reviews and pictures, and commenting on others. Soon, with more people joining the community, PakWheels became Pakistan's largest community of automotive enthusiasts.

In the early years of PakWheels, the few users from outside Pakistan were mostly non-resident Pakistanis residing abroad but having deep ties to Pakistan's auto scene. To develop bonding among the members of PakWheels, Bhatti and Pahuja organised PakWheels' first get-together in Karachi, which was a huge success. Soon, members in other cities also started organizing "Pakwheel Meets" in their cities as well.

Within five years of inception, Pakwheels.com had become one of the few leading brands in Pakistan's internet economy based on good overall business performance driven by an increasing online community and soaring website traffic. Their business model was quite basic, it did not charge the visitors, but some fee was charged for banner advertisements on the website. They were so committed to developing the community that they kept on investing back into the website. Besides this, PakWheels also spent a small amount to distribute stickers among community members for promotion of the portal.

ACQUISITION

Though Bhatti and Pahuja wanted PakWheels to grow but they did not have the requisite resources and time to devote, and felt the need for extra hands to manage the rapidly growing community. Fortunately for them, two young entrepreneurs in Lahore, both LUMS[3] alumni, were looking for new ventures to invest in. They were Muhammad Raza Saeed, a technology entrepreneur, and his friend Suneel Sarfaraz Munj, a car enthusiast and a businessman.

In US and Europe, businesses had started using paid vertical classifieds[4] on internet, e.g., job sites and free horizontal classified[5] sites like Craigslist,[6] eBay[7] etc. Although there was potential for similar opportunity in Pakistan, there was no Craigslist and eBay in Pakistan. Pakwheels.com, built on the same model as horizontal classifieds, seemed a perfect fit for Munj and Saeed, given their relevant

---

[3]Lahore University of Management Sciences (LUMS) is a privately owned institute based in Lahore, Pakistan. It is one of the top ranked universities in Pakistan (source: www. lums.edu.pk).

[4]A vertical classified market: vendors offer goods and services specific to an industry, trade, profession or a group of customers with specialized needs.

[5]A horizontal classified market: vendors offer a wide range of goods and services to a large group of customers with a wide range of needs.

[6]Craigslist is a horizontal classified advertisements website devoted to jobs, housing, personals for sale, items wanted, services, community, gigs, résumés, and discussion forums. It started from San Francisco bay area and then expanded to other U.S. cities in 2000, and now covers 70 countries.

[7]eBay Inc. is an American multinational corporation and horizontal ecommerce company, providing consumer to consumer and business to consumer sales services via internet. It is headquartered in San Jose, California with operations localized in over thirty countries (source: www.ebay.com).

backgrounds with cars and software development. After numerous interactions with Bhatti, the duo acquired Pakwheels.com in December 2008. The office was shifted from Karachi to Lahore.

Led by Munj and Saeed, PakWheels grew to a 250 employee company in July 2015 with over 350,000 registered members, and the website receiving every month 20 million hits[8] from two million visitors[9] and 45,000 automobile listings. Thus, PakWheels had become the most credible website for buying and selling of automobiles, and related news.

INDUSTRY SNAPSHOT

In 2015, there were approximately 3 million cars in Pakistan with 170,000 new cars added each year in addition to imported cars.[10] Annually, more than 600,000 of these cars were traded, with about 20% of these trades being done online. Almost 75% of PakWheels' listings were from Karachi, Lahore, and Islamabad, the three major cities of Pakistan.

With the advent of 3G/4G services, the current 30 million internet users in Pakistan are expected to grow to 100 million by 2020.[11] Also by 2020, current per capita car ownership of thirteen cars per 1000 people is expected to grow from it's to sixteen–seventeen cars per 1000 people, according to the World Bank analysts. So this growth in auto industry and internet population could provide excellent growth opportunities for automotive portals of Pakistan.

CONVENTIONAL "USED" CAR TRADE

Before the advent of online car portals in Pakistan, people traded their cars by relying on used car dealers, newspaper classified ads, and weekly used car markets. According to All Pakistan Motor Dealers Association

---

[8] Hits: an individual landing on the website through online advertisement or any other online sources and then leaving.

[9] Visitors: people who actually browse and spend time exploring various sections of the website.

[10] http://www.pama.org.pk/statistical-information/historical-information/annual-sales-production/ and http://data.worldbank.org/indicator.

[11] http://knoema.com/atlas/Pakistan/Internet-users-percent-of-population and http://knoema.com/atlas/Pakistan/Internet-users-per-100-inhabitants.

(APMDA), there were 4000 car dealers in Pakistan dealing in both new and used cars, as on January 2015. These car dealers mostly worked on three different business models:

1. **Broker Model**: The seller got his/her car listed at the dealer's showroom. The dealer acts a broker and tries to find a buyer and when the sale is made, the dealer charges a commission.
2. **Investor Model**: The dealer buys the car from a seller and tries to sell it at a profit to a buyer, thus making money on the transaction.
3. **Importer Model**: This is similar to the investor model where the dealer imports used cars from different countries and sell at a profit to buyers.

However, conventional car trade provided lot of challenges for the buyer and the seller. The buyer has to visit multiple dealer showrooms to find the desired car and pay a higher price than actual market value because of the dealer's margin. Similarly, the seller has to leave the car with the dealer for an extended period of time till it found a buyer or sell the car to the dealer at a discount to the actual market value.

Using newspaper classified meant that buyers had to sift through thousands of advertisements with no proper categorisation. As there was no detailed picture in the classifieds, often the buyers faced disappointment as actual inspection of the car did not meet what they wanted. For sellers, sometimes the advertisements were not noticed due to clutter and many unwanted calls were received to see more details, which were not possible to be included in the advertisement. Classified advertisements in newspaper (see Exhibit 1a) costs an average of Rs. 500 per twenty words and Rs. 25 per subsequent word, so often the price paid did not provide the value sought.

Weekly car markets ran only on Sundays, which meant that buyers and sellers have to take a complete day off, without any guarantee whether it would lead to a fruitful deal. Also, these markets had no categorization of car make and model, so there is a chance of the same type of car being available in better condition and less price in another part of the market, making the buyers miss out on a good bargain.

Further, as there was no rating or review system for dealers and individual sellers, there was lack of transparency and reliability. Some of the dealers also engaged in illegal and unethical behaviors by reversing the

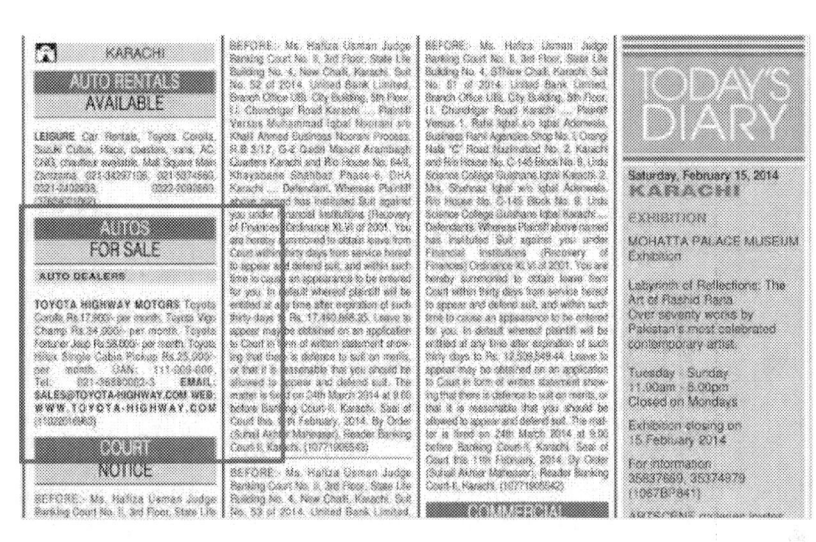

Exhibit 1 **a** Newspaper vehicle classified in 2008 (*Source* Online DAWN news classifieds from archives). **b** Pakwheels.com screenshot from 2008 (*Source* Company data)

car odometer reading to show that car has run less kilometres and thus fetch a better price. So buyers had no reliable way to evaluate the car's quality other than relying on their own judgement.

PRODUCT DEVELOPMENT

Since Pakwheels.com was designed in 2003, there have been few changes and features added to the website until 2008 (see Exhibit 1b), but the basic technology has not been updated from the obsolete ASP/ Windows, which was inflexible to new changes. Soon after acquisition in 2008, the technology was upgraded to modern web development. This dramatically changed the appearance of PakWheels making it more user-friendly and modern, without affecting the core features of vehicle listing remained unchanged (see Exhibit 2).

Over the years, based on user experience, PakWheels had completely redesigned the platform to create certain changes, as follows:

1. to enable easier access, launched mobile applications for all major platforms (iPhone, Android, and Windows);
2. to enable users to access the website from their smartphone, enabled the website for smartphone browsers;
3. to increase user conversion, simplified advertisement posting process; and
4. to ensure the highest quality listings only, improved the advertisement verification process through automated tools.

Also, to enhance the user experience of searching for cars, multiple functionalities were added such as on-road price tool (calculates total cost of ownership including taxes and registration charges), car comparisons, expert reviews, car specs, and prices, etc.

Currently, PakWheels had the most comprehensive automotive content available on the internet. These product features and technology upgrades have led Pakwheels.com to win many prestigious awards such as *Local Brand of the Year Award 2013, IT National Excellence Award Teradata 2013 and Teradata 2014,* and *International Arabia 500 Fast Growth.*

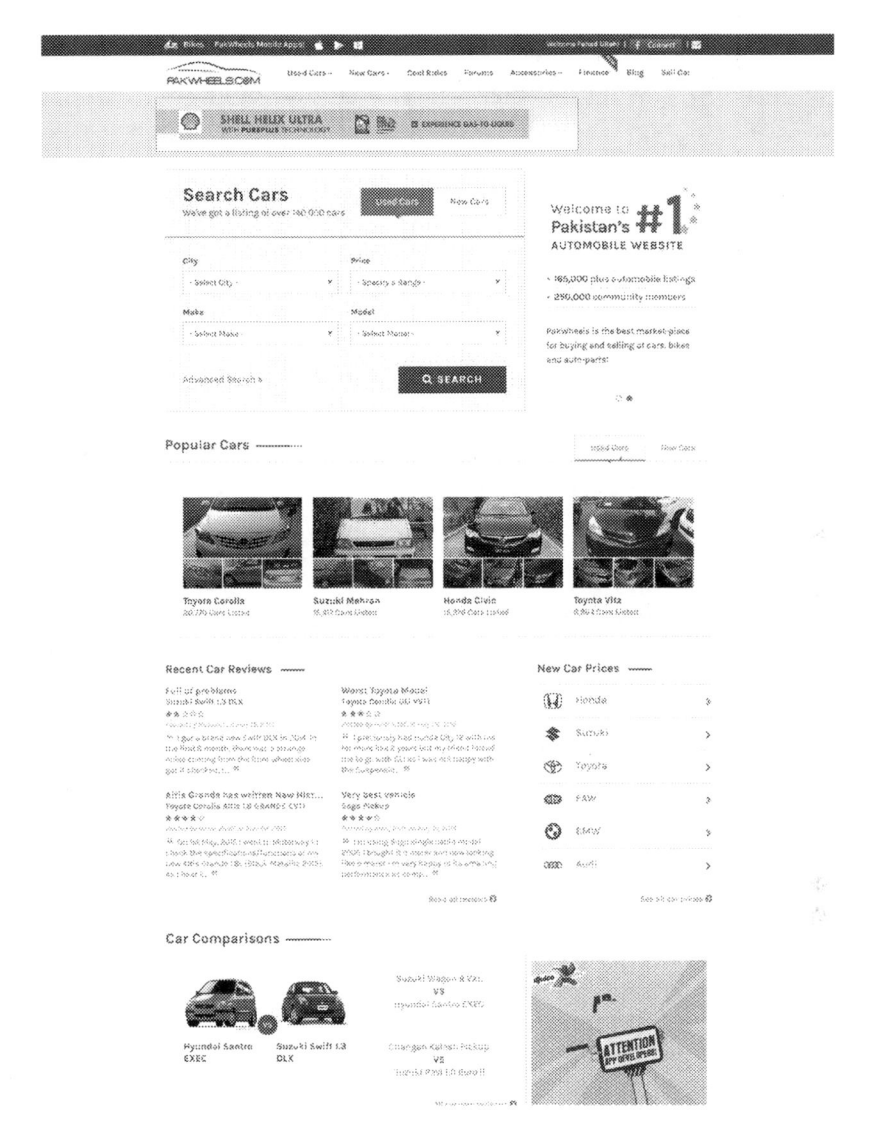

Exhibit 2 Pakwheels.com screenshot from 2015 (*Source* Company data)

Value Creation Through Customer Engagement

"When we bought the website, people discouraged us because trading online, especially such a high involvement product like cars and bikes was unheard of locally. However, we believed that this problem could be overcome by social interaction. In Pakistan, especially, it is crucial to have trust in the people you are interacting with", Saeed recalled.[12] Therefore, to enhance customer engagement, PakWheels introduced social interaction through Facebook and Twitter, ability to see pictures and videos, and mobile apps to access from any Windows, iOS, or Android device.

PakWheels team also considered that the quality of the content they created was critical for success. At the time of acquisition, advertisements were not reviewed so inaccurate information was getting uploaded. To safeguard the quality of the content, every single advertisement and pictures before it went live was reviewed and approved by a dedicated six-member team, created for this purpose. Also the authenticity of the user was verified before every listing went live. The website also had an option of reporting digital abuse (e.g., indecent comments, wrong information, etc.), which was a huge problem in the classified businesses. So it was not possible on PakWheels to post anything or provide a fake phone number, in contrast to other local horizontal classifieds (such as OLX, Dekho, Asani, etc.). Also, through Facebook Connect, PakWheels could indicate whether the buyer and seller have any common contacts. This created a trust in the system. To create trust amongst the customers, PakWheels also introduced a review and rating system for car dealers.

The majority of Pakwheels.com traffic (i.e., visitors) came for classifieds. However, the user forums provided the differentiation and were pivotal in PakWheels' growing. These user forums brought automobile enthusiasts a place to connect with each other and share their passion about cars and discuss problems related to their cars.

PakWheels launched an auto blog that was managed through hired professional auto journalists and content editors. The blog posted car reviews, news, opinions, and other information that resulted in creating significant awareness about PakWheels brand. In different cities, PakWheels also organized multiple large scales auto shows annually and

---

[12] https://aurora.dawn.com/news/1140680.

small meets fortnightly so that the users could know each other personally. PakWheels also started partnering with other auto-related events that saw large turnout of 30,000–40,000 people. All these activities reinforced PakWheels' community development efforts.

To increase listings on the PakWheels platform, it was decided to engage with the car dealers. The dealers in Pakistan controlled the largest inventory of used cars but most had very low awareness about internet and technology. PakWheels focused on educating dealers that by posting their used car inventory on PakWheels website they would get more customers as buyers would have a larger pool of cars to choose from.

"As an individual you do not buy a car every day, you buy one, and then you come back after three years. So how do we retain you?" Munj stated and then reflected about their engagement strategy. The website allowed keeping the maintenance history that would then remind the consumer about maintenance requirements. This feature was built into the mobile apps (both Android and iOS), for the "marketplace" and for "forums and blog" (see Exhibit 3). Additionally to help people with buying decisions, PakWheels had developed blogs and plenty of content in their new car section. Saeed commented, "we believe that the more choices the customers have, the more it will become necessary to research and PakWheels is trying to cater to this at every phase: research, transaction, maintenance, and finally sales. In maintenance, we have launched a 'road runner service,' new feature in trial mode, in which the customers have a PakWheels representative pick up the road tax documents and do the filing by charging a nominal fee. The idea was that anyone who planned to, or owned a vehicle should have a reason to come to PakWheels."[13]

Despite launching all these services, a key hurdle of buying and selling car was the inability to find out the optimal price and quality of a used car. So in February 2015, PakWheels started work on developing "CarSure" (certification) to provide a comprehensive car inspection report for the benefit of the car buyers. This program has now been launched in three major cities and was bringing in good results. "What matters the most in our business is that you have a critical mass of buyers

---

[13] https://aurora.dawn.com/news/1140680. Excerpt from an interview by Raza Saeed.

 App Store

Pakwheels: Buy and Sell Cars | App Store | Free |

Pakwheels Forums App Store | Free

Exhibit 3 Separate logos for Pakwheels marketplace and community forums (*Source* Company data)

Profiles		Brand Awareness
Forums		Engagement
Activity Streams		Lead Generation
Social Graph	accelerate and	Lead Qualification
Collaboration	transform	Sales Operations
Social Analytics		Customer Service
Tagging and Bookmarking		Innovation
Blogging		Product Development
Messaging		Supply Chain Mgmt

Exhibit 4 Digital marketing model for PakWheels (*Source* Company data)

and sellers. We are not quite there yet in Pakistan, but we're definitely on our way, and these loyal followers are our biggest assets, and we would do everything to keep them around." Munj said assertively.

BUSINESS MODEL OF PAKWHEELS

From a standalone website, PakWheels upgraded itself to become a comprehensive vertical automotive portal that deals primarily with used car classifieds and community forums.

PakWheels' business model created value by reducing search and transaction costs in the interactions happening between vehicle buyers and sellers. As a portal, PakWheels created an ecosystem for auto services—all information on buying, selling, researching, auxiliary services, etc. one should find at Pakwheels.com. With the advent of connected technology (e.g., smartphones, 3G services, etc.), the networked ecosystems enabled PakWheels' business model to scale-up, which was not possible for a traditional used car dealer model.

Majority of PakWheels' revenue came from website services that were used by related businesses like local car dealers, and advertisements from corporate clients like Shell, Zic, General Tyres, etc. The customer to customer (C2C) interaction was facilitated as a free business model keeping in mind user convenience. So, PakWheels made almost no money from the C2C interactions. PakWheels focus was on value creation through the delivery of services and products, rather than on profits.

For businesses related to automobiles, Pakwheels.com's traffic was the direct target segment for their businesses' messages and products. So sponsors came to PakWheels on their own, without PakWheels having to go out in search of sponsors. PakWheels attracted traffic by focusing primarily on listings, on-line blogs, content formation, tools for comparison, price reviews etc., and then generated multiple streams of revenue, as shown below.

On-Site Advertising: Pakwheels.com used on-site advertising to generate a steady stream of revenue. On-Site Advertising was done in two ways. **Google Advertisements**: Using Google AdSense,[14] PakWheels

---

[14] AdSense (Google AdSense) is an advertising placement service by Google. The program is designed for website publishers who want to display targeted text, video or image advertisements on website pages and earn money when site visitors view or click the ads.

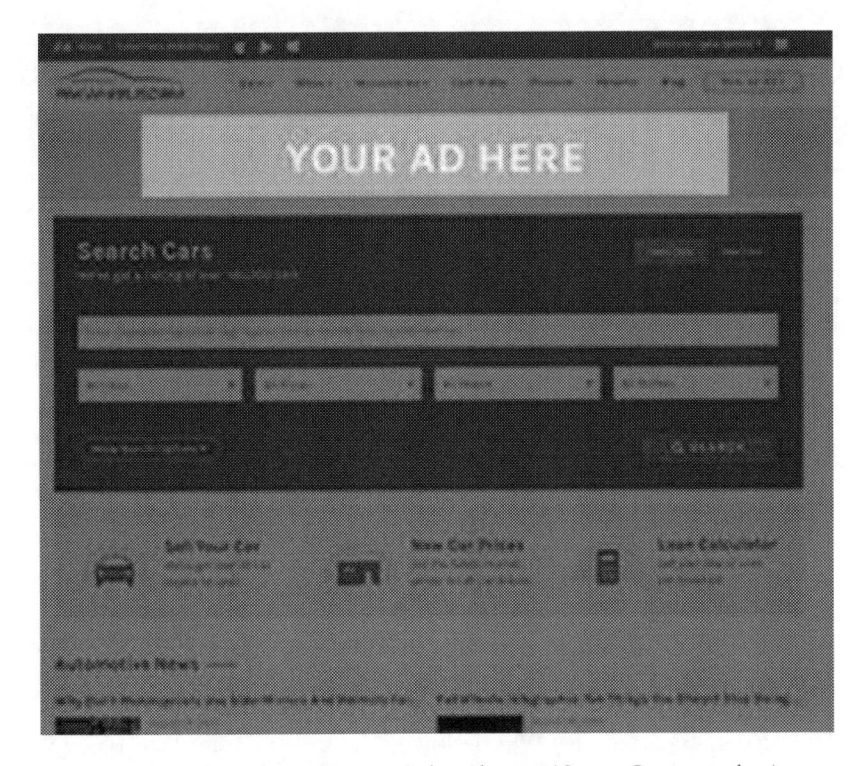

Exhibit 5   CTA sample position on Pakweels.com (*Source* Company data)

allowed Google to display advertisements of its partners. PakWheels provided the banner space and Google decided on the nature of advertisement content to be displayed for each user, based on the user's browsing history profile. **PakWheels Managed Advertisements**: PakWheels sold banner space directly to its partners/sponsors. Here, PakWheels exercised full control over these advertisements and what was shown was not dependent on user's browsing history but on PakWheels' discretion.

Lead Generation: PakWheels allowed different institutions and corporates to strategically place their call to actions (CTAs) on various sections of the PakWheels website (see Exhibit 5). This helped the institutions generate lead for their business. For example, "book a test drive" tab on Honda Pakistan's website provided link to a form that the potential buyer fills out to book a test drive.

Featured Advertisements: This allowed sellers to get maximum attention from the potential buyers by having their car advertisement highlighted for a week, PakWheels charged a small fee (e.g., Rs. 1000) for this service. The Featured Advertisement remained on the website's main page for a week and also got displayed in the top search results.

Dealership Packages: According to Munj, "Car dealers had very different needs than normal users when it came to selling their cars." To keep the dealers on board, PakWheels offered tailored packages to car dealers to grow their businesses as partners of PakWheels. These packages include making websites for the dealers with their desired domain name linked directly to the back end of PakWheels website. This allowed PakWheels to get automatic update of dealer's inventory. PakWheels also helped dealer's setup Facebook page for a dealer which allowed the dealer post updated information.

Content Marketing through PakWheels Blog: By partnering with international and local automakers and auto-parts manufacturers, PakWheels provide them an opportunity to connect with their customers through PakWheels website. For example, PakWheels had a Tyre Guide section sponsored by General Tyre Limited, and an Oil Guide section sponsored by Shell Pakistan. PakWheels' editorial team promoted sponsored and branded content to educate the blog readers.

Offline Advertisement through Auto Shows: Annually, auto shows were organized by PakWheels in six cities across Pakistan, that attracted hundreds of vehicles and visitors. These auto shows provided excellent branding opportunities and thus were sponsored by various brands. Some of the major sponsors of these auto shows in the past were Telenor, Warid, Shell, Mobilink, Pepsi, and Punjab[15] Government.

KEY METRICS FOR EVALUATION

As PakWheels had decided not to charge for website transactions, they evaluated performance not based on profits and revenue generation but based traffic generation and customer engagement, which would eventually translate into higher growth and profits. The following key performance indicators (KPIs) were used for the internal evaluation:

---

[15] Punjab is the biggest province of Pakistan.

1. **Sessions**: The number of people using the website during a given time period (e.g., hour, day, week, etc.). A higher number thus signified good performance of the website. The number of sessions per month had increased from approximately 0.2 million in 2008 to over 2.8 million by January 2015.
2. **Page Views**: The number of times a web page was viewed. More page views were considered desirable as it gave a website and its advertising partners more exposure. In a given month, PakWheels received more than 20 million page views on average. For PakWheels, the average number of page views per session was between seven and eight.
3. **Listings**: The number of used cars uploaded for sale on PakWheels website by the sellers. More the number of listings, more the number of options that was available to buyers to find their preferred choice. Currently, PakWheels has over 150,000 listings on its website with an average monthly turnover of 50,000 cars. While at the time acquisition in 2008, PakWheels only had 1800 cars listed.

PROMOTIONAL ACTIVITIES

According to the PakWheels team, digital marketing was not only about technology but also about creating engaging experiences for visitors through innovative ideas. It was about providing useful services and products to consumers rather tham creating a marketing slogan or jingle. Thus, PakWheels promotion was planned keeping the end customer in mind, such that promotional activities and delivery of services became virtually inseparable.

To have a better understanding of its end customer, in 2013, PakWheels conducted a survey of 6000 of used car buyers. The 2014 edition of the survey was a big improvement over that of 2013, with almost double the number of respondents. The objective of the survey was to better understand market trends like top consideration before buying cars, what attributes customers preferred, most popular lubricants, insurance companies, etc.? (See Exhibit 6). For example, the survey identified that in Pakistan, 76% of the cars were uninsured, and very few cars had a tracker system. These type of trends provided opportunities for PakWheels' to exploit for new business options.

The survey captured users' perceptions about different car brands, which gave an insight into how people perceived different brands

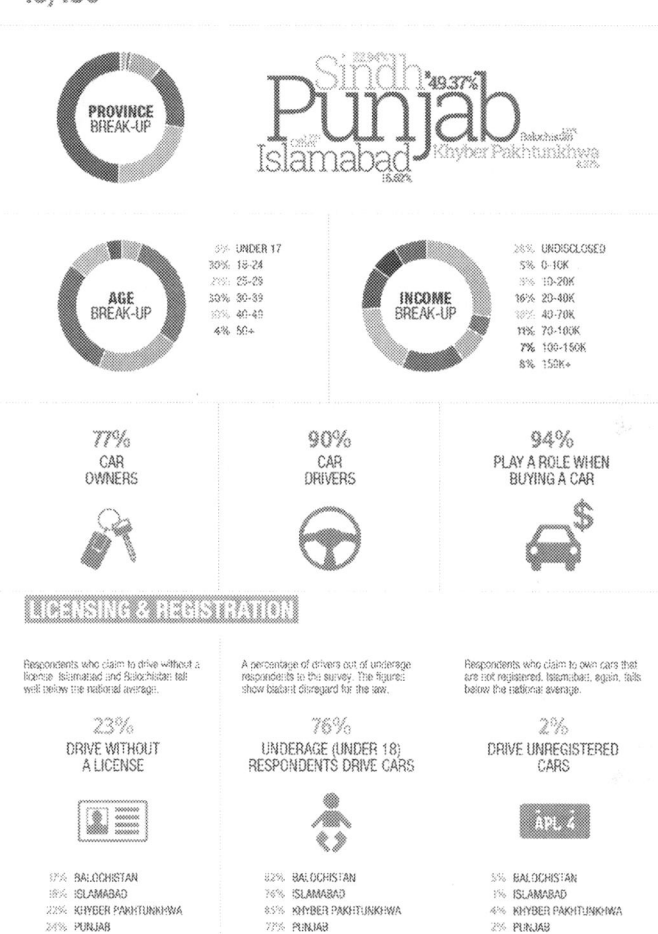

Exhibit 6 **a** Automobile industry survey results 2014. **b** Automobile industry survey results 2015. **c** Automobile industry survey results 2014 (*Source* http://www.pakwheels.com/awards/2014/survey)

IMPORTANT ASPECTS WHEN CHOOSING A CAR

Participants were asked to rate the importance of the following 11 aspects when buying a car. Contrary to popular belief, resale scored less than safety and fuel efficiency.

1. DRIVE/RIDE QUALITY
2. FUEL EFFICIENCY
3. COMFORT

4. VALUE FOR MONEY
5. SAFETY
6. INTERIOR FEATURES & ACCESSORIES
7. INTERIOR DESIGN

8. EXTERIOR DESIGN
9. RESALE
10. COST OF OWNERSHIP
11. AFTERSALES SERVICE

PRICES & SPENDING

55%
USE SECOND
HAND CARS

32%
USE BRAND
NEW CARS

24% NEW CARS WERE BOUGHT THROUGH CAR FINANCING OR A LOAN

65% NEW CARS WERE BOUGHT THROUGH FULL CASH PAYMENT UP FRONT

SPENT ON BUYING A CAR

50% SPENT < PKR 1 MILLION
30% SPENT < PKR 2 MILLION
7% SPENT < PKR 5 MILLION
3% SPENT > PKR 5 MILLION
10% DID NOT DISCLOSE THIS INFORMATION

80% of respondents spent under PKR 2 Million on buying a car. Only 10% spent over PKR 2 Million.

Exhibit 6   (continued)

available in Pakistan. The data provided useful information regarding consumer behavior in Pakistan's automobile industry, and helped PakWheels formulate customer-driven marketing strategies and communication[16] (see Exhibit 6).

PakWheels carried out digital marketing campaigns (see Exhibit 4 *for web-based activities*). In-house experts at PakWheels employed proven techniques like SEO,[17] paid search marketing,[18] and remarketing[19] to

[16] https://www.slideshare.net/PakWheels/pakwheels-autom?qid=a-4fa7430-255c-44f8-8345-ee29c1badc83&v=&b=&from_search=2 (company documents).

[17] Search engine optimization (SEO): process of improving traffic to a given website by increasing the site's visibility in search engine results (source: www.businessdictionary.com).

[18] Paid search marketing: company advertising within the sponsored listings of a search engine or a partner site by paying either each time the company's advertisement is clicked (*pay-per-click—PPC*) or when the company's advertisement is displayed (*cost-per-impression—CPM*) (source: www.econsultancy.com).

[19] Remarketing: to re-engage with site visitors based on their behaviour on prior visits by using a banner advertisement on a third party site, e.g., google.com (source: www.support.google.com)

minima competition faced, PakWheels did not require to use above the line (ATL) promotion (e.g., TVCs, Ads in newspapers and magazines, etc.). In 2014, PakWheels had a budget of about $0.3 million for online marketing.

PakWheels marketing campaigns also involved below the line (BTL) activities like sponsorships, events, public relations. In 2014, PakWheels budgeted $0.4 million for BTL activities and branding of car dealers' showrooms in Lahore, Karachi, and Islamabad/Rawalpindi, with the objective to have visibility and top of mind (TOM) recall amongst buyers and sellers. Till December 2014, approximately 3800 dealer showrooms across Pakistan were co-branded with PakWheels colours and logo. Similar co-branding was done for auto workshops, spare part dealers, and parking plazas. Every car sold by a partner dealer was provided with a PakWheels' sticker to create visibility for PakWheels. According to PakWheels' team, "It was reassuring to observe that every third car/bike in Lahore on average had PakWheels bumper sticker." Due to these successful BTL campaigns, PakWheels was gaining visibility in major cities.

In 2012, a classified magazine was also launched to support online sales. The magazine was made available for free at all popular cafes, petrol stations, metro outlets, etc. To build greater visibility, BTL initiatives involving taxi branding, rickshaw branding, marketing collateral deals with institutes, and agencies were also initiated. To fully capitalize the online opprtunity, external agencies were hired to evaluate online campaigns. PakWheels' spent approximately $0.7 million annually on its marketing budget, including car shows and road trips.

Combining ATL advertising and BTL promotion and exploring more than one medium of marketing would be have been prohibitively costly for PakWheels in the past. However, with the foreign investment, PakWheels can now think about doing so to take on the competition.

COMPETITIVE LANDSCAPE

Internationally, a $110 billion plus business, classified websites were fast becoming the new form of how sellers and buyers found each other. Websites like Rozee.pk (new employee), Hafeezcenter.pk (sell mobile phone), Zameen.com (buy plot or new home), OLX, and now Pakwheels.com were increasingly becoming a popular choice. The fact that all these websites were easy to use and free of transaction fee, made them very valuable to both potential buyers and sellers. So industry analysts were foreseeing stiff competition and an explosive growth of online businesses in the coming years in Pakistan.

As a vertical classified portal (specialised automobile portal), PakWheels had not faced any direct or indirect competition since its inception. Only in 2009, it faced real competition with the entry of OLX in the local market. OLX was a general classified website funded by South African mega media group—Nasper. Subsequently, this was followed by the entry of other classified websites like Asani, Daraz.com, Keymu, foodpanda.com, Carmudi, etc. (see Exhibit 7a, b).

Raza strongly believed that reaching a critical mass of buyers and sellers is the real challenge, than creating a website or marketplace. According to Raza, "some of these sites were just going to the power sellers (the dealerships) to accumulate listings, but that did not help. The portal could not have sellers without buyers because eventually the sellers would stop coming to the site. There was ApniGari, Carmudi, Autotrader, etc., but PakWheels was light years ahead of them. The real competition was from the horizontal classifieds like OLX."[20]

According to a tool called Similarweb.com,[21] other than the newspaper websites, PakWheels was the largest indigenous Pakistani website larger than all the other verticals, including Rozee[22] and Zameen.[23] OLX was the only non-news/media site that was larger than PakWheels (see Exhibit 8).

OLX was a global classified portal operating in 100 countries. In Pakistan, OLX was the leader with 5.2[24] million visitors every month compared to PakWheels' two million visitors. Being a horizontal portal, though OLX did not pose a direct threat to PakWheels' but it's used-car section was becoming popular, and had become the third-largest Section (15,784 ads), after mobiles and tablets (34,562 ads) and electronics and computers (22,688 ads). In Pakistan, OLX had invested majorly in TV-based marketing and advertising to target the non-internet users.

---

[20] https://aurora.dawn.com/news/1140680.

[21] Similarweb.com is an information technology company founded in March 2009. They provide services in web analytics, data mining and business intelligence for international corporations. It uses big data technologies to collect, measure, and analyze and provides user engagement statistics for websites and mobile apps.

[22] A vertical job classified website.

[23] A vertical real estate classified website.

[24] 5.2 million were the users of the entire horizontal portal, which included job classifieds, real-estate classifieds, auto classifieds and others such as electronics, households, etc.

Exhibit 7   a Competitive landscape snapshot—international investment groups and their brands. **b** Selected local start-ups (*Source* Excerpts taken from "The Digital Start Up Report, Pakistan 2014" http://www.slideshare.net/fullscreen/ WorldStartupReport/pakistan-startup-report/17)

Traffic Overview (Estimated Visits in Past 6 months)

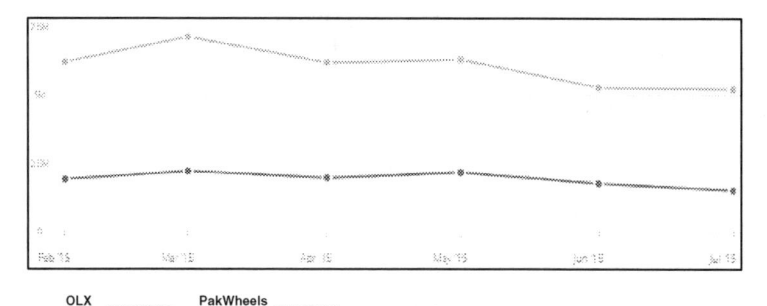

OLX .... PakWheels ....

Engagement

	PakWheels	OLX
Visits	1.5M	5.2M
Time Spent on-site	00:09:06	00:11:42
Page views	6.14	9.61
Bounce rate*	38%	19.2%

Traffic Sources based in May–July 2015

OLX ※ Pakwheels

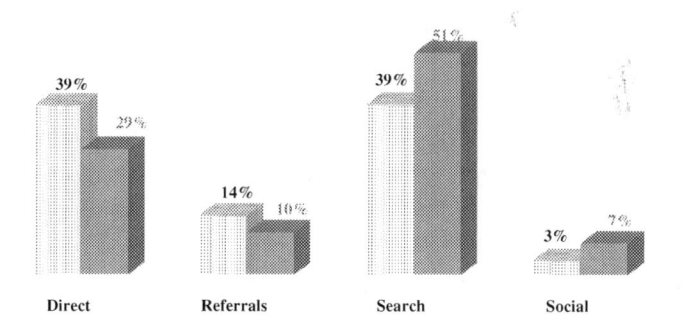

Direct Referrals Search Social

Exhibit 8 a SimilarWeb comparison between OLX and PakWheels (*Bounce rate: the percentage of visitors to a particular website who navigate away from the site after viewing only one page). **b** SimilarWeb Comparison between OLX and PakWheels (*Source* Author's data using the www.SimilarWeb.com tools available online)

One such advertisement campaign was "*Bech Dey*" (means sell it), at a cost double that of PakWheels' entire annual promotion budget, had created a strong impression on Pakistani buyers and sellers.

There were rumours that OLX was planning to launch its used-car section with a three-week campaign focused on TV, radio, and outdoor branding. OLX's policy was not to spend much on services or building content but spend heavily on TVC creation and other mainstream media. Whereas, PakWheels had a clear advantage over OLX and any other car classified portal because of its strong community and user-generated comprehensive content.

Recently, it seemed that the goal of OLX was to gain enough traction (critical mass) to generate a positive network effect. Ideally, they would want to have a large pool of buyers and sellers to create a strong business model. After a decent traffic, the portal would grow even faster because the more buyers they get, the more sellers would be attracted, and vice versa. If they are able to do this early, then it would become very difficult for other online platforms to replicate their model easily. "Although we feel we have reached that stage, the majority of internet users will come in the years ahead—about three-fourths of internet users are not online yet (based on previous figures). We need to ensure that while we are a leader in the current situation, we also continue to dominate the space in the next few years, which will be a super explosive time for the internet".[25] Munj suggested in a recent interview.

CONCLUSION

Investors were seeking ambitious targets like increases in revenue by 25%, traffic by 30%, and listing by 40%, respectively. For Saeed and Munj, the fundamental question was what approach should PakWheels take to meet these tough targets? This question was complicated enough but making it even more difficult to tackle was the range of options which were now available to the company as it moulded a business strategy going forward.

Saeed and Munj debated concerning two critical strategic opportunities, but did not reach any solid conclusion:

[25] https://aurora.dawn.com/news/1140680.

Option 1:
There were speculations about the new law; some industry analysts said it might get delayed for a few years and even if it did get executed soon they would not foresee the strict implementation knowing the country's current status of e-commerce-related laws. "Perhaps it won't be a major cause of concern in the near future so one option would be to wait and see how things would get affected in the future and then take the appropriate action," Saeed exclaimed. He added, "But there is no way we can delay a response to the OLX upcoming media campaign". The rationale for responding to OLX was clear. PakWheels needed to gain critical mass and soon. It's BTL and social media campaigns had only been effective to a certain point. Over the time, the returns/traffic would reach a state of little or no change after a period, and they will slowly start losing valuable traffic to OLX or any other new market entrant with deep pockets and the right products. Currently, close to 50% of the internet population of Pakistan visited Pakwheels.com during a year, which left almost 50% internet users who did not use PakWheels up till then. Moreover, with OLX gaining popularity and aggressively marketing their brand, this competition could be detrimental to Pakwheel's future.

While it was true that setting up an online business was not capital intensive, scaling required a significant amount of capital. To move to the next level, PakWheels had to invest in traditional ATL and BTL methods. There was a large portion of the population that they could not target with their online advertising as they were not available on online forums. The integration of ATL with the social media marketing might be the right approach going forward. However, this option involved a focused marketing initiative by the company which would essentially mean setting up a proper marketing department from scratch, recruiting managers and their teams, hiring creative and media agencies. For that matter, they needed to (almost) double the existing promotion budget and with a spending of about $1.5 million in three major cities (Karachi, Islamabad, and Lahore), PakWheels might counter the effects of OLX mega marketing campaign.

Option 2:
Although the implementation of law might be weak in Pakistan, PakWheels should not take the risk of waiting it out. Saeed and Munj had not forgotten the fate of YouTube and some other websites, which were banned under such discriminatory laws in the past. PakWheels

should use this opportunity to figure out an intelligent way to separate the community forums from the website and still sustain their competitive advantage. One way of doing that would be to have a separate routing address for the "marketplace" and a separate platform for "discussions forums and blogs". Some pertinent concerns with this options included, how could this be achieved practically? What sort of costs was involved? What were the negative effects on the traffic, listings, or other key metrics?

If PakWheels did separate its community forums from its marketplace site, it could ensure that any activity as the aftermath of the new law will not damage the brand and its business directly. Already PakWheels had two separate phone apps with slightly varied logos for forums and marketplace. "Pursuing this strategy will damage our core business" Saeed had warned. However, supporters had argued, "By having a strong position in the buying/selling services to the auto industry, the company could enhance its core services as a middleman in the buying process free of cost while the community forums/website can generate revenues for them independently".

This option also suggested that PakWheels' team should not recognize OLX's media campaign as a threat, instead, continue with their existing marketing model while strengthening their value-adding products and services. They had some promising programs in their infancy stages like the dealer programs and the CarSure certification program. It would be wise to invest in them and get maximum benefits from their strong online presence in the market. If they would redirect their budgets and efforts on matching OLX's marketing strategy, they might lose their focus on the current projects.

Was PakWheels' team willing and capable of continuing spending hefty budgets on media campaigns once this first round of funding was exhausted? There was a chance they might not get uniform funding opportunities in consecutive years.

"Pakistan's internet user base is expected to grow to 100 million users by 2020, and we want to be the go-to place for anything and everything to do with wheels for this online population. This round of funding will help us strengthen our leadership position, improve existing services, and build new offerings. Think Wheels, Think PakWheels," Saeed stated.

It was 9 p.m., 30 July 2015 and the dynamic duo was still in office contemplating which one of these options would be their best strategy to move forward, as the future of PakWheels depended upon that.

TEACHING NOTE

Synopsis

Pakwheels.com was a vertical automotive portal, founded in 2003 and acquired by entrepreneurs Raza Saeed and Suneel Munj in 2008. Over the last 12 years of its operations, Pakwheels.com had helped millions of Pakistanis buy and sell cars and bikes, read automotive reviews and news, check automotive prices, and find solutions to their automotive needs. Despite the introduction of competing classifieds websites by giants like OLX and other international internet firms like carmudi.com, PakWheels had managed to grow its market share. It happened largely because of its cult-like following of a very loyal user base.

In Dec 2014, PakWheels had closed one of the largest venture capital investment deals into a Pakistan technology startup. Frontier Digital Ventures, a Malaysia-based venture capital fund focused on online classifieds businesses in the emerging markets, had invested $3.5 million into their web portal. However, when they were ready to develop an aggressive growth strategy, their legal counsel informed them about the possibility of a discriminating cyber-crime prevention bill called PECA, which was in the approval process by the national assembly of Pakistan. Moreover, there was a speculation about OLX, mega media campaign to introduce its used car section. It was expected that their main competitor OLX would be launching a huge and expensive media campaign of about $0.5 million to introduce its used car section in the local market. Going forward, Raza and Suneel would have to decide the best way to scale up their business by utilizing the investor money in an efficient manner. But before that might happen, they knew they needed to lay out a clear and compelling strategy which would create the most value for the business and its stakeholders by asking some tough questions. What should PakWheels team do to retain community engagement culture if PECA 2015 gets implemented in the country? Should they match OLX media budgets and respond with their own ATL campaign? Or maybe just wait and strengthen their basic product and technology and see how the market changes in the future. PakWheels was aiming for exponential growth in the coming year, and the founders were looking beyond, to when the company's revenues and valuation would allow them to raise a large amount of growth capital and reach critical mass.

As Raza Saeed stated, "Pakistan's internet user base is expected to grow to 100 million users by 2019 and we want to be the go-to place

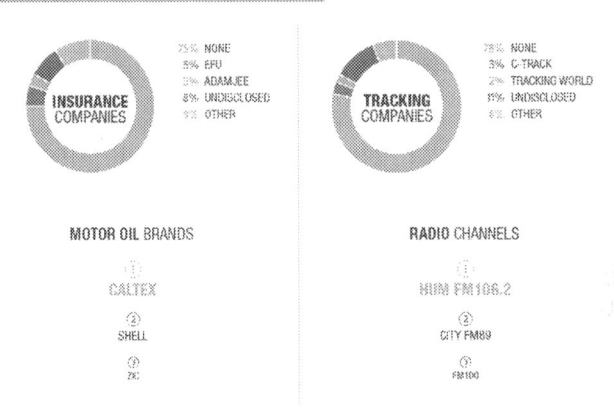

Exhibit 6 (continued)

maximize the website's visibility to the target audience through multiple online channels. Meaningful content was created to engage audiences through reviews, articles, videos, etc. PakWheels also advertised their website using social media and digital PR building, leading to more traffic for the website and meaningful conversions. Till date, due to for anything and everything to do with wheels for this online population. This round of funding will help us strengthen our leadership position, improve existing services and build new offerings. Think Wheels, Think PakWheels."

Teaching Objectives

This case study can be taught in a "Channel Development" module of Marketing Strategy course designed for MBA and EMBA programs. It can also be taught in "Entrepreneurial Marketing" and "Disruptive Innovation" Courses. The following key objectives can be achieved through case discussion:

- To illustrate the development of an entrepreneurial start-up and how a small company disrupts the existing channel and create value for its customers and itself.
- To explore the different ways by which value can be created and appropriated in the digital setting.
- To investigate the challenges associated with managing multiple sets of customers and stakeholders across multiple channels.
- To illustrate how channel and promotional activities have merged in the digital setting.
- To highlight the issues involved in managing a business that is experiencing a changing competitive environment and how the management adapt to the changing environment.

Assignment Questions

1. How does Pakwheels.com create value for its customers? How is it different from existing/traditional car dealer models?
2. How do you assess the company's business model? What are the strengths and weaknesses?
3. Which of the two options should the company choose in order to scale up, using the investor funding going forward?

Q1: How does Pakwheels.com create value for its customers? How is it different from existing/traditional car dealer models?

Before online car portals in Pakistan, buyers and sellers used to rely on used car dealers, classified Ads in the local newspapers and weekly used car markets to trade their cars. According to APMDA, in Jan 2015, there were 4000 car dealers in Pakistan who dealt in both new and used cars. These car dealers mostly worked on three business models:

- **Broker Model**: The seller contacts one of these car dealers and lists his/her car at the dealer's showroom. The dealer then finds a buyer for the seller's car and connects both the buyer and the seller and charge a commission on that sale.
- **Investor Model**: The dealer buys off the car from seller at a lower price than market and sells it at a profit to one of the buyers and makes money on the transaction.
- **Importer Model**: The dealer imports used cars from different countries and sell these cars on a profit to buyers and makes money on the transaction. This model is very similar to the investor model. The only difference here is that the dealer imports the car instead of buying it locally.

Conventional car trade options came with its own set of problems, it had an inefficient value chain with a surplus of information in the used car industry—it's a large market with significant fragmentation multiple independent buyers and sellers who operate independently and with almost no transparency. Some of the most pertinent issues are explained below:

For buyers:

- Sunday car markets were inconvenient, time consuming and involved a lot of hassle in searching the right car.
- Paying an extra or premium above the price of the market price as dealer commission.
- Multiple negotiation and visits required to dealer showrooms for finding the right car.
- Newspapers classifieds did not contain enough information and required making multiple queries to shortlist cars and there was a high rate of disappointment when the physical inspection of the car was made.
- In general, trust issues existed as the car specifications were mostly claims by the dealer or seller, there was no authentic proof or original paperwork to justify their claims, e.g. about the accurate meter reading. Here, based on their experience students might include

some other real life such as paint job, accident history and mainte-nance and mechanical status of the car.

For sellers:

- Inconvenient, time consuming and hassle involved in taking the car to each individual dealer at weekly markets.
- The seller had to leave the car with the dealer for extended periods of time to get a good offer for it.
- Through newspaper classifieds, sellers usually faced a lot of clut-ter and their Ads did not get enough attention or value for their money. (Each classified costs Rs. 500 per 20 words and additional Rs. 25 for every extra word, and the life of the ad was only 1 day.)
- When the car was sold through the dealer, they kept their commis-sion which was usually 1% of the price of the car, so it reduced the profit margins, if any for the seller.

In case there was an urgent need to sell the car, the seller had to take a price cut and sell it to the dealer for less than the market price (Investor model). In order to solve the problems faced by consumers in the cur-rent used car industry, PakWheels provided substantial value through multiple technology based innovations.

PakWheels provided a unique point of contact/platform where higher efficiencies are created by reducing asymmetry of information between sellers and buyers, increasing speed of information exchange and instill-ing trust in the process by making it more transparent. It brought buy-ers and sellers together by providing content in the form of information, knowledge and experience related to automotive industry of Pakistan. PakWheels eliminated the need to access dealers, newspaper classifieds or weekly markets for selling or buying used cars. It provided direct online access to find a suitable match for both buyers and sellers with the hassle of an intermediary. Thus making the process much more efficient, con-venient, hassle free and more price effective. As the Ad placement on the website is free and both sellers and buyers get a fair market price quoted which results in a better business deal for them. PakWheels attempted to remove the trust issues of individual consumers by introducing "CarSure" verification program, where PakWheels experts (Industry analysts/mechanical engineers/paint crew) bring considerable know-how and experience to the car selling/buying process by providing the following facilities to both buyers and sellers:

- Identifying and grading cars
- Price comparisons
- Paint check
- Engine performance
- Meter reading authenticity
- Registration and other paperwork authenticity

PakWheels had become synonymous with a gateway for automobile enthusiasts—a major focal point for users where they get to stay connected with news, innovation and views of other likeminded individuals and businesses. Their community engagement forums and tools had created an un-precedented value in the form of customer loyalty. It focused on numerous partnerships (for example: Shell, Mobilink etc.) on maintaining extensive content and promoting the site and its services to potential car buyers and sellers.

Because of its innovative business model, PakWheels was the fastest growing facilitator of automobile industry specific content for B2B and C2C commerce on the net and bringing buyers and sellers together. With services like latest news, online directories, personalized advertisements, targeted email newsletters of products and services and a facility to create an individual company website within the main portal makes it a major commerce facilitator for the car dealers nationwide. PakWheels presence in the local online market has brought efficiency to the industry. In addition Pakwheels.com encourages healthy competition, increases options for buyers and brings down undue costs. Here students might highlight the other advantages, especially with respect to dealers e.g. they don't need to maintain physical inventories thus reducing their costs.

Q2: How do you assess the company's business model? What are the strengths and weaknesses?

As claimed in the case by PakWheels management, revenue is not the major priority for them yet, as they are still in their start up stage. PakWheels has not yet reached their maximum potential and they claim to be building the business for the longer run. Revenues to support the company are mostly derived through business partnerships and advertising while maintaining the free business model and user convenience of the site. PakWheels made almost no money off the C2C interactions that occurred on the classifieds of the website. Majority of their revenue was derived from portion of the website targeted at related businesses like the local car dealerships, corporate advertisement from clients like Total, Shell, Zic and General Tires etc. So, essentially, PakWheels never focused on profits but rather on value creation and delivery of the services and product to ensure C2C interaction being kept meaningful and engaging to keep them coming back for more. PakWheels is continuously improving its website, customer product experience and fine tuning various tools and options available to its customers.

The strategy is simple; PakWheels will have to continue to offer the best user experience on its website. PakWheels has to ensure maximum traffic placing ads on its site and also expand their geographic spread to all the large cities. And as the advent of 3G and 4G has just begun in Pakistan they must offer the right mobile experience also for its business growth.

Thus PakWheels introduced an innovative business model to monetize its offerings. The instructor can start putting up the ideas on the board related to different business models for online sites. And then he/she can introduce these labels (Which are not given in the case). Following are the salient features of its business model:

- **Advertising model**: (on-site advertising) they make money off paid advertisements. At the same time they are careful that ads are as desirable and unobtrusive as possible. They don't cover the core content, play music automatically or otherwise disrupts their end user experience.
- **Freemium model**: (featured ads) A pricing model in which the initial service is free but upgrades, advanced features and/or virtual goods cost a small fee. In order to make this model successful PakWheels has to make sure that the premium offering is worth the money paid for it. Their featured ads offer the facility of taking the seller/buyer ad at the top of the search listings if purchased for a marginal fee.
- **Lead Generation model**: A model that collected user information and then markets that information to other companies that would be interested in selling or talking directly to them. In return PakWheels offers quality experience and consumer engagement

through its community forums, video blogs and testimonials to lend credibility to their site. And because it's an asymmetrical business model (it is not asking the main user base for money) it is easy to get a large user base fast.

- **Community model**: (Content marketing through blogs and offline advertising through auto shows) the viability of his model is based on user loyalty. Users have a high investment in both time and emotion. Revenue is based on the sale of additional products and services or voluntary contributions; or revenue is tied to contextual advertising and subscriptions for premium services. Internet is inherently suited to community business models and in recent times this is one of the more fertile areas of development, as seen in the rise of social networking. PakWheels provides individuals with the ability to connect to other individuals along a defined common interest: i.e. cars!

Some of the strengths and weaknesses of its current business model are explained below:

Strengths:

1. Since the business is in the infancy stage, "free for all" is a very attractive product offering in the local industry. It attracts maximum users and Ad placements. It also ensures that it highlights the user convenience in the process.
2. This model does not alienate its loyal PakWheels enthusiast community which has been with PakWheels since its inception and it is not willing to pay for advertising on the website.
3. This free C2C business model allows the PakWheels team and the users to focus on creating fun and meaningful engagement through the PakWheels community forums and off line events like auto shows, vintage car events and other spontaneous events. The inclination of logging in and spending time on Pakwheels.com is totally organic and intrinsic right now, not driven by any paid sponsorship or any other ulterior agenda.
4. The current business model is not only helping Pakwheels.com to engage customers and earn revenue it is also developing the online automotive industry in Pakistan.

Weaknesses:

1. The biggest negative with this model is that it is going to take considerable time to mature and start becoming profitable, and till then the PakWheels team has to secure outside investment if they want to grow the business and strengthen their basic product.
2. This model also depends a lot on size of its user base in order to attract relevant and large sponsors for Ads.
3. The current business model mainly depends heavily upon consumer engagement with Pakwheels.com especially through PakWheels forums. Therefore, if anything happens to the forums such as censorships from the government, the main stream of earning or pakwheels, which is heavily dependent upon, consumer traffic would be threatened.

The sustainability and scalability of the business in the long term depends on lead generation. For businesses, they would be providing different packages, tools and services to dealers, new car manufacturers, importer and anybody we are generating leads for. For this, PakWheels first need to get that critical mass where they are clearly a leader in the entire user space. While it is true that setting up an online business is not capital intensive, scaling requires significant amount of capital. For example heavy investment would be required for a more consumer responsive website and more tools to improve consumer search experience and capability.

Q3: Which of the two options should the company choose in order to scale up, using the investor funding going forward?
Option 1: Delay responding to the cybercrime bill but OLX entering into the used car market with their $0.5 million advertising campaign should be considered as serious threat to PakWheels future and thus should be reciprocated with an aggressive marketing campaign.

Proponents of option 1 might make the following points in the class discussion:

As the case suggests that there were speculations about the new law, some industry analysts said it might get delayed for a few years and even if it did get executed soon they did not foresee very strict implementation knowing the country's current status of e-commerce related laws. So one option that the PakWheels management could consider was just to wait and see how early and how seriously this law might be implemented.

Also the argument is very valid that separating the PakWheels website in two separate sites might result up in losing their loyal founding members and customers. This would alienate their fan following and might end up confusing and disappointing them with the way new websites would be run.

Rationale behind responding to OLX is very clear, PakWheels needed to gain critical mass and soon. Their BTL/social media campaigns had only been effective to a certain point. Over time the returns/traffic would plateau and they will slowly start losing valuable traffic to OLX or any other new market entrant with deep pockets and the right products. And with OLX gaining popularity and aggressively marketing their brand, this competition could be detrimental for PakWheels future. To move onto the next level and strengthen the brand, PakWheels team plans to invest in advertising and traditional ATL methods as there is a significant portion of population that cannot be targeted with just online advertising since they don't believe in online buying and selling.

With the investor funding, this would be the right time to make the heavy investment in setting up a marketing department, hiring creative and media agencies and making a competitive TVC to respond to OLX. Rough budget calculation by the PakWheels team had revealed a staggering figure of $1.5 million for creating and rolling out a responsive campaign against OLX in the major cities. Because while it is true that setting up an online business is not capital intensive, scaling up requires significant amount of capital.

Option 2: PakWheels should not attempt to respond to OLX as a threat and just focus on their own vertical product development and community engagement strength. And the cybercrime bill should be taken as a serious threat to the business and responded to in an intelligent way.

Proponent for option 2 might present the following points in the class discussion:

OLX is a horizontal portal with international standing, experience and deeper pockets than PakWheels. It doesn't make sense to compete head to head with OLX because OLX is operating on a different business model and targeting a wide range of diversified consumers, whereas PakWheels has a very sharp focus on only automotive related news, activities, and consumers. This should be considered its strength and PakWheels should not get involved in a media race.

PakWheels stream of funding might not be uniform in nature and to sustain such heavy campaigns focusing on only communication would be a very risky maneuver. Creating TVC and buying media in Pakistan industry is an expensive task and with so many new initiatives by PakWheels in its infancy stage, would not be wise to shift all resources and attention towards an un-necessary media involvement.

Till date PakWheels team has not spent large marketing dollars, which portrays its entrepreneurial and tech savvy mindset. Their annual marketing budget for 2014 was a total of $0.7 million ($0.3 Digital marketing and $0.4 BTL) compared to OLX campaign which was ready to spend $0.5 on a 3 week long launch campaign only. More importantly, taking into account the fact that PakWheels team has no experience with creating and conducting ATL marketing campaigns in the past, an aggressive media plan might backfire.

Instead of marketing PakWheels should focus more on improvement from product teams by shifting focus from just traffic, to liquidity/traction, better categorization, better hyper localization and content quality.

People need richness of experience for specific categories where a large sum of money or trust is at stake. And that is why despite the horizontal classifieds platforms (such as OLX) investing huge amount of money on TV will pose absolutely minimum threat to vertical sites (such as PakWheels). The instructor can perform a simple exercise to make an emphasis that creating awareness of online websites might not result into actual transactions on those sites. The instructor can ask the students how many have heard of any online classifieds and then ask if they have ever sold or bought anything from that website. So this exercise will highlight the fact that TOM might not have a very strong connection with actual consumer transaction on online portal as compared to retail channels.

The new cybercrime should definitely be considered a threat and the PakWheels team should work towards avoiding it in a smart way. The fate of YouTube and some other technology based businesses that were closed down over night have not been forgotten by many in Pakistan.

As the case explains, for its mobile site access, PakWheels was maintaining two parallel channels with slightly separate logos, a marketplace for buying and selling exclusively and the other one catering to the chat forums and communities only (refer to Exhibit 3 in the case). The same could be done for the parent website. This would minimize the risk of losing out on their main business leg in case the cybercrime law did post threats to the website.

The Expansion of Online Travel Portal—MakeMyTrip

Abha Rishi, Kiranpreet Kaur and Natasha Mahawar

INTRODUCTION

Great holiday packages at reasonable prices. Customer support level is average, but still a good option for online booking
                                   – Customer review for MakeMyTrip

MakeMyTrip, with its commitment and providing full satisfaction to its customers, has become an online leader in India, with its share being more than 50% of all online sales. According to surveys and feedback, MakeMyTrip users are usually satisfied and delighted. MakeMyTrip has a strong customer support system which is available round the clock. In 2016, it had its workstations in 20 cities in India besides having two offices in cities like New York and San Francisco, which makes it capable to be just a click away from

A. Rishi (✉) · K. Kaur · N. Mahawar
Birla Institute of Management Technology, Greater Noida, India
e-mail: abha.rishi@bimtech.ac.in

K. Kaur
e-mail: kiranpreet.kaur16@bimtech.ac.in

N. Mahawar
e-mail: natasha.mahawar16@bimtech.ac.in

A. Sikdar and V. Pereira (eds.), *Business and Management Practices in South Asia*, https://doi.org/10.1007/978-981-13-1399-8_8

the customers. MakeMyTrip, which is number one in India as an online travel company, after changing and developing the Indian market with its complete range of offers, had decided to cross the national boundaries with its complete set of travel solutions in the South Asian market.

Tour and travel companies like MakeMyTrip have been successful due to the increased penetration of e-commerce sector throughout the globe. With the help of e-commerce portals, new opportunities for growth are now available with the tour and travel industry all over the world. The tourism sector has a huge potential to expand, thus internet and e-commerce provide them with a platform to excel further. With the advancement in technology, there has been a wider scope for further development in the e-commerce websites and these changes have affected both the consumers and the industry. Now customers have more choices when it comes to travel and compare the most affordable option. According to a survey, approximately 95% internet users have searched for tour and tourism related information before going in for the best possible option. Around 93% people used established online travel portals to acquire information about booking and travel (Xinran et al. 2006). In the present times, consumers can access information from technologically advanced gadgets such as smartphones, tablets, laptops, etc., and they have aided in improving the overall consumers' travel experience.

INDIA—THE OCEAN OF OPPORTUNITIES

E-commerce in India has taken a huge leap. It is expected to cross the mark of $16 billion by the end of the present fiscal year. Among the top 20, India ranks as one of the developing countries due to the increased usage of internet and smartphones.[1] The travel and tour sector accounts for the highest share in the Indian e-commerce sector (Fig. 1).

Earlier, travel agents acted as mediators to help the customers in deciding tour destinations and arranged tickets for them. Customers considered the ticket booking system as a complicated process. But with the innovation of direct ticket reservation system, customers got an easier and more convenient process for booking tickets. Further, the internet made this task much easier. Middlemen got removed, and the customers became free to contact the company directly.

The wave of advancements in technology had hit the Indian continent. Internet had penetrated deeply into the Indian market, and the customers sought convenience in their daily lives. The travel and tourism

---

[1] According to Global Retail Development Index 2014, by A.T. Kearney.

Fig. 1 Share of travel industry in e-commerce in India (*Source* IMRBI—Cube 2014, All India estimates, December 2014)

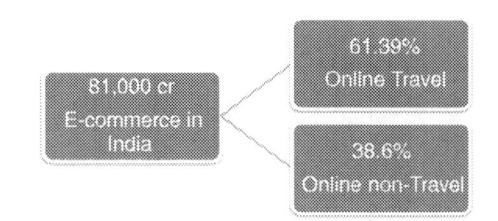

industry tapped this opportunity to further expand their online commercial portals realizing the fact that India had a huge potential of prospective clientele. The online travel portals started serving the Indian customers and together were called the Online Travel Agencies (OTAs). Only one of these companies has been publicly listed—MakeMyTrip, but even the rest are also showing tremendous growth.

MakeMyTrip—One Stop Solution for Travellers

MakeMyTrip limited has been started by Deep Kalra in 2000 and now it is India's largest online travel company having its headquarters in Gurgaon, Haryana. The growth in the travel sector started gaining pace from early 2000, and now in the present times, it is at its peak.

The reason for the growth of such online travel companies was the rising demands for economical, convenient, and consumer friendly options for booking of the hotels, checking the status of railways and flight bookings. The expansion of companies like MakeMyTrip gained momentum due to the Indian Railways Catering and Tourism Corporation's (IRCTC's) online business model which was appreciated by the customers from India, as it helped them to book tickets without standing in long queues and the online operations saved travellers' time.

With the noticeable growth in the Indian aviation industry, in September 2005, MakeMyTrip started its Indian operations dealing in the booking of flight tickets of Indian travellers. In order to expand the company's portfolio, the company also started focusing on holiday packages and hotel bookings. MakeMyTrip made its mark by being listed on the NASDAQ on 13 August 2010 and made an entry into the US market.

With the purpose of growth, MakeMyTrip in the year 2011 and 2012 made a strategic expansion via new channels and markets to parts of Southeast Asia. For the same reason, the company has also launched its app for the mobile devices to make it convenient for the customers to utilize its services at their convenience. In addition to the app, which provides full-time service to its customers, the company has also made its presence through 59 retail stores across all the major cities in India and also has its international offices in cities like New York City and Sydney.

MakeMyTrip did not want to portray itself just as an online portal so it developed the growth of its offline businesses like its affiliates and franchisees. It also worked on building a strong company's retail base. Today, MakeMyTrip is an online one-stop travel portal that deals in a broad range of travel and tourism products and services in India.

PRODUCTS AND SERVICES

The URLs www.makemytrip.com and www.hoteltravel.com are the websites of the company. MakeMyTrip assists travellers in booking in all major international and domestic airlines, whether it is to or from India. It helps to access more than 100,000 hotels outside India and gives access to more than 11,000 hotels and other boarding houses in India, and bookings in the railways and other Indian bus operators. The services offered by MakeMyTrip include:

- **Flights Tickets**—MakeMyTrip makes bookings of airline tickets for travelling in all major international and domestic flights. The company also looks after the flights coming to India from other nations like Canada, Singapore, UAE and US.
- **Rail and Bus Ticket Services** —MakeMyTrip helps in the booking and selling tickets to customer's online, providing those services like easy cancellation of tickets, automatic generation of alerts and information about the updates on the status of tickets. It arranges bus tickets to Indian customers in various types of buses.
- **Cab Services**—In 2010, MakeMyTrip also included the facility of hiring cars through its website for Indian customers. It provides car hiring facilities along with holiday package bookings.
- **Hotels and Packages**—MakeMyTrip has tie-ups with a wide range of hotels in India and worldwide, and helps customers make easy hotel reservations. There are more than 13,000 guesthouses and hotels available in India for booking. MakeMyTrip also gives the option of comparing the prices of other online portals with the website of

MakeMyTrip itself. The hotel's accommodation varies from economic to luxury. In order to increase the number of rooms and to provide better services to its customers, MakeMyTrip has acquired My Guest House Accommodation in 2012. With the acquisition of easytobook.com, MakeMyTrip now holds a wider range of hotels to choose from even outside India with access to more than 18,000 hotels. With MakeMyTrip, one has the convenience of getting customized travel packages to well-known destinations.

- **Solutions via Mobile Phones**—In the year 2012, MakeMyTrip launched its app for all smart phone devices. The online application enables its users to track, book and avail deals in services like holiday packages, hotel reservations, bus bookings, flight bookings and trip packages. It also provides other services like making easy and convenient cancellations, tracking the process of refunds, enabling e-ticket services and other travel alerts.
- **Route Planner**—MakeMyTrip route planner guides its customers on all details of more than one million routes in the country.

The key differentiating factors which add to the brand equity[2] of MakeMyTrip have been listed as follows:

1. **Broaden Hotels and Packages Service Business**
   Hotels and packages contribute more to MakeMyTrip's revenue margins than their air ticketing business, and their objective is to enable more hotel suppliers to be effortlessly connected to their website with the latest advancements in the approach.
2. **Expand The Product Portfolio to Improve Cross-Selling Opportunities**
   MakeMyTrip actively markets additional features to the travel services for their customers. For example, it promotes non-air provisions to customers once they have booked the air tickets.
3. **Enhance Service Platforms by Investing in Technology**
   To augment and enhance the features of the services offered on the MakeMyTrip platform, the company is investing quite a bit in technology. In lieu of this focus, MakeMyTrip is integrating

---

[2] Brand equity can be defined as an association of the brand product or service with the brand recall or recognition by the customers, market share of the brand, and loyalty of the customers towards it.

the hotel booking systems across various websites. A high level of application of user feedback is also on the strategy radar and the company is planning to use this feedback to create more user-friendly bookings for their customers.

4. **Expand into New Geographic Markets**
   MakeMyTrip is well structured for growth in markets across the boundaries, especially in those countries that have a large number of the non-resident Indian population as well as places close to India, which are adored and admired by Indian travellers.

On 17 August 2015, MakeMyTrip announced a mobile app for booking in trains. This app allows the site users to search and book for their tickets in English and regional languages like Malayalam, Tamil, Gujarati and Telugu. The user can book general tickets and Tatkal (immediate booking for travel within 24 hours) tickets to different places in India with the help of its mobile app. It is also the only train booking app in India that has the facility of return ticket bookings. Rail or train travel has been the fastest growing segment when it comes to travel in India. According to statistics, in 2014, online rail booking penetration was nearly forty-three percent. Mobile rail booking app further accelerated the growth and adoption of online rail-bookings.

Make my trip has also added Pay Pal as a payment option for non-residents and it recently began selling opaque fares in which the traveller cannot see the name of the airline disclosed until a purchase is completed.

The company has three strategies:

- Increasing its business through smart phones.
- Maximizing revenue from the high-margin non-flights business such as selling hotel rooms and holiday packages.
- Buying up more early-stage start-ups in travel-related space.

MAKEMYTRIP IN UAE

Scenario of E-Commerce in UAE

More than half of the UAE residents use the internet for commercial purposes. There is around 61% internet penetration and the citizens of UAE have been waiting for an efficient online Travel Agency. Research has shown that global e-commerce in 2012 was around $13 trillion, which included 850 million people all over the globe. It is expected that the UAE market for e-commerce revenues is likely to go up. Industry watchers have predicted an annual growth rate of e-commerce in the Gulf at 20% in the present scenario.

The reasons given by the **Chief Marketing Officer of MakeMyTrip, Mr. Mohit Gupta,** for the business opportunity and making a strategic investment in the UAE market are:

- NRI's are maximum in number in UAE, after the US.
- UAE market has shown favorable growth trends in the hospitality and travel sector, especially from India into the UAE.
- One of the largest networks available in inter-country flight system in the world is UAE–India.
- As Dubai is a popular travel destination around the world, it makes it profitable to invest and set up business.
- The UAE local operators also provide adequate help to MakeMyTrip set up its operations around hotels and other localized products, which will ultimately benefit the customers.

Capturing the UAE Market

There is a lot of scope of MakeMyTrip to expand in Hotel and Packages segment in UAE. The company is building their strong presence in emerging markets such as UAE and South East Asia through organic and inorganic expansion.

MakeMyTrip in Emirates is the first travel portal which provides customers all the facilities and comfortable at just one click, it offers services which were earlier unavailable to the local UAE travellers, such as

- The local travellers in the UAE can access various services in a convenient manner and they can also compare the availability and price of different services at one place easily.
- MakeMyTrip allows them to make safe and secure online payments easily by following simple processes. The payments can be made in the local AED currency and no additional transaction cost needs to be paid.
- The local people get a wide range of options to select from various services like flight and railway ticket bookings, hotels reservations and customized holiday and trip packages for both international and only within India.

MakeMyTrip—India's largest online travel company came to the UAE market with a partnership with **SNTTA**, a travel service provider company, which has a network of around 20 outlets across UAE. As per this partnership, SNTTA's travel division will look after MakeMyTrip's products for outbound holidays, while SNTTA Emir Tours, which is SNTTA's DMC division, will look after all the necessary arrangements for its inbound leisure travellers.

With the help of this partnership with SNTTA, the local citizens of UAE will be able to enjoy the various set of services provided by MakeMyTrip such as online bookings for flights and trains, hotel reservations, easy payments, competitive pricing and access to retail outlets. UAE citizens can reach out to SNTTA to benefit from MakeMyTrip's exclusive trip and holiday packages, both domestic and international.

MakeMyTrip and SNTTA's association is a branding boost for MakeMyTrip and is something which will provide it with a platform to enter and expand the company's workings and operations in the UAE market.

According to **Mr. Keyur Joshi, Co-founder & COO, MakeMyTrip**, *"As MakeMyTrip is one of the most successful Online Travel portals in India, we see a clear opportunity for our offerings in the Emirates market. This will be helpful mainly to NRIs who can plan their last minute travel in India on a single portal, being able to book international and domestic flights and also make hotel reservations."*

Cleartrip is the market leader in the travel services providers in the UAE market as it was the first to come into the market. At second place comes MakeMyTrip followed by Yatra which is a distant follower. The ranking is in terms of both for revenue earned and the number of bookings done.

MakeMyTrip in Singapore

Singapore is Southeast Asia's most tourist-friendly destination with an area of 716.1 square kilometres and a population of around 5.39 million. Unlike other destinations in Southeast Asia which are cramped and congested, Singapore is fresh and open. Singapore as a tourism destination is just like a delicious preparation on one single platter and tourists get the royal feel once they start exploring Singapore through the fashion emporiums of Orchard Road and go antique shopping in China town. Singapore has around 300 parks, 63 islands and 4 nature reserves thus making it a huge tourist destination.

Singapore is cool during December and January with an average temperature of 23 degrees. It is hottest in the month of May and June with an average temperature of 34 degrees. Tourists can visit Singapore throughout the year but ideally tourists visit during the festive season.

Singapore has a blend of many cultures. There are 74.2% Chinese, 13.3% Malaysians and 9.2% Indians in the country. Thus Singapore is a perfect destination for any organization to begin its operation in the field of Hospitality, Travel and Tourism. Singapore is considered as the high-income economy. Petroleum and Pharmaceuticals are the leading sectors of the country which also attract a lot of business travellers.

Singapore is a democratic country and the country also enjoys a low political risk in the continent. Among the ASEAN countries, Singapore has the highest per-capita income. Singapore is highly corruption-free city which supports and attracts the business environment in the country. The government as an active and imperative player has invested with an intention to bring in diversity in the economy due to which industries like Tourism and pharmaceutical are flourishing. Labor is cheap when compared with the neighbouring countries. The Ministry of Environment of the country works relentlessly to maintain its environmental factors. There was a period when Singapore was one among the most carbon dioxide emitting economies, but now it is known for its progressive policies.

The IT-Infrastructure in Singapore is remarkable as a whole. The penetration rate for the Internet in the masses is over 70% which have resulted in the use of E-commerce and Eb2c models. The Government of Singapore has the belief that regulations and legislation which are transparent and market-favorable will spur the growth of E-commerce. In tune with this idea, for its cross-border businesses, Singapore has introduced policy initiatives.

MakeMyTrip acquired almost 80% stake in a Singapore based travel agency, **Luxury Tours and Travels Pvt. Ltd.**, for almost $3 million in 2011. It enabled MakeMyTrip to have a stronger hold in countries like Malaysia, Hong Kong and Thailand. Luxury Tours and Travels was basically involved in hotel reservations, excursion tours and inbound-outbound travel.

In 2012, MakeMyTrip acquired **Hotel Travel Group** for about $25 million. The company had an existence of over a decade, having approximately 140,000 hotels all over the world. The company employs highly trained professionals from more than twenty countries, who have expertise in both travel industries and internet related services (Table 1).

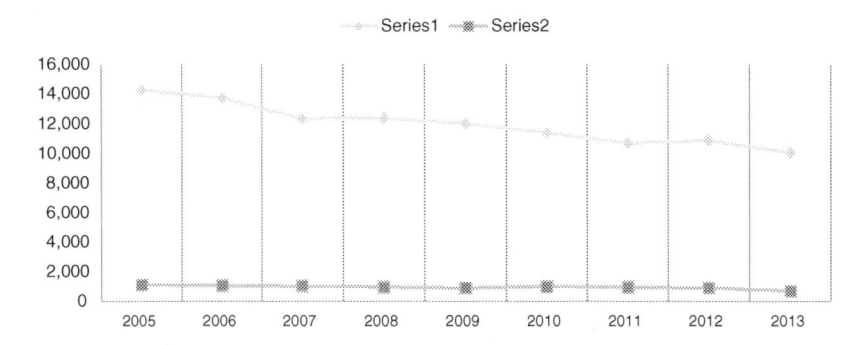

Fig. 2 Number of domestic and international trips, reported and represented, 2005–2013

There is a high expectation from the US market for international and domestic trips. According to this survey by U.S Bureau of Labor Statistics,[3] both domestic (series 1) and international (series 2) travel decreased during the recession period (2007–2009). The decline continued during the recovery period too, but international trips managed to grow in 2011 and domestic trips showed a temporary rebound in 2012.

Internet Penetration

By 2013, almost 84.2% of the US population had an access to internet and were comfortable working with it. This was a lot higher than that of China, which had internet penetration of only 45.8% of the total Chinese population. Although there was a drastic difference in the Chinese and the US scenario, UK and US had an almost equal score, with the UK having the upper hand. The internet penetration in the UK was almost 89% of the total population. Out of 322,583,006 people in the U.S.A., 279,834,232 people were using internet which comes out to be 84.2% of the population (Table 2).

---

[3] This federal body, known as The Bureau of Labor Statistics is responsible for measuring and analyzing the working conditions for labor, activities in the market, and the fluctuations in the prices in the country.

Table 2   Expenditure on domestic and international trips

Average travel expenditure per trip

Year	Domestic ($)	International ($)
2005	440	1991
2006	492	2449
2007	513	2742
2008	535	2826
2009	496	2633
2010	517	2583
2011	538	2874
2012	580	2872
2013	583	3273

There are 2 main reasons for higher expenditure in international trips:

- Duration of an international trip.
- Higher airfares and other costs.

Higher expenditure means more opportunities for the companies to expand. Expenditure on both domestic and international trips shows an increasing trend.

Return on Investment

Oxford Economics managed to develop a relationship between business travel and industry performance over time with the help of an econometric model. This model produced a range showing an acceptable level of confidence (95%). Taking the median of that range, it tells that every dollar invested in business trips will generate a revenue return of 9.5% and a profit of 2.9%.

Entry Strategy

Inspirock was founded by Anoop Goyal and Prakash Sikchi in 2012. It covers major destinations in the U.S. and Europe. It monetized through revenue sharing model by facilitating users to book tickets from different providers. MakeMyTrip raised $3 million in seed funding acquiring 18% of its share.

The Way Ahead

The emerging trends in the online travel portals have further given impetus to the websites like MakeMyTrip to ponder over their future line of action. Observing their present working scenario, the company needs to decide how it has to further expand itself outside India. MakeMyTrip can either expand its product portfolio in its existing working locations in countries like UAE, Singapore and USA, the countries where it is already present or it could enter into areas nearby India as it has got a resounding success in the home turf, thus it has bright chances of getting fast growth in the South-Asian countries because the factors are more or less the same. A third case can also be adopted in which MakeMyTrip can plan to enter into a completely new market after doing an analysis of the favorable factors needed for the online travel company and the economy as a whole. The company also needs to understand the following questions, viz., which products and services portfolios and countries can the company profitably enter into? When there is so much of cut throat competition amongst the different online portals, how will MakeMyTrip be able to maintain its customer loyalty? What more benefits in terms of "holiday *pe* holiday offer" or prepaid foreign exchange card or providing the service of long-term immigration visas/work permits for corporates, is it going to offer to its customers?

Thus, MakeMyTrip needs to define its present and future functioning based on the fact how much it can differentiate itself from its competitors, how user-friendly their app and website can be, and how easy, convenient and affordable the offerings can be made by the company. Besides the customers in general and corporates, in particular, now want that all their travel requirements may get fulfilled under one roof. Providing them better services comprehensively and in an eclectic manner will ensure that MakeMyTrip comes out as a face in the crowd and will help carve its unique niche in the group of travel companies.

Teaching Note

Synopsis

MakeMyTrip is a revolutionary venture started in India in the year 2000 which changed the way the customers perceived about booking and reservation for travel. Earlier it was a time consuming job as most of the booking had to be done on a physical basis. During its journey, the company has entered into a lot of services like reservation of flight and train tickets, hotel bookings, tour and travel packages etc. With its success in the Indian Continent, MakeMyTrip plans to cross the national boundaries and establish its roots in other developed and emerging economics such as Singapore, UAE and United States of America. The case deals with the countries MakeMyTrip have entered into along-with the market scenario and the entry strategies. Understanding the fact that MakeMyTrip is not the sole online travel portal and that it faces huge competition from various companies across the globe, MakeMyTrip has evolved dynamically in the past 15 years. But despite all this, it has not yet been listed in the top 10 online travel portals of the world. Considering these factors, what does MakeMyTrip need to do to speed up its growth trajectory?

Teaching Objectives
This case illustrates a number of concepts like marketing challenges in emerging markets, including expansion strategies, e-commerce and marketing and issues in conducting business. Although developed for post graduate students, it is also appropriate for executive education programs in "emerging markets," business growth and strategy.

Teaching Plan
The suggested teaching plan is to divide a ninety minute class into five sections: an analysis of the acquisition and the company's success factors (15 minutes), a broader discussion about emerging market conditions (20 minutes), a critique of the issues (20 minutes) and an evaluation of possible paths forward for sustaining the brand (20 minutes). The last fifteen minutes can be used to summarize the main points.

Analysis
Emerging vs. Developed Economies
Normally, when students are asked to distinguish emerging markets from developing and developed economies, two types of variants are likely to arise, viz., based on the virtue of their fast economic growth and on the basis as emerging strong competitors for various business processes (especially those being outsourced).

The class discussion will bring out quite a few elements of the challenges of operating a business in many of the emerging markets like frequent policy changes, insecurity of intellectual property rights (IPRs), unreliable product quality, insufficient good quality local talent- despite a huge number of unemployed people, navigating government bureaucracies and the crowning problem of all- corruption which is endemic at all levels.

A wide range of factors play a role in the operations of a business from emerging markets like India, which could include infrastructure bottlenecks, issues related to policies, stability in the financial markets, growth in the country's disposable income, tourism related challenges, ecommerce laws, depreciation in the Indian rupee, etc.

Another major difference is the physical infrastructure like roads, ports and communications. This is also a reason why companies are wary when it comes to entering developing economies. Even though MakeMyTrip is leading in its sector, still the internet penetration is still quite nascent. There is more emphasis on creating mobile apps which can reach out to a larger audience.

Entrepreneurs in developed markets rely a lot on a range of institutions to facilitate transactions and manage operations in their home markets. Such infrastructure is usually missing in the emerging economies. If they are not missing, then they are woefully inadequate. Market and consumer data are easily available for many entrepreneurs in developed economies. In a developing economy, especially with the cultural dimensions of India, it is highly complicated exercise, requiring deep knowledge of customer needs and distribution networks. The challenge of transacting in the absence of well-developed market infrastructure can be best illustrated by the Nobel Prize winning economist George Akerlof's example of a used car market. (This can be given as extra reading.)

Strategies for Growth in Emerging Markets
Although due to the problems in many emerging countries because of the slowdown, companies are rethinking their strategies. Some of the questions which can lead to a better class discussion are

1. Are strategies from one emerging market replicable in another market?
2. What are the cultural and socio-economic demands of the growth markets?
3. What are the competencies and capabilities that the company should have to succeed in particular markets?
4. What kind of financial or market metrics should be used for evaluating success?

Succeeding in emerging markets would involve applying the right strategies based on local knowledge and a focus on learning and adapting as the firm grows. The case study would provide an opportunity to analyze how organizations could build more effective and sustainable platforms for growth in emerging markets.

The EPRG framework can also be taught through this case, as the global expansion of MakeMyTrip is following this framework.

EPRG Framework

EPRG (Ethnocentric, Polycentric, Regiocentric, and Geocentric) orientations describe an organization's process of evolution towards internationalization. Initially firms begin by being Ethnocentric where they emphasize their domestic market in the decision making. As firms gain experience and involvement through exporting they start to focus on their host market in the decision making and thus become Polycentric. As the number of host markets increase, the firm starts to emphasize on a region (e.g., South Asia, North America) in the decision making and thus become Regiocentric. Finally, the firm becomes Geocentric when it emphasizes multiple regions in their decision making and become globally oriented.

Based on the original works of Perlmutter (1969) and Wind et al. (1973), Keegan (1995) suggested an enriched model comparing the stages of internationalization as presented in Table 3.

Table 3   Stages in the evolution of the TNC (Transnational Corporation)

S. No.	Stage and company	Strategy	View of world	Style/Model	Orientation
1.	Domestic	Domestic	Home country	NA	Ethnocentric
2.	International	International	Extension markets	Coordinated federation	Ethnocentric
3.	Multinational	Multinational	National markets	Decentralized federation	Polycentric
4.	Global	Global	Global markets or resources	Centralized hub	Regiocentric
5.	Transnational	Global	Global markets and resources	Integrated Network	Geocentric

Source Adopted from Keegan, W. (1995). *Global Marketing Management*, 5th Edition, p. 363

Growth Through Adjacencies

Growth through adjacencies is a very effective way for MakeMyTrip to achieve repeated bursts of new growth. It will help the firm identify and rank promising opportunities for expansion that are outside, but closely related to, their core business.

REFERENCES

Keegan, W. (1995). *Global Marketing Management* (5th edition). Prentice Hall.

Perlmutter, H. V. (1969). The Tortuous Evolution of the Multinational Corporation. *Columbia Journal of World Business*, vol. 4, no. 1, pp. 9–18.

Wind, Y., Douglas, S. P., & Perlmutter, H. V. (1973). Guidelines for Developing International Marketing strategies. *The Journal of Marketing*, vol. 37, no. 2, pp. 14–23.

Xinran, L., Dae-Yong, K., & Alastair, M. (2006). The Effect of Prior Destination Experience on Online Information Search Behaviour. *Tourism and Hospitality Research*, vol. 6, no. 2, pp. 160–178.

Web References

http://www.greenworldinvestor.com/2011/10/22/top-online-travel-agenciesportalssites-in-india-list-and-review-best/.

http://dazeinfo.com/2015/03/19/e-commerce-industry-india-worth-13-5-billion-2014-will-cross-16-billion-2015/.

http://www.inc.com/encyclopedia/brand-equity.html.

http://www.sitejabber.com/reviews/www.makemytrip.com.

http://articles.economictimes.indiatimes.com/keyword/makemytrip.

http://articles.economictimes.indiatimes.com/2015-08-14/news/65524418_1_rajesh-magow-makemytrip-ceo-india.

http://yourstory.com/2014/07/online-travel-india/.

https://www.questia.com/library/journal/1P3-1889954271/impact-of-e-commerce-on-travel-and-tourism-an-historical.

http://online-travel-sites-review.toptenreviews.com/.

http://techcrunch.com/2015/06/24/inspirock/.

http://www.inspirock.com/aboutus.

http://www.similarweb.com/country/united_states.

http://www.investors.makemytrip.com/phoenix.zhtml?c=238356&p=irol-irhome.

http://www.bls.gov/opub/mlr/2015/article/travel-expenditures-2005-2013-domestic-and-international-patterns-in-recession-and-recovery.htm.

https://www.ustravel.org/research/domestic-research.

https://www.ustravel.org/sites/default/files/Business_Travel_ROI_Study_Key_Messages.pdf.

Table 1   Competitors of MakeMyTrip in Singapore

Wego	Wego.com is a Singapore based travel site and has its regional offices in Bangalore, Jakarta, Australia and Dubai. It is a leading travel site in the Asia Pacific and the Middle East. It was founded by Craig Hawett and Ross Veitch. They were the former executives of Intercontinental Hotel Group and Yahoo. It covers more than 700 travel sites. Users can easily compare and book flights, hotels or make other deals. It is available in more than 50 countries and in over 30 different languages. It also converts prices to 42 different currencies
Chan Brothers	Chan Brothers is one of the leading travel and tour operators of Singapore, giving their customers a wide range of choices for holiday destinations. Chan Brothers has been in this business for the last five decades. It offers bookings for flights, hotels, cruises, packaged tours and customized holidays. They also offer travel gift vouchers and travel insurance
Zuji	Zuji is one of the leading travel portals in Singapore. Zuji is actively involved in operations in Singapore, Hong Kong and Australia. It began its business in 2002 and is currently associated with more than 150,000 hotels, approximately 400 airlines across the world, and vendors for car hiring and insurance purpose. There are 60,000 unique visitors on an average per day on the website

MakeMyTrip in USA

After leaving their own mark in its category as a brand known for transparency, affordability and reliability in India, MakeMyTrip stacked its success in 2005 in the US by launching its operations.

Major Products are:

- Tickets of domestic and international airlines
- Bus and rail ticket provisions for domestic networks
- Private taxi
- Car rental provisions
- Meetings, conferences and exhibitions
- B2B Services
- Incentives.

Why USA

The travel and tourism industry generated approximately 1.5 trillion in 2013. This industry has created 7.8 million jobs and contributed around 9% in U.S exports. Americans have a higher frequency of travelling as compared to the rest of the world (Fig. 2).

Reliance Jio—Late, but the Latest and Later?

Swati A. Kulkarni and K. Prakash Vel

Evolution of Indian Telecom Industry

The licence for setting up telephone exchanges was given to a British company called 'Oriental Telephone Company' in 1881. This company constructed telephone exchanges in different cities of India like Calcutta (now Kolkata), Madras (currently Chennai) and Bombay (now Mumbai). Once India became independent from British rule in 1947, India's Ministry of Communication formed the Department of Post, Telephone and Telegraph by nationalizing different foreign telecom companies.[1] It completely enjoyed its monopoly for a substantial time in providing telecom services in India. Private companies had to be satisfied only with the production of telecom equipment in India.[2]

[1] Press Information Bureau, Government of India 2017, Accessed 30/08/2017, http://pib.nic.in/newsite/mainpage.aspx.

[2] Indian Telecom Industry, Telecom Industry, Telecom Industries, 2017, Accessed 2/09/2017, http://www.indianmirror.com/indian-industries/telecom.html.

S. A. Kulkarni (✉)
SIES College of Management Studies, Navi Mumbai, India
e-mail: swatik@sies.edu.in

K. Prakash Vel
University of Wollongong, Dubai, UAE
e-mail: prakashvel@uowdubai.ac.ae

© The Author(s) 2019
A. Sikdar and V. Pereira (eds.), *Business and Management Practices in South Asia*, https://doi.org/10.1007/978-981-13-1399-8_9

Later, Indian Government separated Department of Telecommunication (DoT) from Department of Post. DoT was given all the rights to take regulatory decisions and was made responsible for planning, implementing and managing telecom services in India. In 1986, Videsh Sanchar Nigam Limited was established by the Government of India to take care of International Telecommunications.[3] 'National Telecom Policy' in 1994 allowed private companies to provide telecom services in India. To ease the functioning of telecom service providers, India was divided into 23 service areas including four metros.

Kolkata witnessed the first cellular call of India which was made in July 1995 over Global System for Mobile (GSM) network.[4] In continuing the progress of telecom services in India, mobile services were launched shortly in the capital of the country, Delhi, and also in the financial city of India, Mumbai. Different mobile services helped the country in faster communication. To monitor different issues related to telecom and internet service providers, an independent body was needed and hence in 1997, Telecom Regulatory Authority of India (TRAI) was established. The main responsibility of this body is to handle different regulatory issues in telecom industry (see footnote 2).

Government of India (GoI) launched a policy for Internet Service Provision which opened the doors for private players as Internet service providers. With the new telecom policy in 1999, Government encouraged these private players by allowing them a revenue sharing model in place of fixed licence fee.[5]

Private companies started providing domestic as well as International long distance calls in the year 2000. It was the time for telecom service providers to gain more popularity in the consumer market and hence in 2003, TRAI made a strategy to lower down the cost of calls made from mobile phones. It introduced a model called 'calling party pay model'.[6]

[3] Tata Communications History, Tata Communications Information – *The Economic Times*, 2017, Accessed 30/08/2017, http://economictimes.indiatimes.com/tata-communications-ltd/infocompanyhistory/companyid-11992.cms.

[4] History of Indian Telecommunication, History of Indian Communication, Accessed 31/08/2017, https://telecomtalk.info/history-of-indian-telecommunication/67789.

[5] New Telecom Policy 1999, Telecom Regulatory Authority of India, *New Telecom Policy 1999*, 2017, Accessed 04/09/2017, http://www.trai.gov.in/about-us/acts-policies/new-telecom-policy-1999.

[6] *The Hindu*, CPP for Cellular Mobile Services, 2017, Accessed 06/09/2017, http://www.thehindu.com/2001/09/25/stories/13250462.htm.

To encourage foreign players' investment in telecom sector of India, FDI limit was raised to 74% in 2009.[7] This increased the competition between Indian telecom service providers as more foreign players entered the Indian market.

Responsibilities of both DoT and TRAI were clear. DoT was responsible for spectrum auctions and TRAI for setting up the prices. Both the regulatory bodies of telecom sector were powerful. 3G and 4G services were auctioned by GoI in 2010. Infotel Broadband Services Private Limited (IBSPL) won the auction for 4G services on a PAN India basis, which was later acquired by Reliance Jio. Consumers by now wanted something more than mere voice calls and text messaging from mobile phones. Their liking changed to data consumption. Telecom Service providers could sense this and changed their efforts in providing more data at lower cost to consumers. Service providers knew that their main revenue will come from data than the voice calls and text messaging. Though, Indian consumers could access internet from their desktop computers or laptops, their preference was more for mobile phones to access internet because of easy accessibility at a lower cost.

Younger generation prefers social media over traditional media to communicate with people. They communicate through Facebook, WhatsApp and Skype instead of text messages or voice calls. By 2013, online retailing and online banking was becoming a trend. It was noted that 18% of overall retail transaction was done online.[8] GoI launched 'Digital India' campaign in 2015 which encouraged further data or internet use for consumers. Main aim of the 'Digital India' campaign was to make India corruption free, knowledge economy and a digitally powerful nation. To support this, GoI was putting more efforts to improve infrastructure for internet connectivity across the nation. GoI wanted Indian citizens to use different digital facilities like DigiLocker, MyGov. in, e-Hospital. In 2015, the Indian E-commerce industry registered a CAGR of 35%.[9] To grab this opportunity, Airtel launched its 4G services

[7] Department of Telecommunication, and Government of India, 2009, Government of India, Department of Telecommunication, 2009–10, Annual Report, Page No 10, http://www.dot.gov.in/reports-statistic/2471.

[8] PwC India, 2017, Evolution of E-commerce in India Creating the Bricks Behind the Clicks, p. 10, http://pwc.in.

[9] Gadgets Now, 2017, Gadgets Now, Technology News, Latest & Popular Gadgets Reviews, Specifications, Prices, *Mobile Comparison, Technology Videos & Photos*, 2017, Accessed 06/09/2017, www.gadgetsnow.com.

in 14 different telecom circles of India in August 2015. Rising disposable income encouraged the use of smartphones in younger generation of India. Owing to the large number of smartphone owners, transition took place from e-commerce to M-commerce.

COMPETITION IN THE INDIAN TELECOM INDUSTRY

The major drivers behind the growth of Indian telecom Industry include[10]:

1. Internet Penetration and online shopping trends: Every second, three new users are entering in Internet world of India and hence mobile service providers in this industry constantly have to strive in maintaining a competitive edge on the same. India has already become second largest market for Internet globally (Table 1).
2. Per capita income is likely to double by 2025 in India. Indian consumers have shown their interest in online shopping than the traditional shopping. Mobile traffic for major fashion and general merchandise players in 2015 (Table 2):
3. Mobile wallets have become popular in India recently. Paytm, MobiKwik, FreeCharge, JioMoney are few apps which are very popular among Indian masses.[11] These apps have been used for different payments through the smartphones (Table 3). The statistics of the usage of mobile wallets for the last three years are as follows:

Top five wireless broadband services (as of 31 October 2016)[12] are mentioned in Table 4.

Airtel could sense the potential of Indian market and launched its 4G services across 296 towns in 14 telecom circles, first time in India in August 2015. Airtel gained 'first mover advantage' over its competitors in serving consumers of Indian telecom sector with 4G services.[13] Airtel

---

[10]Morgan Stanley, Asia Insight, India Technology, February 12, 2016.

[11]Morgan Stanley, The Next India, India's Digital Leap—The Multi Trillion Dollar Opportunity, September 26, 2017.

[12]TRAI Report, January 9, 2017.

[13]Bharti Airtel commercially launches 4G services in India's 296 towns, August 6, 2015, Accessed 02/09/2017, https://telecom.economictimes.indiatimes.com/news/3g-4g/bharti-airtel-commercially-launches-4g-services-in-indias-296-towns/48372755.

Table 1 Predicted internet penetration and online shopping trends

	2015	2020e
Internet penetration (%)	32	59
Online shoppers (million)	50	320

Table 2 Mobile traffic across fashion and general merchandise players

Company	Percentage
Myntra	100
Voonik	80
Flipkart	75
Snapdeal	75
ShopClues	70
Craftsvilla	70
Paytm	70
Alibaba	68
Amazon India	60
Yepme	60
ASOS	56
Zalando	50
Jabong	50

also gained the attention of consumers as it launched its 4G services at the same price of its 3G services.[14]

Airtel also offered free up-gradation of 3G SIM cards to 4G SIM cards. It was the strategy of Airtel to encourage its subscribers to move to 4G from its 3G services. 4G services are the main revenue source for Airtel. Airtel got into agreement with handset manufacturing companies like Samsung to manufacture 4G-enabled handsets for them. This was helping consumers to get 4G-enabled handsets. It was a win-win situation for Samsung as well as Airtel. To compete with Airtel, Vodafone also launched its 4G services in different cities like Mumbai, Delhi, Kolkata and different states like Karnataka and Kerala in February 2016.[15]

---

[14] Difference between 3G and 4G: 4G is 10 times faster in speed than 3G.

[15] *Live Mint*, May 11, 2016. http://www.livemint.com/Companies/qen0d15MIxn-0MFK92hmtUM/Vodafone-says-second-phase-of-4G-rollout-will-cover-4-new-ci.html.

Table 3 Payments through smartphones

Sr No	Year	Breakdown of funding				
		Payments (%)	Mobile POS (%)	Lending (%)	Wealth management (%)	Insurance (%)
1	2015	84	4	2	9	1
2	2016	55	0	37	5	3
3	2017	86	3	9	1	1

Table 4 Top 5 wireless broadband services

Company	Market share (in millions)
Bharti Airtel	46.22
Vodafone	40.19
Reliance Jio	35.44
Idea	29.76
Reliance Communication	16.95

Overall penetration in Indian market of smartphone users was less than 30% by February 2016.[16] India is the second largest country in the world in terms of population which shows that telecom service providers still have a very large scope to reach a wide set of untapped Indian consumers. Out of total population of 1.3 billion of India, only 220 million people are using smartphones. But with this number also, India is second in the list of smartphone users whereas China is at number one position.

In March 2016, Idea Cellular launched its 4G LTE[17] services in 10 telecom circles and reached to 50% of mobile users in India. This was in competition with earlier providers of 4G services like Airtel, Vodafone. To compete, Airtel expanded its 4G services to next 8 telecom circles by acquiring 4G spectrum from Aircel for INR 35 billion in April 2016. Finally, Reliance Jio launched its services on September 5, 2016 to change the dynamics of entire telecom industry of India.

[16] *The Hindu*, February 3, 2016, http://www.thehindu.com/news/cities/mumbai/business/with-220mn-users-india-is-now-worlds-secondbiggest-smartphone-market/article8186543.ece.

[17] 4G LTE is most advanced network for speed.

RELIANCE JIO'S ENTRY IN TELECOM INDUSTRY

Mr. Dhirubhai Ambani observed that postcard was the cheapest and most used communication medium in India. His vision was to make communication cheaper and faster than a postcard in the country.[18] To reach his goal, Reliance Industries ventured into communication industry and formed its subsidiary Reliance Communication (RCOM), in December 2002. Reliance Communication became the first telecom operator which provided CDMA and GSM with digital voice clarity.

Sometime later, it was observed that India was suffering from missed call syndrome.[19] To help consumer combat with this problem, RCOM launched its Dhirubhai Ambani Pioneer Offer which made incoming calls free for consumers. RCOM reached to 118 million customers and became India's leading telecom company. Not only that, it soon got listed on both stock exchanges of India at Mumbai, NSE and BSE. It also became one of the leading companies of the Reliance group.

In 2005, because of family disputes, Reliance group of companies got separated. RCOM was given to Mr. Anil Ambani and elder brother Mr. Mukesh Ambani became the owner of Reliance Industries Ltd. In 2010, to provide telecom services in India, Mr. Mukesh Ambani acquired Infotel Broadband Services Pvt. Ltd (IBSPL). IBSPL was the only company which won the bid for its 4G services on PAN India basis. IBSPL was acquired by Reliance Industries Ltd in 2013 and relaunched as Reliance Jio Infocomm Limited (RJIL).

After Hon. Prime Minister Mr. Narendra Modi came into power in 2014, he announced his Digital India campaign. Government of India (GoI) was giving large importance to infrastructure development and service quality. Better infrastructure and better service quality encouraged people to use various digital platforms or spend their money online. This scenario really helped RJIL to expand their market.

On 27 Dec 2015 on the 83rd birth anniversary of Mr. Dhirubhai Ambani, RJIL launched its Jio network services among its own and group company employees. Launch of RJIL marked re-entry of Mr. Mukesh Ambani in telecom business. The commercial launch was

---

[18] http://profit.ndtv.com/stock/reliance-communications-ltd_rcom/reports.

[19] Outgoing and incoming calls were chargeable for mobile phone subscribers in India but incoming calls were cheaper than outgoing calls. Hence, subscribers used to give a miss call as they were charged less for the incoming call than an outgoing call.

scheduled in March 2016 earlier, but got delayed and was finally launched on September 5, 2016.

Mr. Mukesh Ambani invested INR 1.5 lakh crore in his RJIL project. Jio crossed 100 million subscribers by end of February 2017. In just INR 309, people are getting free outgoing calls and 1 GB data free every day with 2 months' validity. Text messaging is also offered absolutely free.

Currently, Jio owns spectrum in 800 and 1800 MHz based in 10 and 6 circles, respectively, out of the total 22 circles in the country, and also owns PAN India licence for 2300 MHz spectrum. This spectrum is valid till 2035. RJIL has a network more than 250,000 km of fibre-optic cables in the country. In July 2016, RJIL launched Lyf brand of smartphones in country's metropolitan area with 4G-enabled Jio SIM cards.

CHANGING NATURE OF COMPETITION

Mr. Mukesh Ambani changed the dynamics of Telecom Industry of India. RJIL announced very different and economical schemes compared with its competitors and gave many choices to customers. Other major players of Indian telecom industry like Airtel, Vodafone and Idea had to find new strategies to compete with RJIL and also to sustain in this competitive market.

Jio was always on its toes to grab the market share faster. Since, RJIL launched 4G services; Jio was losing out on buyers who had mobile phone compatible only to 2G or 3G. To help such customers, Jio has come up with a device that upgrades 3G mobile phones to 4G services.

Since, Indian market is a price sensitive market; every customer prefers a service provider who offers a quality service at a lower cost. Additionally, Indian telecom industry has many players, and hence, switching cost for buyers from one service provider to another is extremely low. Hence, customers can easily move to another subscriber where they get a high-quality service at a lower cost. This has increased more competition in Indian Telecom sector.

Another reason for this intense competition among different telecom service providers is the number of users of smartphones. India has large number of young population with higher disposable income. As a result of which, almost every household has a smartphone in India. With such a huge consumer database, Indian mobile market is almost saturated. There is hardly any chance for any new player to enter the market. Each player has to struggle for its market share. In such scenario, if Jio wants to expand its market, it has to grab share from the competitors. It is extremely difficult for any player to exit this industry, because of the huge investment made to enter into the industry. Hence, the only choice left for every telecom service provider is to stay and fight out the competition.

To survive in Indian telecom market and grab more market share, Bharti Airtel is planning to invest Rs. 32,000 crores in 2018–19. In 2019–20, Airtel is planning to expand its network to offer quality service to its subscribers. With this investment, Airtel is expecting to grow its market share from 34 to 39%. Importantly, Airtel is not planning for more price reduction in future.[20]

Adding to the competition, Vodafone India and Idea are going for a merger. Both the companies are ranked at two and three, respectively, and will have a huge subscriber base of nearly 400 million users and enjoy 41% market share.[21] All the subscribers of telecom industry are benefited because of intense competition faced by all big players of telecom industry. Customers are enjoying low switching cost and high bargaining power with the service provider. They also enjoy portability, i.e., the subscribers can change their service provider without changing their number. As subscribers are price sensitive, they prefer service providers who offer them a quality service but at low cost. This makes subscribers very powerful.

To grab attention from subscribers in such competitive market, Jio launched its services at almost zero prices. Also, Jio made outgoing calls free for subscribers and offered 1 GB data at no cost, every day. This made it difficult for other players like Vodafone, Airtel and Idea to survive in the market, and hence, they had less bargaining power with customers and had to offer better services at a reasonable price. Result of this was all these big players Vodafone, Airtel and Idea had to slash down their prices by 40%.

[20] *The Economic Times*, September 19, 2017, https://tech.economictimes.indiatimes.com/news/corporate/bharti-airtel-plans-to-spend-over-rs-32000-crore-in-next-two-fiscals/60741008.

[21] *The Economic Times*, March 21, 2017, https://telecom.economictimes.indiatimes.com/news/idea-cellulars-board-approves-vodafone-idea-merger/57726148.

MARKETING MIX OF RJIL

Product Differentiation

RCOM as mentioned earlier, made incoming calls free for customers, way back in 2002 itself. When Jio was launched in 2016, incoming calls were free, but outgoing calls and data were charged at high rates.

RJIL offered its 4G services in 22 telecom circles PAN India using Long-Term Evolution (LTE) technology. RJIL transferred then voice calls over LTE termed as VoLTE, a new technology. VoLTE gave the advantage of free voice calls using the broadband network. Jio offered its customers free voice calls with VoLTE technology. However, VoLTE needed supporting infrastructure like IP Multimedia Subsystem (IMS) to be developed and also LTE-enabled smartphones to offer the best usage to its smartphone users.

RJIL signed agreement with different handset manufacturing companies like Samsung, Apple and Micromax to offer competent handsets for their services.[22] To help customers know more on Jio products and tariff plans, Jio launched its website. On this website, customers can register their interest to buy SIM cards. In order to provide better services to customers in terms of network, RJIL acquired 751.1 MHz quantum of spectrum from TRAI and became the largest liberalized spectrum holder in the country.

To provide the best experience in terms of quality and speed to Jio subscribers, RJIL used both FDD-LTE (on 1800 MHz) and TDD-LTE (2300 MHz) technologies. RJIL, uses 800MHz for 2G and 3G voice call services in as these services gives the best results. 1800 and 2300MHz spectrum bandwidths are used for 4G network services.

Thus, RJIL differentiated its product not only based on network, technology or pricing but also various features offered to customers.

Pricing

Sharp discounts and complimentary services were the strategies of RJIL to face competitor and gain more and more market share. Till March end 2017, Vodafone, Idea and Airtel did not show any difference in their

---

[22] *Business Standard*, 2015, Today's Paper, *Business Standard*, 2015, Accessed 04/09/2017, http://www.business-standard.com/todays-paper.

market share and earned revenue as till that time, RJIL did not book its revenue.

Customer using feature phones for voice calls were encouraged by RJIL to use their 4G services. This changed market equation dramatically. RJIL came out with a relevant offer for them. With this offer, these subscribers can update their services from 2G or 3G to 4G at very nominal rate. This offer gives them unlimited outgoing voice calls for free. While giving so many offers to customers, RJIL could lock their SIM card to the device. It is just to secure itself by not allowing customers to use competitor's phone instead of RJIL phone.

RJIL offered free unlimited outgoing voice calls and SMS (up to 100 SMS every day), 4 GB data along with unlimited data access (during night time) with the validity of 28 days for Rs. 499. To compete with this offer, Airtel offered 2 GB data for Rs. 455 for a period of 21 days. Vodafone's Rs. 497 plan has offered 3 GB data for a period of 28 days. Idea played its card by offering 3 GB of data for Rs. 455 with a validity of 28 days. In the plan of Rs. 999 offered by RJIL, 10 GB data was given to subscribers along with all the goodies like unlimited data at night and free voice calls and SMS (up to 100/day). All these plans were with the validity of 28 days. But Vodafone went little ahead and offered unlimited data, with the speed capped at 40 kbps after consuming the 10 GB data. RJIL again beat this by coming out with Rs. 1499 plan in which subscribers could enjoy 20 GB data. Airtel offers 80 kbps speed between 15 and 17 GB and 40 kbps beyond that, while Vodafone offers 40 kbps speed after exceeding the limit.[23]

Promotion

RJIL was not the only player of telecom services in India when it started its operations. Though it launched its services at value prices, it still had to reach a large number of consumer database and hence promotion was mandatory for RJIL. To add huge credibility to the brand, RJIL got Mr. Shahrukh Khan, the king of Bollywood as Jio's Brand Ambassador.[24]

---

[23] 91 Mobiles, September 1, 2016, https://hub.91mobiles.com/reliance-jio-vs-airtel-vs-vodafone-vs-idea-tariffs-compared/.

[24] *The Hindu*, December 25, 2015, http://www.thehindu.com/news/cities/mumbai/business/shah-rukh-khan-to-be-brand-ambassador-for-reliance-jio/article8028076.ece.

Vodafone and Airtel had a large customer database in the market. RJIL had to increase their brand awareness to gain more market share. To gain more market share, RJIL offered free SIM cards in various college and office campuses and also offered a free subscription till 31 December 2016, supported with advertisement which said these services can be continued if subscribers are registering for the prime membership for just INR 309/-.

To promote Jio, RJIL also became associate sponsors for 7 teams of Indian Premier League (IPL). Only one team was sponsored by Idea Cellular. Players of all 7 teams sponsored by Jio were shown dancing on Jingle 'Jio Dhan Dhana Dhan' (translates to 'live happily my boy'—a psychographic positioning) during IPL and promoting the brand. These seven teams were divided according to the cities but were dancing on one single common tune of Jio, an effective message indeed that was given to audience.

Jio came with another campaign which gave again free service for three months. The campaign offered 1 GB data free every day for 56 days along with free unlimited voice calls for just INR 309/-. INR 399/- gave 1 GB data free for 84 days and INR 501/- gave 2 GB data free for 556 days. In all these tariff plans, unlimited outgoing voice calls are made non-chargeable for subscribers.

Another campaign brought out by RJIL was where Jio offered mi-fi concept (a portable broadband device). This campaign was for people who did not have 4G phones. They can enjoy 4G services on their 2G or 3G mobile phones using mi-fi. RJIL also offered diverse range of Apps like JioMusic, JioTV, JioMags, JioCloud, JioChat, JioCinema, JioXpressNews, JioMoney to name a few. Then Jio started promoting its services to different segments like Jio Health Hub for fitness conscious people, Jio Education for student community. To promote Jio, RJIL also partnered with Samsung by offering free Jio services to customers for period of 90 days on selected Galaxy devices.

RJIL wanted to encash on opportunities arising from launching of Goods and Services Tax (GST) by GoI. RJIL came out with JioFi and JioGST starter kit and also JioGST billing app. JioGST starter kit includes GST software solutions for one year, unlimited outgoing voice calls, 24 GB data for one year, JioFi device and GST billing App. This starter kit came with the pricing of INR 1999/- and RJIL claimed to have offered benefits of INR 10884/- in the kit. GST was launched in July 2017. After that all business people were in need of GSTIN number to file their taxes and returns. This Jio kit will help business people to file their GST and also can file returns.

To fight this basket of applications and discount offered by RJIL, Airtel came out with its own promotional strategy. Airtel was promoted by Sasha Chhetri, the Airtel Girl along with her friends in a new promotional campaign designed by Airtel. In this campaign, Shasha is trying to promote Airtel for India's fastest Mobile network. The fastest mobile network offered by Airtel is approved by Okla—the global leader in mobile broadband testing and web-based network diagnostic applications. Also, this campaign is 360 degree media mix led by TV and will be supported in outdoor, print, radio and digital medium.[25]

People

Before RCOM, Reliance Industries were mainly into B2B. Reliance Industries started their own retail store (Ex. Reliance Fresh started in 2006[26]). This new venture gave them the fair idea of dealing with consumers.

Since Reliance has a big name in the market, getting skilled and knowledgeable people was never a problem for RJIL. Additionally, people who were with RCOM and retail business of Reliance are the pillars of RJIL. Thus, RJIL is an organization with people who are loyal to Reliance group, familiar with Reliance culture and also are familiar with telecom market in India. They exactly know what consumers need and how to reach to them. RJIL has offered attractive schemes for its vendors to keep them happy. RJIL have made it sure that its vendors are also loyal to RJIL.

CHALLENGES FACED BY RJIL

As discussed earlier, Airtel was the first Telecom Service Provider who offered 4G services and then other players came in. So, RJIL could not enjoy the 'First Mover Advantage' for its 4G services. RJIL really had to have a strong strategy backed by good product differentiation and quality services to grab the market share. It was a major challenge for RJIL.

---

[25] Press Release, Airtel, March 15, 2017.

[26] https://relianceretail.com/reliance-fresh.html.

Getting network throughout the country was another major challenge as India is still a developing country as far as infrastructure goes.

'Low cost means low quality', is the perception of Indian consumers. Since Jio was offering services at very low cost, it was difficult to convince people for RJIL's good product as well as service at affordable prices. Changing perception of a consumer was another major challenge faced by RJIL.

Dealing with regulatory bodies, following their norms and finding right balance between regulations and customer needs was one of the major challenges for RJIL. Government of India is also taking a lot of initiatives for the betterment of telecom sector of India. TRAI is focusing on identifying various issues faced like licence acquisition, spectrum allotment by different telecom service providers. GoI is also planning to auction 5G spectrums in bands like 3300 and 3400 MHz to promote different application based on Internet in different smart cities of India.[27]

Also, on 20 March 2017, Vodafone–Idea merger was announced. There are few more mergers that are in pipeline. Bharti Airtel will be buying Telenor India's operations, MTNL (Mahanagar Telephone Nigam Limited) is seen to be merged with Bharat Sanchar Nigam Limited. So it is clear that Indian Telecom Industry is heading towards an oligopoly, where three to four players together will control over 90% of the market.[28] This may occur as a big challenge for RJIL.

FUTURE OF RJIL

RJIL was continuously taking feedback about its product and services by talking to people, by encouraging people to go to Jio centres which are set up in 800 different towns of India just to help customers with their grievances. In August 2017, RJIL launched its first phone which is a substitute to featured phone of other competitors. This phone can be possessed with an initial payment of just INR 1500/-. RJIL is planning to return this initial payment in future. In two days' time, 5 million bookings were already done for this phone. RJIL is also planning to have a tie-up with Apple in future, so that it can acquire these subscribers too.

---

[27] IBEF Report, 2017, IBF Report, 2017, https://hub.91mobiles.com/reliance-jio-vs-airtel-vs-vodafone-vs-idea-tariffs-compared/.

[28] Scroll.in, April 3, 2017, https://scroll.in/article/833434/deals-like-the-vodafone-idea-merger-are-the-way-forward-for-the-telecom-industry-and-the-consumer.

Table 5   Data and Voice call usage across age groups

Age group	On data (Rs/month)	On voice calls (Rs/month)	% of total spent on data in a month
<15 years	166	29	85
15–24 years	210	104	67
25–34 years	239	119	67
35–44 years	235	142	62
>45 years	275	277	50

Table 6   Data consumption across different demographic profiles

Age	Gender	Region	Occupation/ marital status	Activity	Time spent (min/day)	Total data consumption (GB/month)
<18 years	Male	Metros	Student	App/games downloads	160	6.7
18–24	Female	Metros/ Minimetros	Single	Social networking	263	2.77
25	Female	Minimetros	Married	Making calls	84	1.4
Up to 24 years	Male	Minimetros/ lower	Student	Games, videos, music, browsing	211	2.9

Next plan is to make many college campuses of India Wi-Fi free so that students can have easy access to internet at affordable prices.

In 2011, 430 million of population of India was in age group of 15–34 and it is predicted that by 2020, India will be the world's youngest country with 64% of its population in the working age group.[29] Also, the statistics show that younger generation spend more time accessing data than voice calls (Tables 5 and 6).[30]

The data consumption on smartphones and Demographics of the younger generation.

Given the above trends, the current strategies of RJIL providing a long-term success and its sustainability remain to be looked at.

[29] *The Hindu*, April 17, 2013, India is set to become the youngest country by 2020.

[30] *Live Mint*, Wed, May 17, 2017, http://www.livemint.com/Money/xWFJ353DGq1WZOceuXPSrO/How-much-are-you-spending-on-mobile-data.html.

TEACHING NOTE

Synopsis

Mr. Mukesh Ambani has fulfilled the dream of his father, Mr. Dhirubhai Ambani, founder of Reliance Group of Industries in July 2016 by launching Reliance Jio Infocomm Limited (RJIL). Mr. Dhirubhai Ambani, a visionary could sense the market much before anyone else could actually do it. His every step was towards make India better and powerful. Launch of RJIL drastically changed the dynamics of Telecom Industry in India. RJIL empowered people by giving them free unlimited voice calls and data at low cost. RJIL has been a big helping hand to achieve the Prime Minister's dream of corruption free Digital India. RJIL being late entrant to the telecom market has been successful to grab 150 million subscribers of the country. Other players like Vodafone, Airtel and Idea are struggling to survive in the market. RJIL came out with different technologies like VoLTE to give quality services to its customers. RJIL made communication convenient for its subscribers at a low cost. However, is the success of RJIL sustainable?

Learning Objectives

- To be able to do Industry analysis and exploit the emerging opportunities for achieving business objectives.
- To be able to carry out critical analysis of the marketing mix of an organization.
- To be able to understand the competitive advantage.

Questions for Discussion

1. **List the competitive drivers of this industry in recent times. How did RJIL plan to leverage these key drivers for its business advantage?**

There are three key drivers behind the growth of online retail in India (see footnote 10):

1. Internet Penetration: Every second, three new users are entering in Internet world of India. India has already become second largest market for Internet globally.

2. Online shopping has been continuously increasing in India (see Table 1).
3. Per capita income is likely to double by 2025 in India. Indian consumers have shown their interest in online shopping than the traditional shopping. Mobile traffic for major fashion and general merchandise players in 2015 are shown in Table 2.

Mobile wallets have become popular in India recently. Paytm, MobiKwik, FreeCharge, JioMoney are few apps which are very popular among Indian masses (see footnote 11). These apps have been used for different payments through the smartphones. The statistics of the usage of mobile wallets for last three years are as follows:

Top five wireless broadband services (as of 31 October 2016) (see footnote 12) are mentioned in Table 4.

In 2011, 430 million of population of India was in age group of 15–34 and it is predicted that by 2020, India will be the world's youngest country with 64% of its population in the working age group (see footnote 29).

Also, the statistics show that younger generation spend more time accessing data than voice calls (see footnote 30).

The data consumption on smartphones and Demographics of the younger generation.

Airtel could sense the potential of Indian market and launched its 4G services across 296 towns in 14 telecom circles, first time in India in August 2015. Airtel gained 'first mover advantage' over its competitors in serving consumers of Indian telecom sector with 4G services (see footnote 13). Airtel also gained the attention of consumers as it launched its 4G services at the same price of its 3G services.

Mr. Mukesh Ambani spent INR 1.5 Lakh crore in his RJIL project. Jio crossed 100 million subscribers by end of February 2017. In just INR 309/-, people are getting free outgoing calls and 1 GB data free every day with 2 months' validity. Text messaging is also offered absolutely free.

Currently, Jio owns spectrum in 800 MHz and 1800 MHz based in 10 and 6 circles, respectively, out of the total 22 circles in the country and also owns PAN India licence for 2300 MHz spectrum. This spectrum is valid till 2035. RJIL has a network more than 250,000 km of fibre-optic cables in the country. In July 2016, RJIL launched Lyf brand of smartphones in country's metropolitan area with 4G-enabled Jio SIM cards.

RJIL announced very different and economical schemes compared with its competitors and gave much choice for customers. Other major players of Indian telecom industry like Airtel, Vodafone and Idea had to find new strategies to compete with RJIL and also to sustain in this competitive market.

RJIL offered its 4G services in 22 telecom circles pan India using Long-Term Evolution (LTE) technology. RJIL transferred then voice calls over LTE termed as VoLTE, a new technology. VoLTE gave the advantage of free voice calls using the broadband network. Jio offered its customers free voice calls with VoLTE technology. However, VoLTE needed supporting infrastructure like IP Multimedia Subsystem (IMS) to be developed and also LTE-enabled smartphones to offer the best usage to its smartphone users.

2. Critically analyse the positive and negative aspects of the Marketing Mix of Reliance Jio

Product Differentiation

RCOM as mentioned earlier made incoming calls free for customers in way back 2002. RJIL offered its 4G services to its subscribers at nominal rate and unlimited outgoing calls for free of cost. Also, RJIL signed agreement with different handset manufacturing companies like Samsung, Apple and Micromax to offer competent handsets for their services.

Pricing

Sharp discounts and complimentary services were the strategies of RJIL to face competitor and gain more and more market share. This offer gives them unlimited outgoing voice calls for free. It also offered daily 1 GB data free for customers with some validity period. RJIL came out with different prepaid and post-paid schemes along with boosters.

Promotion

To add huge credibility to the brand, RJIL got Mr. Shahrukh Khan, the king of Bollywood as Jio's Brand Ambassador (see footnote 24). To gain more market share, RJIL offered free SIM cards in various college and office campuses. To promote Jio, RJIL also became associate sponsors for 7 teams of IPL. RJIL wanted to encash on opportunities arising from launching of GST by GoI. RJIL came out with JioFi and Jio GST starter kit and also JioGST billing app. RJIL also offered different schemes for subscribers at very economical prices.

People

Since Reliance has a big name in the market, getting skilled and knowledgeable people was never a problem for RJIL. Also people, who were with RCOM and retail business of Reliance, are the pillars of RJIL. RJIL has key people who are loyal to Reliance group, familiar with Reliance culture and also are familiar with telecom market in India. They exactly know what consumers need and how to reach to them. RJIL has offered attractive schemes for its vendors to keep them happy. RJIL have made it sure that its vendors are also loyal to RJIL.

3. Discuss the challenges RJIL may face in future

RJIL really need to have a strong strategy backed by good product differentiation and quality services to grab the market share. It was a major challenge for RJIL. Getting network throughout the country was another major challenge as India is still a developing country as far as infrastructure goes. Since Jio was launched at zero prices and was offering services at very low cost, it was difficult to convince people for RJIL's good product as well as service at affordable prices. Changing perception of a consumer was another major challenge faced by RJIL. Dealing with regulatory bodies, following their norms and finding right balance between regulations and customer needs was one of the major challenges for RJIL.

Government of India is also taking a lot of initiatives for the betterment of telecom sector of India. TRAI is focusing on identifying various issues faced like licence acquisition, spectrum allotment by different telecom service providers. GoI is also planning to auction 5G spectrums in bands like 3300 MHz and 3400 MHz to promote different application based on Internet in different smart cities of India and this will further add to the competition.

To sustain and grow in the Indian telecom industry, maintaining and enhancing service quality is a key factor for RJIL. Offering a quality service in terms of networking and maintaining good customer relationships can be pre-emptive measures which RJIL can plan for the future.

Also, RJIL should start marketing for their products like 'Lyf' phones, 4G SIM cards aggressively since telecom market will be controlled by only 3–4 big players in future.

Since, RJIL is already in partnership with various mobile manufacturers like Samsung, Intex and they are also planning to have partnership with Apple, strengthening partner relationship management can also be a strategy for RJIL. Different manufacturer of mobile phones can help RJIL to grab a major market share in Indian Telecom Industry.

Overseas Courier Services, Pakistan: Logistics Operations at Central Region

Muhammad Naiman Jalil and Eesha Shah

INTRODUCTION

'We need to reduce operational costs. Our network operations are inefficient and costly. We are spending more than what we're earning. It is simply not sustainable', said Ashhad Ullah. 'Every day, I receive numerous complaints from our corporate customers in Karachi, stating that parcels are not delivered to their relevant customers in Lahore, Rawalpindi, Faisalabad, Islamabad and Peshawar on time'.

It was 26 December 2012. Ashhad Ullah—General Manager of OCS Pakistan Pvt. Ltd. was chairing a meeting at central region's headquarter in Lahore. Rising fuel costs and increased competition were worrisome as these had resulted in smaller industry-wide profit margins. Customers were increasingly demanding greater efficiency and timeliness for parcel and cargo delivery services.

In today's meeting, Taimoor Ahmed—(Regional Operational Manager) was also present. 'Our primary operational costs are transport costs for inter-city and intra-city transportation. We can perhaps try

M. N. Jalil (✉) · E. Shah
Suleman Dawood School of Business,
Lahore University of Management Sciences, Lahore, Pakistan
e-mail: muhammad.jalil@lums.edu.pk

A. Sikdar and V. Pereira (eds.), *Business and Management Practices in South Asia*, https://doi.org/10.1007/978-981-13-1399-8_10

reducing them. But I'm afraid, that this may lead to further deterioration in parcel delivery performance. Moreover, our regional headquarter is located in a congested area. We should follow TCS (the industry leader) as an example and move the regional headquarter near the airport, outside the city', Taimoor said in a slightly frustrated manner as this argument had been repeatedly presented to no avail.

Ashhad pondered about the potential capital expenditure involved, but said: 'Make a business case and I promise that I shall seriously look into it'.

A Brief History

Overseas Courier Service (OCS) first originated 50 years ago in Tokyo, with the main purpose of providing quick delivery for newspaper publisher's publications. OCS's, quality courier services are spread across 240 countries delivering 70 million business packages annually. In 1986, OCS Pakistan (Pvt.) Limited began operations as an independent courier services company. Currently, OCS Pakistan is delivering across 100 countries and 240 worldwide destinations. Its primary focus is parcel and cargo handling services within Pakistan. Currently, it has around 212 pick-up points in Pakistan with services ranging from overnight, same day, bulk shipment delivery, etc. OCS has always been known for its efficient premium quality and quick delivery system.

OCS Services

OCS provided parcel and cargo delivery services to its business and private customers. The parcels are generally small size packages whose size and weight is limited to 500 grams. Any item exceeding the weight or size limit is transported via cargo delivery services.

For domestic parcel shipments, OCS provides same day express services, next day delivery services and second day delivery services. For international shipments, OCS has partnered with international parcel delivery services to provide competitive services. The parcels are mainly collected from corporations and individuals. A major chunk of these corporations include banks and other institutions, sending parcels to individuals and other organizations. Furthermore, a large portion of these corporations have headquarters located in Karachi. OCS was well aware that this customer segment is quite time sensitive and, required all deliveries to be made before 10 a.m.

OCS also handless less than truckload (LTL) cargo and containerized cargo for its private and business customers and provides door-to-door, door-to-port and port-to-door delivery services to its cargo customers. The delivery time deadlines for cargo services were not as speedy or stringent as parcel services, but in general, OCS committed to delivering within 3–7 days.

Logistics Network

The logistics network of OCS has been designed in alignment to their strategic vision. OCS aims to provide quick delivery service, efficiently. To manage the efficiency and quick delivery requirements, it designed its logistics network to operate in a hub and spoke manner. The OCS office locations and parcel and cargo pick-up locations are spread across the country. Exhibit 1 shows the distribution of OCS office locations all over Pakistan.

For efficient management, OCS has subdivided the entire serving region (i.e. Pakistan) into three regions:

1. Northern region: Northern region headquarter (HQ) was located in twin cities of Rawalpindi/Islamabad with HQ serving cities such as Peshawar, Murree, Muzaffarabad, Abbottabad, Kohat and etc.
2. Central region: Central region's HQ was located in Ichhra Lahore. This region included surrounding cities of Okara, Kasur, Multan, Faisalabad, Vehari, Bahawalpur, Dera Ghazi Khan, Jhang, Sargodga, Gujrat, Khushab and etc.
3. Southern region: Southern and south eastern cities of Pakistan such as Quetta, Kalat, Gwadar, Hub, Karachi, Hyderabad, Larkara, and Sukkar were organized under the regional HQ located in Karachi.

Cargo and parcels shipments were collected from each pickup point and aggregated at each office location. Subsequently, these shipments were routed according to their destination. For example, parcel shipments collected from pickup points in Sukkar city were first aggregated in Sukkar office location and sorted into two: within Sukkar and outside Sukkar deliveries. The shipments bounded for Sukkar city were then routed through intra-city transportation network, whereas outside Sukkar city shipments were sent to regional HQ in Karachi for sorting and would then be delivered using intercity transportation network (Exhibit 2).

Exhibit 1 OCS locations across Pakistan

For intra-city and inter-city transportation, OCS utilized a variety of transportation modes, such as motorcycle riders, delivery runners such as Suzuki Ravi pickup, and larger cargo trucks such as Hyundai Shehzore truck as well as air cargo services.

For intra-city transportation network, OCS used a combination of motorcycle riders and runners. Long haul, intercity transportation was generally managed by using larger capacity trucks and runners. Additionally, OCS also utilized existing train facilities at different routes. In specific cases, where the distances were large and delivery service requirement was stringent, OCS utilized air cargo services. For example, parcel movements between Southern Regional HQ-Karachi and Central

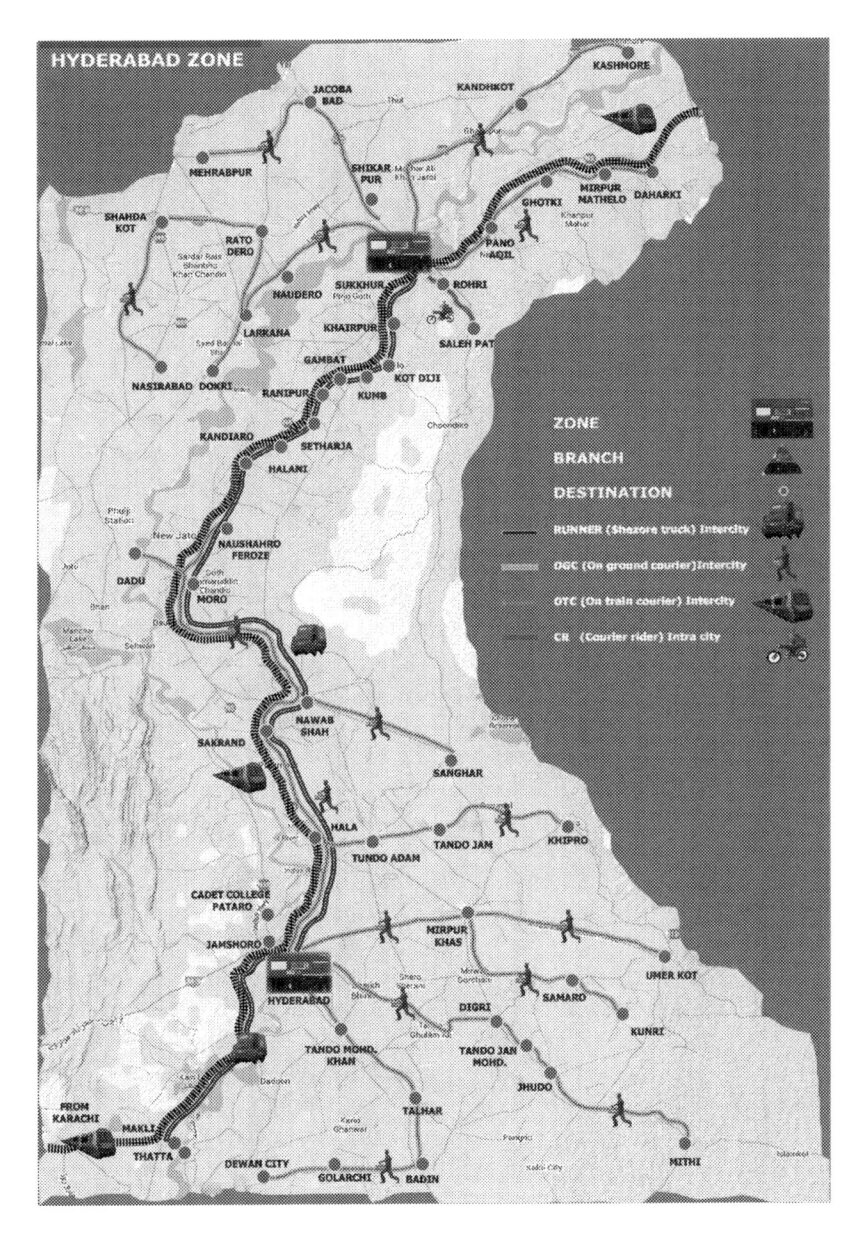

Exhibit 2   Intercity routing

Regional HQ-Lahore were managed by using Shaheen Airlines flights. OCS has a permanent contract with Shaheen Airlines where Shaheen Airlines was bound to carry 2000 kg of OCS shipments every night between Karachi and Lahore. The shipments from Southern Regional HQ-Karachi and Northern Regional HQ-Rawalpindi/Islamabad were also transported first to Central Regional HQ-Lahore via Shaheen Airlines flight and then moved from Lahore to Northern HQ by using Hyundai Shehzore trucks.

OCS utilized the above mentioned transportation and logistics network infrastructure to provide cargo and parcel shipment services. The exact choice of transportation mode and logistics network varied as per physical characteristics (weight and size) and delivery service requirements of the shipment.

Cargo Shipment

OCS takes special care of handling heavy shipments and bulky cargo. Cargo shipments often include personal furniture and corporate shipping. The cargo services of OCS can be classified as Personal cargo, Industry Solutions and containerized cargo. OCS is a certified IATA cargo agent, providing freight forwarding services as well as transportation services. Cargo shipments are collected through the help of trucks and consolidated at warehouses. These shipments are then shipped through air to domestic warehouses of the region of delivery. Shipments are charged according to their weight; in case of excess weight the standard IATA approved formula is used.

[Height (cm) × Width (cm) × Length (cm)]/5000 = volumetric weight

OCS's current cargo strategy can be inferred from the following example:

In the industrial capital, Karachi, heavy shipments are collected from all pickup locations in Karachi by utilizing Suzuki Ravi runners. These shipments are then aggregated and sorted at regional HQ—Karachi. The shipments that are bounded for within Karachi are dispatched using Suzuki Ravi runners. The outbound shipments that are destined outside Karachi are consolidated and shipped via Suzuki Ravi runners or Hyundai Shehzore trucks to the destination city offices or other regional HQs.

Parcel Delivery

The parcel delivery system of OCS is unique in terms of routing. A combination of riders classified as CCR and PCR are used to provide delivery within 48–72 hours. Apart from other minor distinctions, CCR is basically contractual staff with remuneration based on unit rates whereas PCR is permanent getting fixed monthly salary. Fuel costs were paid to the rider on km travelled basis, where petrol prices were Rs. 107 per liter and each rider's motorbike on average travelled 50 km/liter.

Parcel collection and delivery was available for inter as well as intra-city routes. For intra-city collection of parcels, riders performed milk-runs to collect the parcels from OCS offices and customer locations and aggregated the parcels at city office for consolidation, sorting and routing to its destination. Intra-city delivery of parcels was performed each morning by the riders, who performed milk-runs throughout the city on their motorbikes. Each rider had a special inbuilt case in his motorbike where he could carry a maximum of thirty-two (32) kg load. Picked up parcels were delivered by the riders to the city offices or regional HQs in case of Lahore, Karachi and Rawalpindi/Islamabad. At each location, consolidation, sorting and routing of parcels and cargo was done.

CURRENT SCENARIO

Sitting in his office, Taimoor deliberated where OCS could easily save on cost. He and his assistant Khalid had recently completed an exercise on inter-city transportation for transport cost savings. So he was not very sure if much can be saved there. Last mile transportation or intra-city transportation however, was a different story. Utilization of contractual workforce in parcel pickups had resulted in an extensive gaming behaviour among the CCRs as their unit rate based remunerations meant higher pay if they could visit customers with higher mail loads. Hence, riders actively lobbied to secure such potential city locations in their routes. Over the years, the routes at which riders travelled evolved organically while accommodating for all the intellect and biases of riders and their supervisors.

He thought perhaps a starting point could be to analyze a small subset of routes in the vicinity of Lahore HQ office. 'Khalid, can you provide me some data?' Taimoor called.

'What do you need?' asked Khalid.

'Get me the route data for four or five riders in the vicinity of our office. I need customer locations covered in these routes, each customer's average monthly or daily parcel loads, effective travel distances and travel times between all these customer locations and our office,' said Taimoor.

'Give me a few minutes,' replied Khalid.

After a few minutes, Taimoor heard Khalid saying, 'Here you go. I just sent you everything in email. What are you going to do with this data?' (Refer to Exhibits 3, 4 and 5)

'I am going to see if we can save on intra-city routing costs. Particularly the fuel costs. I feel our routes for our pickup riders may be quite inefficient,' replied Taimoor.

'Good idea. You do realize that if we are to save in routing or last mile distribution, we would need to have operational managers at all regional and city office locations onboard.' said Khalid.

'True, but first we need to see the extent of potential savings. That is why I am thinking to first analyze a small subset of routes in Lahore', replied Taimoor.

'Agreed, do you need anything else from my side?' said Khalid.

Taimoor thought for a moment and said. 'The boss has asked me to prepare the business case for the HQ location options'.

Exhibit 3   Client sample

Client no.	Coordinates		Daily parcels	Daily weight
	X-coordinate	Y-coordinate		
1	31.511	74.344	13	7
2	31.512	74.284	13	7
3	31.531	74.295	10	5
4	31.555	74.321	13	7
5	31.546	74.317	13	7
6	31.482	74.302	17	8
7	31.569	74.290	20	10
8	31.531	74.312	17	8
9	31.529	74.337	17	8
10	31.585	74.317	27	13
11	31.482	74.311	20	10
12	31.462	74.292	27	13
13	31.522	74.345	17	8
14	31.528	74.329	13	7

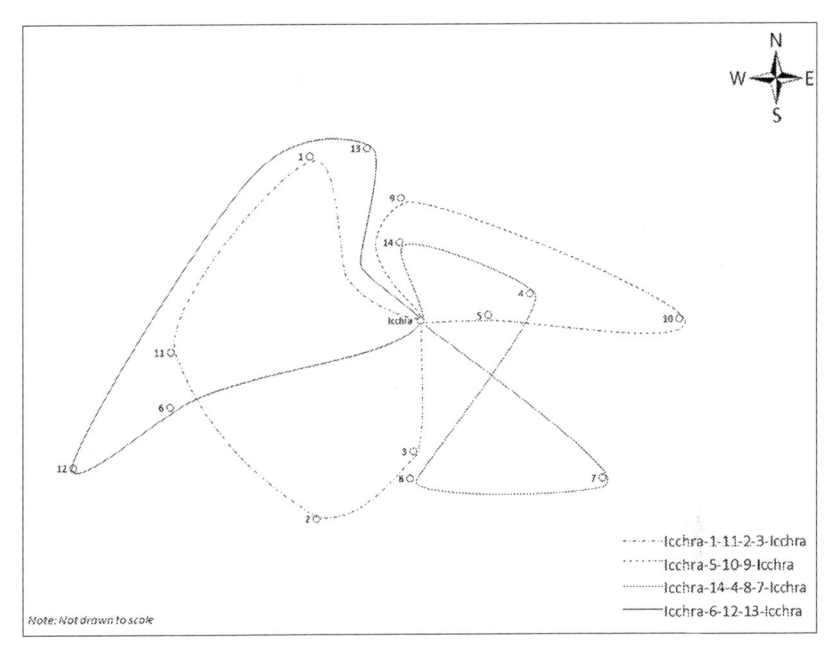

Rider 1:29 kg Icchra-1-11-2-3-Icchra

Rider 2:28 kg Icchra-5-10-9-Icchra

Rider 3:32 kg Icchra-14-4-8-7-Icchra

Rider 4:29 kg Icchra-6-12-13-Icchra

Exhibit 4　Rider's current routes (for clients in Exhibit 3)

'Is he serious?' exclaimed Khalid.

'Apparently yes, I'm thinking about analyzing the airport as opposed to our current office location in Icchra.' said Taimoor.

'Not a bad idea. Also think about Saghian too, as an option. A challenging problem though. How are you going to analyze it? On what basis are you going to compare them?' asked Khalid.

Taimoor thought for a moment and smiled. 'You see, the senior management thinks in terms of money. So I think, we should definitely show them how much it's going to cost.'

Exhibit 5   Distance and time matrix

Distance matrix	1	2	3	4	5	6	7	8	9	10	11	12	13	14
Ichhra	5 km / 10 min	4.9 km / 12 min	2.7 km / 8 min	3.4 km / 8 min	3.8 km / 7 min	9.1 km / 14 min	6.6 km / 17 min	0.9 km / 3 min	3.2 km / 8 min	7.1 km / 19 min	7.1 km / 21 min	11 km / 18 min	11 km / 18 min	2.2 km / 6 min
1	0	7.4 km / 14 min	6.3 km / 16 min	6.8 km / 12 min	5.9 km / 10 min	5.8 km / 10 min	9.9 km / 23 min	5.1 km / 12 min	2.9 km / 7 min	11.8 km / 24 min	6.5 km / 12 min	9.2 km / 15 min	2 km / 5 min	4 km / 9 min
2	9.6 km / 16 min	0	3.9 km / 9 min	9.1 km / 19 min	5.8 km / 10 min	7.9 km / 18 min	11 km / 22 min	4.2 km / 11 min	7.4 km / 12 min	14.4 km / 30 min	6.3 km / 13 min	7.1 km / 14 min	8.1 km / 14 min	7.5 km / 13 min
3	8.1 km / 18 min	3.9 km / 9 min	0	4.9 km / 12 min	6.4 km / 16 min	5.5 km / 13 min	6.7 km / 17 min	1.9 km / 6 min	6 km / 13 min	8.6 km / 18 min	8.6 km / 19 min	10.6 km / 22 min	6.7 km / 14 min	6.1 km / 15 min
4	8.1 km / 14 min	9.1 km / 19 min	4.9 km / 12 min	0	4.1 km / 10 min	4.6 km / 10 min	9 km / 22 min	3.8 km / 9 min	5.3 km / 10 min	5.8 km / 15 min	10.4 km / 18 min	14 km / 23 min	6 km / 11 min	3.8 km / 10 min
5	7.2 km / 13 min	8.3 km / 17 min	6.1 km / 12 min	1.9 km / 7 min	0	1.9 km / 6 min	5.6 km / 15 min	4.2 km / 9 min	4.6 km / 8 min	7.4 km / 16 min	10.9 km / 18 min	13.7 km / 20 min	5.3 km / 9 min	3.1 km / 8 min
6	5.8 km / 10 min	5.8 km / 13 min	5.5 km / 13 min	10.3 km / 19 min	1.9 km / 6 min	0	13.9 km / 27 min	8 km / 20 min	7.9 km / 12 min	15.8 km / 29 min	13.1 km / 25 min	16.2 km / 29 min	7 km / 12 min	8.1 km / 12 min
7	9.9 km / 23 min	11 km / 22 min	7.9 km / 18 min	3.9 km / 14 min	11.6 km / 17 min	13.9 km / 27 min	0	6.5 km / 16 min	9.1 km / 19 min	5.1 km / 14 min	8.2 km / 14 min	11.5 km / 22 min	11.4 km / 20 min	9.2 km / 20 min
8	6.5 km / 14 min	4.2 km / 11 min	6.7 km / 17 min	4.3 km / 12 min	5.7 km / 14 min	8 km / 20 min	6.5 km / 16 min	0	4.2 km / 8 min	8.6 km / 19 min	7.9 km / 14 min	10.4 km / 16 min	4.9 km / 9 min	4.3 km / 10 min
9	3.9 km / 8 min	7.5 km / 13 min	1.9 km / 6 min	6.7 km / 11 min	4.6 km / 10 min	7.9 km / 12 min	10.6 km / 19 min	4.2 km / 8 min	0	10.6 km / 19 min	14.2 km / 29 min	19 km / 32 min	1.4 km / 3 min	1.2 km / 4 min
10	13.4 km / 25 min	14.5 km / 30 min	5.9 km / 14 min	6 km / 15 min	6.9 km / 18 min	18.3 km / 29 min	4.8 km / 11 min	8.6 km / 19 min	9.2 km / 19 min	0	16.5 km / 30 min	19 km / 32 min	10.6 km / 21 min	9.6 km / 21 min
11	6.4 km / 12 min	6.3 km / 13 min	11.2 km / 27 min	10.4 km / 18 min	11.2 km / 18 min	1.1 km / 2 min	13.1 km / 25 min	8.8 km / 16 min	8.4 km / 15 min	16.5 km / 30 min	0	17.7 km / 30 min	14.2 km / 29 min	9.6 km / 21 min
12	9.6 km / 15 min	7.1 km / 14 min	10.1 km / 19 min	13.5 km / 23 min	13.7 km / 20 min	3.3 km / 8 min	16.2 km / 29 min	11.8 km / 19 min	10.4 km / 16 min	19 km / 32 min	17.7 km / 30 min	0	10.6 km / 16 min	11 km / 20 min
13	1.7 km / 5 min	10.4 km / 15 min	10.6 km / 22 min	6 km / 12 min	5.3 km / 10 min	8.6 km / 20 min	9.8 km / 20 min	4.9 km / 9 min	1.4 km / 3 min	10.3 km / 23 min	16.5 km / 30 min	9.9 km / 16 min	0	9.9 km / 18 min
14	3.5 km / 9 min	7.7 km / 15 min	6.7 km / 15 min	5 km / 11 min	3.5 km / 9 min	7.5 km / 14 min	10.4 km / 19 min	4.6 km / 13 min	1.2 km / 4 min	10.7 km / 23 min	10.7 km / 23 min	10 km / 16 min	10.6 km / 16 min	0

'True, but I guess we only need to see how the transport cost within Lahore and from Lahore HQ location to the exit points shall be affected. As transportation costs outside Lahore will not change,' said Khalid.

'Agreed, the boss is particularly concerned about the delays in delivering parcels originating from Karachi. Although, I think it's mainly because of delays in Shaheen Airlines,' said Taimoor.

Khalid added, 'I think we should focus more on deliveries originating from Karachi for our time based analysis'.

'Correct! Now let me think about this proposal in depth. I'll catch up with you for further ideas later,' said Taimoor.

OCS Central Region's Headquarter—Lahore

OCS's central region's headquarter was located in Icchra, Lahore. A bustling metropolis, Lahore, has gone through extensive population and infrastructure expansion over the years. A consequence of rapid expansion was that infrastructure expansion was lagging in comparison to population expansion, resulting in traffic congestions and delays. OCS's current regional HQ was located at Icchra, where all inbound shipments from Lahore and within Lahore were received. Similarly, all outbound shipments to Lahore and outside Lahore were made from Icchra.

Icchra, a central region in Lahore city, is one of the most densely populated areas in Lahore. Despite being the focus of major infrastructural developments such as Metro Bus and construction of Ferozpur road, it faced severe traffic congestions and delays.

Infrastructure developments within Lahore had begun taking place since the early 1990s. Abundant infrastructure expansion, modernization and development projects were introduced by successive governments. Lahore Canal bank road, Ferozpur road and Ring road were noteworthy projects. It was apparent that the government wanted to reorganize the city transportation by creating roadways that would promote faster connections among various Lahore suburbs while bypassing the congested central region. Similar developments also took place in inter-city highways that connected Lahore to other major urban centers in the wider region. This led to the availability of new exit points that can be accessed for long-haul inter-city parcel and cargo movements.

Exhibit 6 shows the current OCS location in Icchra, a potential HQ site near Airport, and a potential HQ site near Saghian. It also shows major exit points from Lahore. Saghian was at the junction of major

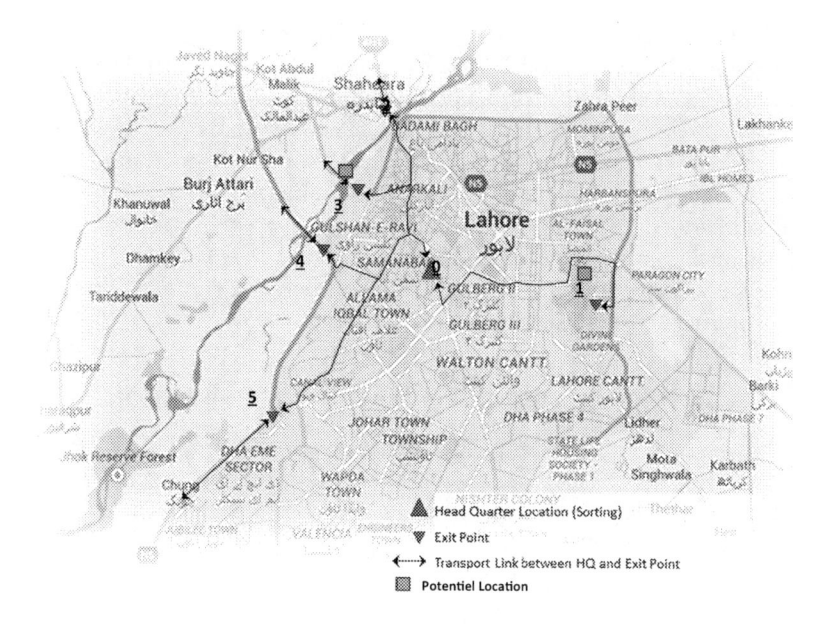

Notations

0	Icchra	**3**	Saghian
1	Airport	**4**	Motorway
2	Grand Trunk Road	**5**	Multan Road

Exhibit 6 Current, potential locations and exit points

highways such as Lahore-Sheikhupura expressway that could be used to travel to cities like Faisalabad. Similarly, the Motor Way was being used to travel to cities like Mianwali and Dera Ismail Khan (Exhibit 7). Exhibit 8 shows the travel distances and travel times of current and potential HQ sites from all exit points in Lahore. These exit points are:

1. Saghian
2. Motor Way (MT)
3. Grand Trunk Road (GT)
4. Airport (for air freight movements via Shaheen Airlines)
5. Multan Road

Exhibit 7   Exit points

Destination city	Exit points (Lahore)
Faisalabad	Saghian
Mianwali	Motorway
Dera Ismail Khan	
Safdarabad	Grand trunk road
Rawalpindi	
Mirpur, Azad Kashmir	
Narowal	
Karachi	Airport
Bhai Pheru	Multan road
Multan	

Exhibit 8   Exit point distance and time matrix

Distance matrix (km)

Exit points	OCS (Icchra)	Airport	Saghian
Saghian	9.45	30.4	0
MT	10.2	33.5	5.8
GT	12	26.3	6.9
Airport	25.8	0	28.4
Multan road	29.15	48.2	21
Total	103.4	157.9	89.4

Time matrix (min)

Saghian	14	30	0
MT	15	35	12
GT	18	23	9
Airport	31	0	26
Multan road	27	45	20
Total	120	161	101

Furthermore, Exhibits 9 and 12 provide the cost matrix for each of the modes of transportation. For shipments within Lahore and outbound shipments from Lahore, the details of the annual number of runners, trucks and riders are depicted in Exhibits 10, 11, and 14. Details of the effective distances from the assigned clusters are provided in Exhibit 13.

Taimoor knew that in order to make a decision, inter and intra-city cost analysis for each of the locations was necessary. He wasn't sure how

Exhibit 9   Cost per runner/truck

Runner		Trucks	
Average km covered/liter	9.0	Average km covered/liter	8
Diesel rate	110.0	Diesel rate	110

Exhibit 10   Annual runners from/to Lahore HQ

Exit Points	Outbound runners per exit point	Inbound runners per exit point	Total per route
Multan road	720	720	1440
GT	2160	2160	4320
MT	720	720	1440
Saghian	360	360	720

Exhibit 11   Annual trucks from/to Lahore HQ

Exit points	Outbound trucks per exit point	Inbound trucks per exit point	Total per route
Multan road	318	318	636
GT	270	270	540
MT	72	72	144
Saghian	0	0	0

Exhibit 12   Rider cost

Riders	
Average km covered/liter	50
Petrol rate	107

the choices would affect the inter-city costs. Taimoor thought that as the Airport and Saghian were located in the periphery of Lahore as opposed to Icchra, intra-city costs may go up. An alternative could be to follow TCS's hybrid approach.

Exhibit 13   Cluster distances

MID-POINT	OCS (Icchra)	Airport	Saghian
Davis road and Mall road	15.6	36.3	24
Shadman	6.3	41.6	26.1
Model Town and Garden Town	22.2	44.8	41.1
Badami Bagh and Allama Iqbal Town	10.8	46.1	12
DHA, Cantt and Gulberg	26.4	34.4	45
Total	81.3	203.2	148.2

Exhibit 14   Annual riders from/to Lahore HQ

Cluster	Inbound	Outbound	Total per route
Davis road	7560	3240	10,800
Model Town/Garden Town	3600	1800	5400
Gulberg/Cant DHA	7200	4320	11,520
Allama Iqbal/Badami Bagh	4680	2160	6840
Shadman	1800	720	2520

HYBRID APPROACH

Currently, TCS-their competitor, was using a hybrid approach. They had a regional warehouse near the airport from where they would sort all their deliveries, and only local deliveries were transported to their local warehouse where riders would perform milk-runs. This perhaps saves time and costs for Lahore bound and outbound deliveries; however there were no concrete numbers.

To use TCS as an example OCS could either use Saghian or the Airport as their HQ location, keeping Icchra their local collection and delivery point. Taimoor knew that if this were to be implemented, he would need to have a runner permanently touring between the regional HQ location and local delivery location in Icchra, Lahore many a times a day. According to Taimoor, this runner will cost around Rs. 220,000 annually.

Taimoor, was now lost, he had to sort intra-city routing as well as locate a viable new HQ location keeping all costs and travel timing in mind.

Teaching Note

Synopsis

While managing transportation and logistics operations, managers need to tread carefully between the conflicting objectives of operational cost and customer service. Often, these performance indicators are a result of strategic, tactical and operational decisions made by the managers. This case involves operational cost and customer service issues that OCS encountered in 2012. OCS is a major player in parcel and cargo services industry in Pakistan. Its services include parcel and cargo pickup and delivery for its private and business customers. The purpose of this teaching case is to expose class participants to the strategic, tactical and operational aspects of network planning and transport fleet planning within transportation and logistics industry. It involves analysis for route planning of transport fleet and selecting headquarter location for OCS's central region.

Teaching Purpose and Objectives

This case can be used to highlight transport network design and planning issues at MBA, executive and undergraduate levels. It can be used in various courses such as supply chain management, transportation and logistics management, and distribution management. The network design problem presented in this case can also be used to highlight the use of mathematical programming techniques (such as mixed integer programming based network planning models) for design and analysis of transport networks.

Discussion Questions and Analysis

Question 1: Develop a route plan for customer pickup locations identified by Taimoor. What are the primary cost and customer service drivers in route planning?

Question 2: Should OCS keep using its current location in Icchra as a central region headquarter (HQ) or follow the example of industry leader (i.e. TCS) and shift its central region HQ?

Question 3: The case also indicates the use of Hybrid approach for network planning. What is it? Is it preferable? Why or why not?

Question 1:

Develop the route plan for customer pickup locations identified by Taimoor. What are the primary cost and customer service drivers in route planning?

Analysis:

This question involves establishing route plans for pick from identified customer locations and in doing so the objective is also to determine the performance drivers in route planning. Various heuristics are available in literature for route planning. As a first step, one needs to establish a baseline for comparison. For this purpose, we can use the data provided in Case Exhibit 5. The exhibit provides the distance and travel time information between Icchra and each customer. Case Exhibit 4 provides the current routes that are in place. OCS used four riders to arrange the pickup from each customer location. Given the route information in Case Exhibit 4 and travel time and travel distance information in Case Exhibit 5, one can deduce the travel time and travel distance for each route as shown in TN Table 1.

Case Exhibit 11 provides information on fuel consumption and fuel costs for riders. Using average fuel costs per km, one can also deduce as shown in TN Table 1. It is easy to argue that in place routes are inefficient by observing the graphical depiction of routes in Case Exhibit 4. Current routes overlap each other, thus inducing inefficiencies as more than one rider is being used to coverage similar regions. This discussion is likely to lead the participants to understand that in order to reduce costs, the riders total travel distance needs to be reduced.

TN Table 1   Travel time, distance and costs for each rider in existing routes

	Total weight (kg)	Route	Total distance	Total time	Total cost
Rider 1	29	0-1-11-2-3-0	24.4	52	52.22
Rider 2	28	0-5-10-9-0	23.6	50	50.50
Rider 3	32	0-14-4-8-7-0	24.1	59	51.57
Rider 4	29	0-6-12-13-0	34	56	72.76
Total			106.1	217	227.05

Routing by Sweep Heuristic

Here, the instructor can point out a simple technique in route planning to include the customer locations in routes in clockwise or anticlockwise manner. This technique is called sweep. For example, to plan in an anticlockwise manner, we can start from +ive y-axis and include the closest customer location, which is closest to y-axis in an anticlockwise manner. The added location is deleted from the location set and the next closest location is added to the route, and in such a manner customer locations are added to the current route till rider's capacity is exhausted. TN Table 2 depicts the routes constructed via sweep method. The analysis shows that considerable savings can be established if sweep method is followed. For example, total travel distance is reduced from 107 to 78.4 km. Similarly, travel costs are reduced significantly from Rs. 227.05 to 167.77.

Despite sweep being a very simple technique, the improvements are significant. It is evident that travel distances play a major role in deducing transportation costs and time efficiencies. At this point, the instructor may ask class regarding other methods to establish route plan. It is likely that some participants may point out that often transport companies try to segment their entire coverage area into smaller clusters and then develop the route plans for customer locations in each cluster.

Geographical Clustering and Routing by Nearest Neighbour Heuristic

How should the entire region be clustered into smaller region? A simple way is to observe the entire region visually and segment it into small clusters of perhaps approximately equal size and equal number of customers. TN Exhibit 1 shows one such clustering. The customers are clustered according to their geographical positioning. For example, the

TN Table 2 Travel time, distance and costs for routes established via sweep method

	Weight (kg)	Route	Total distance	Total time	Total cost
Rider 1	30	0-9-14-13-1-0	12.5	40	26.75
Rider 2	31	0-11-6-12-0	22.5	49	48.15
Rider 3	30	0-2-8-3-7-0	24.1	62	51.57
Rider 4	27	0-10-5-4-0	19.3	52	41.30
Total			78.4	203	167.77

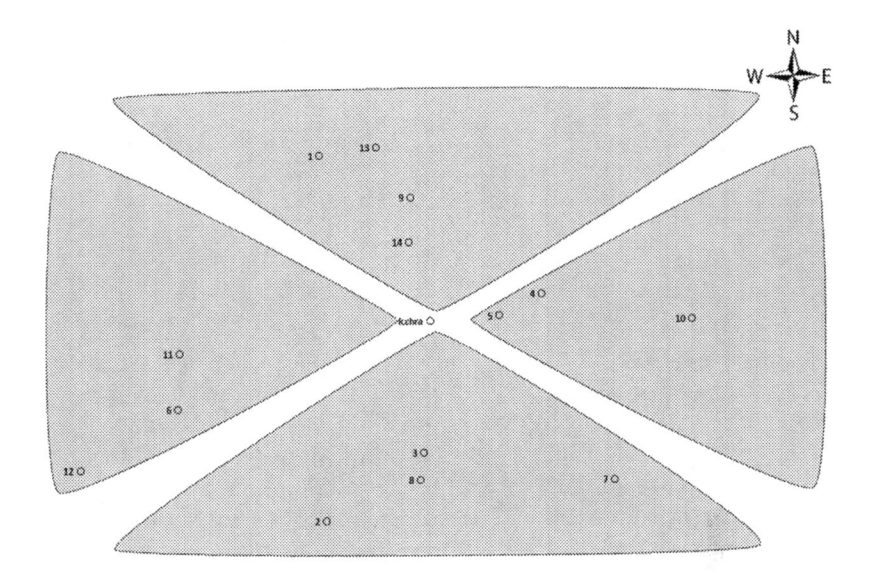

Note: Not drawn to scale

TN Exhibit 1   Customer segments—clusters

customers to the north of HQ are clustered together and so on. Once the clusters are available, routes can be derived for the customers in each cluster by considering the travel distance. A single technique here is often termed as nearest neighbour which involves selecting the nearest location to the current location for inclusion into the current route. For example, in northern cluster our current location is Icchra (starting HQ location). Here the nearest location in northern cluster is customer location 14 so it should be visited first. Now the current location has been updated and the next selection from remaining set is customer location 9 as it is the closest to customer location 14. In such a manner the routes can be constructed for each rider. The result of utilizing geographical clustering and nearest neighbour are shown in TN Table 3. The clustering and nearest neighbour method provides slightly superior results as opposed to sweep method. The negligible difference can perhaps be attributed to the use of a two-step approach.

TN Table 3   Travel routes established via geographical clustering and nearest neighbour routing method

		Total weight (kg)	Total distance	Total time	Total cost
Rider 1	0-14-9-13-1-0	32	11.5	30	24.61
Rider 2	0-11-6-12-0	30	22.5	40	48.15
Rider 3	0-3-8-2-7-0	30	24.4	64	52.22
Rider 4	0-5-4-10-0	27	18.6	48	39.80
Total			77	182	164.78

Probing the class participants on limitations can help instructor deduce the following observations: Clustering technique used in the earlier text is rudimentary and does not involve any considerations of weight limitations of riders. In addition, it did not explicitly consider travel distance of customer locations and Icchra. Further probing may also reveal that the inter travel distances among all customers should also be considered for clustering and route planning as choosing the nearest location from the current location (i.e. nearest neighbour) may not be optimal. The optimal approach must therefore consider all travel distances before choosing the next customer. Here the instructor can introduce the concept of 'Saving Matrix' to deduce the clusters, while considering the inter travel distances of all customers.

Clustering by Saving Matrix and Routing by Nearest Neighbour Heuristic

The saving matrix technique helps to allocate customers to different clusters, while trying to minimize the total distance travelled. Being a heuristic technique, the savings matrix does not provide an optimal solution however gives a solution which is often close to optimal.

The saving matrix technique creates clusters while considering the impact of inter-travel distances of all locations. The main concept stems from the fact that joining two routes into one route may help reduce travel distances. For example if there is an existing route from the origin to a location-x, what shall be the potential savings if we include a location-y in this route as opposed to starting a new route from the origin to a location-y? Thus, in our case instead of the rider going straight from Icchra to customer location 14, we will need to investigate the savings resulting by adding any other customer location into the route. The expression used to construct the saving matrix is the following:

$$s(x, y) = Distance(Origin, x) + Distance(Origin, y) - Distance(x, y)$$

The calculated saving matrix for each customer location is shown in TN Exhibit 2. Larger the value, the more attractive it is to add two customer locations in a single route in terms of cost. TN Table 4 depicts the clusters constructed using the saving matrix:

The different regions formed are graphically depicted in the TN Exhibit 3. An example of how the 6, 12, 11 cluster has been formed is as follows: Looking at TN Exhibit 2, the largest saving is of 16.8 formed by combining customer locations 6 and 12. To get the next point we need to look at the largest savings adjacent to all customer locations corresponding to customer location 6 and 12, this is found to be 15.6 by combining customer location 6 and 11. These three customer locations require a total weight of 31 kg; hence, another customer location cannot be added into the current cluster. This method is then repeated until all the clusters have been formed. Route planning can now be performed among customer locations in each cluster. For example, we first show the use of nearest neighbour approach to establish routes. TN Table 5 depicts the routes established by Saving Matrix—Nearest Neighbour technique as associated performance indicators.

This method yields a total cost of 15,760 which is closer to the previous methods. The advantage of using this method is that the saving matrix forms all the clusters and no manual technique is required to form clusters. However, the nearest neighbour method is still difficult to manage with a large number of customers. This can be resolved by using a formal technique like farthest insert or nearest insert as opposed to nearest neighbour. In the remaining text we discuss the use of nearest insert heuristics for route planning for the clusters identified by using saving matrix technique.

Clustering by Saving Matrix and Routing by Nearest Insert Heuristic
We shall apply nearest insert routing technique on the clusters identified in TN Table 4. In nearest insert, for each route, a new customer location (from the un-routed customer set) with minimum increase in length from all potential points is inserted. Hence, the customer location closest to the current route is inserted and not from the current customer

TN Exhibit 2   Saving matrix

Saving matrix	1	2	3	4	5	6	7	8	9	10	11	12	13	14
1	10.0	2.5	1.4	1.6	2.9	8.3	1.7	0.8	5.3	0.3	5.6	6.8	14.0	3.2
2	0.3	9.8	3.7	1.0	2.3	9.4	2.5	1.6	0.7	−2.4	5.7	8.8	7.8	−0.4
3	−0.4	3.7	5.4	1.2	2.4	3.9	2.8	1.7	−0.1	1.2	1.2	3.1	7.0	−1.2
4	0.3	−0.8	0.0	6.8	5.3	1.9	6.0	0.5	1.3	4.7	0.1	0.4	8.4	1.8
5	1.6	0.4	1.0	5.3	7.6	1.8	4.8	0.5	2.4	3.5	0.0	1.1	9.5	2.9
6	8.3	8.2	3.9	2.2	1.3	18.2	1.8	0.9	4.4	0.4	15.1	16.8	13.1	3.2
7	1.7	0.5	2.6	6.1	4.7	0.6	13.2	1.0	0.7	8.6	0.6	1.4	6.2	−0.4
8	−0.6	1.6	1.7	0.0	2.0	1.0	1.0	1.8	−0.1	−0.6	−0.2	0.4	7.0	−1.2
9	4.3	0.6	0.0	−0.1	2.4	4.4	−0.8	−0.1	6.4	−0.3	2.4	3.8	12.8	4.2
10	−1.3	−2.5	−1.4	4.5	4.0	−2.1	8.9	−0.6	1.1	14.2	0.0	−0.9	7.5	−0.3
11	5.7	5.7	−0.3	0.1	−0.3	15.1	0.6	−0.8	1.9	−2.3	14.2	−0.9	3.9	−0.3
12	6.4	8.8	3.1	0.9	1.1	16.8	1.4	0.1	3.8	−0.9	0.4	22.0	11.4	2.2
13	14.3	5.5	7.0	8.4	9.5	11.5	7.8	7.0	12.8	7.8	1.6	12.1	22.0	3.3
14	3.7	−0.6	−1.1	0.6	2.5	3.8	−1.6	−1.5	4.2	−1.4	−1.4	3.2	2.6	4.4

TN Table 4 Clusters deduced by using saving matrix technique

Saving matrix clusters	Weight
13,1,9,5	30
7,10,4	30
2,3,8,14	27
6,12,11	31

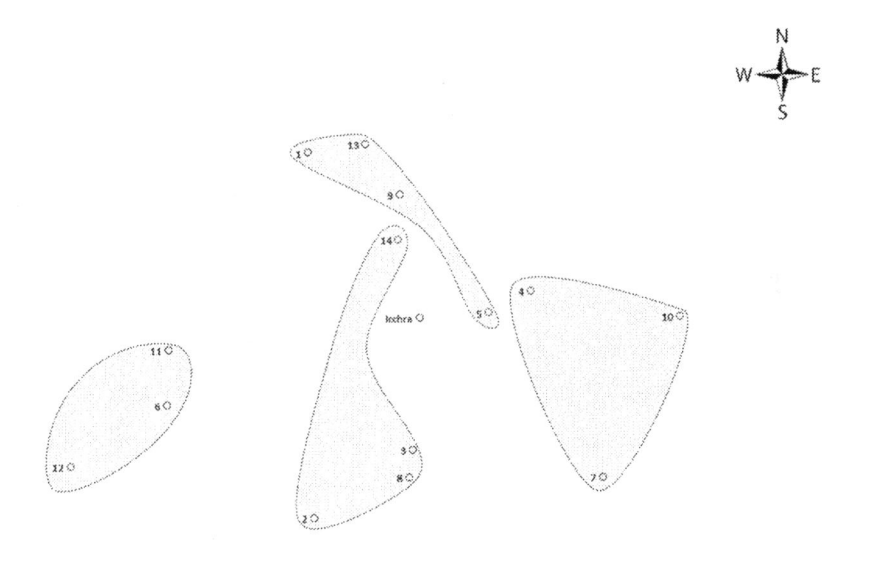

Note: Not drawn to scale

TN Exhibit 3   Clusters formed by using saving matrix technique

location. Thus, the main difference between farthest and nearest insert is that the former always inserts customers that give the highest distance in a given route. The following example summarizes the route for cluster 10, 4, 7 are established using nearest insert routes heuristic.

- Step 1: For each customer location choose the one having the least distance to and from the warehouse. For example, from Ichhra (location 0), customer locations 7, 10 and 4 have a return distance of

TN Table 5 Travel routes established via saving matrix clustering and nearest neighbour routing method

	Route	Weight (kg)	Distance	Time	Total cost
Rider 1	0-5-9-13-1-0	30	16.5	35	35.31
Rider 2	0-4-10-7-0	30	20.6	51	44.08
Rider 3	0-14-3-8-2-0	27	19.2	50	41.09
Rider 4	0-11-6-12-0	31	22.5	49	48.15
Total			78.8	185	168.63

TN Table 6 Travel routes established via saving matrix clustering and nearest insert routing method

	Route	Weight (kg)	Total distance	Total time	Total cost
Rider 1	0-11-6-12-0	31	22.5	49	48.15
Rider 2	0-9-5-1-13-0	30	28	52	59.92
Rider 3	0-4-7-10-0	30	19.6	55	41.94
Rider 4	0-8-3-14-2-0	27	21.5	51	46.01
Total			91.6	207	196.02

13.2, 14.2 and 6.8 km, respectively. Customer location 4 has the least distance to and from the warehouse; hence the rider will visit it first

- Step 2: Keeping customer location 4 fixed, each customer location is inserted next to find the minimum increase in length. For example, the total distance of route 0-4-10-0 is 16.3 km whereas the route distance of 0-4-7-0 is 14 km.

Hence, adding customer location 7 after customer location 4 gives the shortest distance, as only customer location 10 is now left it is added after customer location 7, giving a final route of 0-4-7-10-0.

The above steps are repeated for the rest of the clusters giving the routes shown in TN Table 6.

Summary
Thus far, we have compared the performance of various routing heuristics. It is clear from the analysis that in general the cost efficiencies in routing can be attained by travelling minimum distances with higher capacity utilization. During class discussion, the instructor does not need

to discuss all of the above heuristics, but the focus should be to discuss more than one heuristic so the role of performance drivers (i.e. minimum travel distances and higher capacity utilization) can be highlighted.

Question 2:
Should OCS keep using its current location in Icchra as a central region headquarter (HQ) or follow the example of industry leader (i.e. TCS) and shift its central region HQ?

Analysis:
Before deciding the new location of the regional HQ, all the potential factors that would impact the decision have to be identified. It is clear that from the case discussion that OCS management is interested in an option that saves delivery times as well as overall operational costs.

In order to evaluate each viable location, first, a cost analysis needs to be performed. Currently, the main costs being incurred by OCS for a particular facility are:

1. Capital Expenditure of facility—these costs will remain same as the investment from the current facility will be used to construct a new one.
2. Operational Cost

    (a) Facility running costs—these costs will not change across facilities
    (b) Transportation cost—this cost will change across the location of each facility, and hence is the most important in determining new facility location.

This analysis will entail the transportation cost of each mode used. Currently, OCS uses runners and trucks for inter-city deliveries. For intra-city deliveries OCS only uses riders.

Hence, for each of the identified viable location the total cost of runners, riders and trucks will be computed for inter-city transportation costs. Riders' costs analysis shall be performed for each viable HQ locations to ascertain intra-city transportation costs. This analysis will be done in two parts:

1. InterCity Transportation Cost Analysis using Exit Points
Under this method, the total runner and truck cost will be computed for each of the exit points, and a step by step approach will be provided to arrive at the final cost.

2. Intra-City Transportation Cost Analysis using Clusters

Under this method, Lahore will be divided in 5 different clusters, and for each cluster the total rider cost will be computed for the three viable locations.

InterCity Transportation Cost Analysis Using Exit Points

These exit points connect Lahore city to the wider central region. The exit points of Saghian, Motor way (MT), Grand trunk road (GT), Airport and Multan road are listed in the case. The viable HQ locations for analysis are Icchra (baseline option), Saghian, and Airport.

Case Exhibit 6 plots the different exit points against each of the three viable locations. In order to conduct an exit-point analysis, the cost for each mode of transportation from each exit point needs to be analyzed. Hence, we will calculate Total Runner Cost and Total Truck Cost.

In order to calculate the total runner cost we require distances to and from each exit point (Case Exhibit 8), Cost for each transport mode (Case Exhibit 9) and required number of annual runners for each exit point (Case Exhibit 10).

Using the data listed above, the cost is computed in a simple manner. An example for Airport to Icchra is given below:

- On average 1 liter of diesel covers 9 km
- The required distance to be covered as seen from Case Exhibit 8 is 25.8 km
- Total amount if diesel required is $25.8/9 = 2.87$
- The diesel rate is 110
- Cost from Airport to Icchra per route $= 110 \times 2.87 = 315.47$

Using, the above method the Cost per Runner Matrix is computed in TN Exhibit 4. In order to get the total cost for runners, total numbers of runners travelling towards each exit point are multiplied with cost per runner towards each exit point. TN Exhibit 5 lists total costs per runners from each potential HQ location to each exit point.

Cost per truck and total truck costs are computed in a similar manner. Case Exhibit 8 lists distances to and from each exit point, Case Exhibit 9 lists fuel costs for each transport mode and number of annual trucks travelling towards each exit point are listed in Case Exhibit 11. The cost per truck for each exit point and total truck costs are provided in TN Exhibits 6 and 7 respectively.

TN Exhibit 4 Cost per runner

Cost/runner matrix

Exit points	OCS (Icchra)	Airport	Saghian
Saghian	115.55	371.71	–
MT	124.72	409.62	70.92
GT	146.73	321.58	84.37
Airport	315.47	–	347.26
Multan road	356.43	589.36	256.78
Total	1264.32	1930.72	1093.13

TN Exhibit 5 Total runner cost

Exit points	OCS (Icchra)	Airport	Saghian
Multan road	513,259	848,678	369,763
GT	633,874	1,389,226	364,478
MT	179,597	589,853	102,125
Saghian	83,196	267,631	–
Airport	454,277	–	486,164
Total cost	1,864,202	3,095,388	1,322,530

TN Exhibit 6 Cost per truck

Exit points	OCS (Icchra)	Airport	Saghian
Saghian	129.94	418.00	–
MT	140.25	460.63	79.75
GT	165.00	361.63	94.88
Airport	354.75	–	390.50
Multan road	400.81	662.75	288.75
Total cost	1421.75	2171.13	1229.25

TN Exhibit 7 Truck cost per exit point

Exit points	OCS (Icchra)	Airport	Saghian
Multan road	254,915	421,509	183,645
GT	89,100	195,280	51,235
MT	20,196	66,331	11,484
Total cost	364,211	683,120	246,364

Intra-city Transportation Cost Analysis Using Clusters
Earlier in the case study, routing for 14 customer locations were being studied, giving a very microscopic view for routing in Lahore. However, in reality OCS has a large number of customers encompassing the whole city, and hence routing analysis can no longer be done on a sample of clients. Thus, in our analysis Lahore has been divided into 5 different regions, and for each region the geographical mid-point has been taken giving their effective distances from each of the locations as shown in Case Exhibit 13. The only cost that needs to be calculated for intra-city is the rider cost, thus we will be using the same process as before, however the only difference will be that here clusters will be used instead of exit points.

The cost per rider has been given in Case Exhibit 12, this cost is fixed irrelevant of the route, and using this cost per rider needs to be calculated.

For example cost of a rider from Shadman using Icchra is done as follows:

- On average 1 liter of diesel covers 50 km
- The required distance to be covered as seen from Case Exhibit 13 is 6.3 km
- Total amount if diesel required is $6.3/50 = 0.126$
- The diesel rate is 107
- Cost from Shadman to Icchra per route $= 107 \times 0.126 = 13.482$

Using, the above method the complete Cost per Rider is computed in TN Exhibit 8. This cost is only per rider, and in order to get the total cost the total numbers of riders are required. Case Exhibit 14 gives the

TN Exhibit 8 Cost per rider

MID-POINT	OCS (Icchra)	Airport	Saghian
Davis road and Mall road	33.38	77.68	51.36
Shadman	13.48	89.02	55.85
Model Town and Garden Town	47.51	95.87	87.95
Badami Bagh and Allama Iqbal Town	23.11	98.65	25.68
DHA, Cantt and Gulberg	56.5	73.62	96.3

TN Exhibit 9 Rider cost

MID-POINT	OCS (Icchra)	Airport	Saghian
Davis road and Mall road	360,504	838,944	554,688
Shadman	33,970	224,330	140,742
Model Town and Garden Town	256,554	517,698	474,930
Badami Bagh and Allama Iqbal Town	158,072	674,766	175,651
DHA, Cantt and Gulberg	650,880	848,102	1,109,376
Total cost	1,459,980	3,103,841	2,455,387

TN Exhibit 10 Comparative costs

	OCS (Icchra)	Airport	Saghian
Runner transport cost	1,864,202	3,095,388	1,322,530
Truck transport cost	364,211	683,120	246,364
Rider transport cost	1,459,980	3,103,841	2,455,387
Total annual cost	3,688,394	6,882,349	4,024,282
% Comparison (baseline: Icchra) (%)	100	187	109

annual number of riders required. We can calculate total rider cost by multiplying cost per rider with total riders. Total rider costs are depicted in TN Exhibit 9.

Comparison of Viable Options

Combining all the above solutions, we get a comparative cost analysis as shown in TN Exhibit 10. This analysis gives the total cost for each of the rider, runner and truck for Icchra, Airport and Saghian.

Keeping Icchra our base case, the airport's cost is 1.87 times greater than Icchra whereas Saghian's cost is only 1.09 times greater. Looking at these results alone, one may assume that if not Icchra, Saghian may be a better location to open a regional warehouse. However, in this analysis time is a crucial determining factor.

Moreover, the case study focuses on only relocating outbound deliveries to the Airport and using Icchra or Saghian for intra-city deliveries due to their central location. Hence, it is important to consider the hybrid analysis before making a final decision.

Question 3:

The case also indicates the use of Hybrid approach for network planning. What is it? Is it preferable? Why or why not?

Analysis:

The hybrid solution involves using different locations for intercity and intra-city transportation. The idea is to use either Airport or Saghian location as HQ location for central region where collection and sorting is performed. The intercity shipments originate from these two locations. For intra-city deliveries and pickups through riders, the plan is to use existing location at Icchra (which is in the center of Lahore city) for an origin and destination location. Thus the plan involves movement of Lahore bound deliveries and Lahore origin pickups (intra-city shipments) from Icchra and HQ location (either airport or Saghian) by using a runner.

Base Case

Before considering any other alternative solution we need to evaluate the current scenario. Case Exhibit 6 shows the outline of deliveries from Icchra to all its exit points:

Moving from the left, all deliveries coming from Karachi first arrive at the airport from where they are sorted at Icchra. Similarly, deliveries from Saghian, Motor Way, Grand Truck and Multan Road, which are located on the left of Icchra, are collected at Icchra. Once the sorting has been performed at Icchra, packages for different regions are made and are ready to be delivered. The exits are used for different cities are listed in Case Exhibit 7.

Hybrid Approach

Under the hybrid approach, Icchra will be the local warehouse, and either all deliveries will be collected at Saghian or the Airport. In order to evaluate an alternate solution, two scenarios need to be considered:

1. Sorting all deliveries at the Airport, directly delivering outbound and sending all local deliveries to Icchra,
2. Sorting all deliveries at Saghian, directly delivering outbound and sending all local deliveries to Saghian,

1. All parcels collected at Airport and local parcels to Icchra—The figure in TN Exhibit 11 describes the new route.

Under this method, all outbound and inbound deliveries will first be collected at the airport. Once, this has been done, all deliveries to be made in Lahore will be sent to Icchra, whereas all deliveries to be made inter-city will directly leave from the airport, to their respective exit points via Ring Road. Thus, the only distance and time which will be changing will be when in Lahore, as once the deliveries reach their exit points the distance will remain the same.

If this method is implemented then to each route going towards Icchra 31 min will be added. These 31 minutes represent the time taken to travel from the Airport to Icchra, as all intra-city deliveries will first stop at Icchra and then be delivered from there. Thus, all outbound deliveries will no longer have to enter the heart of the city and therefore, saving time.

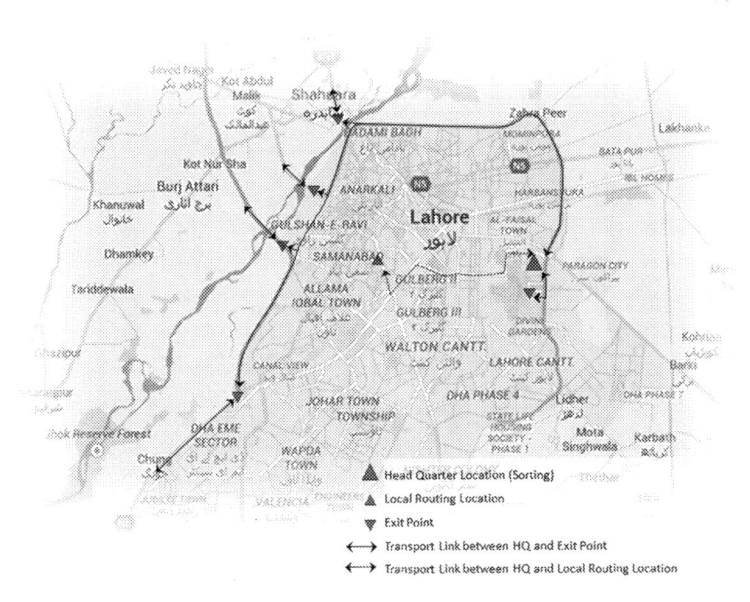

TN Exhibit 11 Hybrid approach option 1: Airport as HQ

2. All parcels collected at Saghian and local parcels sent to Icchra—
   The figure in TN Exhibit 12 describes the new route.

Under this method, all outbound and inbound deliveries will first be collected at Saghian. Once, this has been done, all deliveries to be made in Lahore will be sent to Icchra, whereas all deliveries to be made inter-city will directly leave from Saghian, to their respective exit points. Thus, the only distance and time which will be changing will be when in Lahore, as once the deliveries reach their exit points the distance will remain the same.

If this method is implemented then to each route going towards Saghian, 26 minutes will be added. These 26 minutes represent the time taken to travel from the airport to Saghian. The main reason to consider all routes from the airport is that this analysis is being done for Karachi parcels. Deliveries from Karachi and Lahore make 80% of the revenue hence; they are the core of our analysis. Once, all the deliveries have been accumulated at Saghian, all the parcels for Lahore will be sorted and sent to Icchra. Moreover, all outbound deliveries will be directly delivered from Saghian. Thus, all outbound deliveries will no longer have to enter the heart of the city and therefore, saving time.

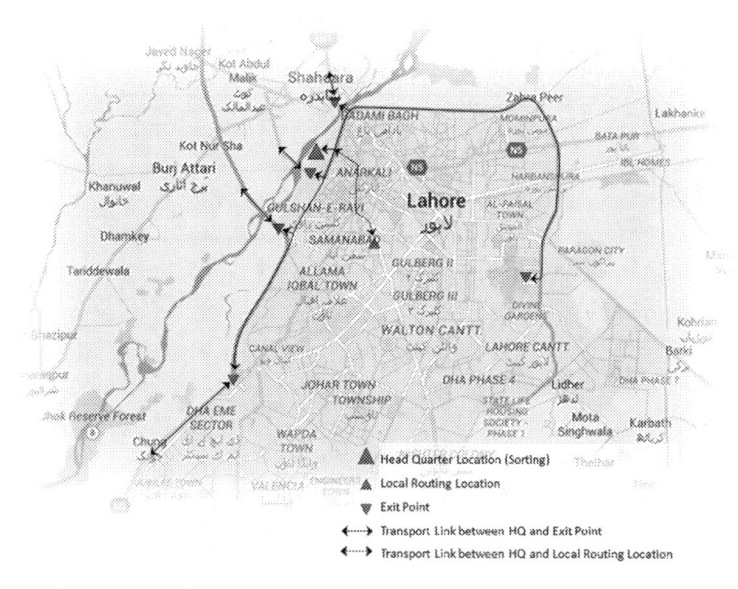

TN Exhibit 12   Hybrid approach option 1: Saghian as HQ

Time Saving Analysis

Thus, to the actual time given before, for all routes towards OCS 31 minutes are added, whereas to all routes towards Saghian 26 minutes are added, as explained above. The main reason to adjust the time is that all deliveries within Lahore will be having a fixed element of travelling from the Airport due to the Karachi deliveries. The adjusted time is shown in TN Exhibit 13.

In order to find which option is better a time savings analysis needs to be done for sending outbound deliveries from Airport and Saghian. No time savings are incurred for the deliveries within Lahore, as in each case Icchra remains the delivery point (TN Exhibit 14)

In TN Exhibit 14 the column airport, represents the savings from only moving outbound deliveries from the airport and inbound deliveries from Icchra. Similarly, the column Saghian represents the savings of moving outbound deliveries from Saghian and inbound deliveries from Icchra.

TN Exhibit 13 Effective time

Effective travel time per runner

Exit points	OCS (Icchra)	Airport	Saghian
Saghian	45	30	0
MT	46	35	38
GT	49	23	35
Airport	31	0	26
Multan road	58	45	46

TN Exhibit 14 Time savings

Time saved

City	Exit points	Airport	Saghian
Faisalabad	Saghian	15	26
Mianwali	MT	11	8
Dera Ismail Khan			
Safdarabad	GT	26	14
Rawalpindi			
Mir Pur Azad Kashmir			
Narowal			
Karachi	Airport	31	5
Bhai Pheru	Multan road	13	12
Multan			

For example for all deliveries going to Faisalabad, Saghian is used as the exit point—

- If deliveries are directly made from the Airport, then 15 minutes are saved (45-30).
- If deliveries are directly made from Saghian, then 26 minutes are saved (26-0).

As it can be inferred from the TN Exhibit 14, greater time savings are incurred by using the airport for sending all outbound deliveries.

Cost Comparison

If the hybrid solution is used, assuming maximum time savings at the airport, then each of the total runner and truck costs are taken for the airport. This is because all outbound deliveries will now be made from the airport. However, for local deliveries Icchra will be used and thus the rider costs will remain same. An additional runner cost will now be incurred, for sending all parcels from the airport to Icchra, and for bringing all parcels from Icchra to the airport. The detailed calculations are shown in TN Exhibit 15. This solution, results in a cost 1.43 times greater than the original cost, however the time savings are significant and cannot be overlooked.

Moreover, a similar cost analysis is also done for Saghian as the HQ and Icchra as the regional warehouse. This results in a cost of 3,069,993 which is 0.83 times of Icchra (TN Exhibit 16).

TN Exhibit 15   Hybrid solution—Airport as a HQ

Hybrid location costs		
Runner transport cost	3,095,388	Airport to exit points
Truck transport cost	683,120	Airport to exit points
Rider transport cost	1,459,980	Transit to last mile delivery
Additional runner fixed cost	220,000	Airport-Transit-Airport
Total annual cost	5, 279,606	
% Comparison with base case	151%	

TN Exhibit 16   Hybrid solution—Saghian as HQ

Hybrid location costs

Runner transport cost	1,322,530	Saghian to exit points
Truck transport cost	246,364	Saghian to exit points
Rider transport cost	1,281,098	Saghian to last mile delivery
Additional runner cost	220,000	Saghian-Transit-Saghian
Total annual cost	3,069,993	
% Comparison with base case	83%	

TN Table 7   Advantages of each HQ location option

Icchra	Saghian	Airport
• Centre of Lahore	• Outskirts of Lahore	• Ring road can be used
• Nearer to inner city routes	• Centre point of GT and MT	• Less traffic
• Densely populated	• Industrial infrastructure	• Time saving, due to direct transportation for inter-city transfers
• Time loss due to traffic	• Cheap land	• Far away from city
	• Inner routes available	

Qualitative Analysis

For each of the three viable locations a qualitative analysis should be performed, which will be an intuitive brain-storming process, as shown in TN Table 7.

SUN Rises from RANBAXY: Supply Chain Strategy of an Indian Pharmaceutical Company

Sushmera Manikandan and Balan Sundarakani

INTRODUCTION

On April 7, 2014, when the deal of $4 billion was successful to merge India's largest pharmaceutical company called 'Ranbaxy laboratories' with 'Sun Pharmaceutical Industries Limited', the Indian-born billionaire and Managing Director of Sun Pharma, Mr. Dilip Shanghvi's dream of making a world class pharmaceutical company came close to reality. The company shares sky rocked since then and Sun Pharma tripled its revenue in the succeeding years of 2015–2016. However, Shanghvi decided to discontinue some of the company's non-strategic business lines in order to foresee long-term synergies from this mergers and acquisition (*The Economic Times* 2015). Was this decision found to be a best strategic move? Did Shanghvi's strategic alignment help the

S. Manikandan (✉)
Swiss Business School, Zurich, Switzerland
e-mail: s.manikandan@student.sbs.edu

B. Sundarakani
Faculty of Business, University of Wollongong in Dubai, Dubai, UAE
e-mail: balansundarakani@uowdubai.ac.ae

© The Author(s) 2019
A. Sikdar and V. Pereira (eds.), *Business and Management Practices in South Asia*, https://doi.org/10.1007/978-981-13-1399-8_11

company move in the right direction? The case unfolds some of these aspects through the study of various secondary reports and data which are presented from this section forward.

Globally, pharma industry plays a vital role and is one of the most research-intensive rapidly growing global industries in this century. It is also a major source of employment generation and foreign exchange earnings for many countries around the globe (Papert et al. 2016). Globalization in this sector has occurred with respect to both distribution of medicines to new markets as well as shifting of their Research and Development (R&D) and manufacturing to lower cost market with growing pharmaceutical manufacturing centres like India, China, Korea, Brazil, Middle East, and Russia. Due to its direct link with the welfare and wellbeing of human development, pharmaceutical industry is of strategic importance for the development of a healthy and productive nation.

INDIAN PHARMACEUTICAL INDUSTRY—A CLOSE OBSERVATION

According to the working group report for the 12th five-year plan, the Indian Pharmaceutical Industry is one of the India's science-based organized industrial sectors, with wide range of drug manufacturing and technology pioneering. India ranked as third preferred country in the pharma drugs contract manufacturing that's ranging from simple pills to sophisticated medicines and the industry is estimated to be worth $4.5 billion, growing approximately between 8 and 9% annually (IBEF 2018). Global region wide pharma trade of India is shown in Fig. 1,

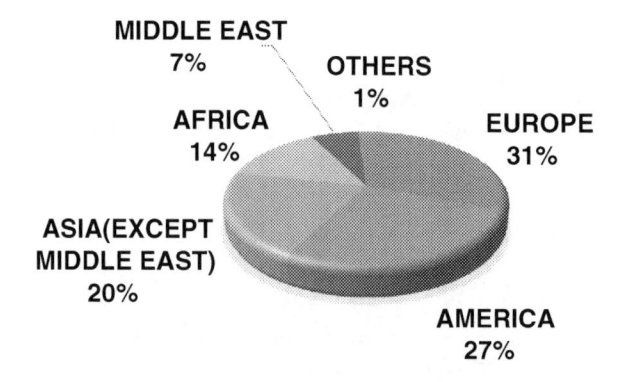

Fig. 1 India's exports of pharmaceutical product across the world (*Source* Directorate General of Commercial Intelligence and Statistics 2012)

wherein Europe dominates receiving 31% India's export product and America gets around 27% of its export product.

India has a tremendous growth for the exports of pharmaceuticals from the year 2006 until now and it's ranked as 12th position in the international pharmaceutical market with a total market share of 1.27% globally, according to Singh et al. (2016). In addition, Indian pharmaceutical Industry has expanded radically for the past two decades with aggressive growth worldwide. India's highly fragmented domestic market with secured Intellectual Property Protection regime drives the industry to succeed in the global market.

Sun Pharma and Ranbaxy—Consolidation

Ranbaxy is one of the leading pharmaceutical Companies in India with a commendable market share of around 5%. Nowadays, Ranbaxy exports its products to 125 countries with overall business operations in 46 and manufacturing facilities in 7 nations. The main motto of Ranbaxy is to enhance its competitive position through secured business strategy and also to focus on customers in order to dominate various therapeutic segments.

The Fig. 2 shows the horizontal product-based organizational structure of Sun Pharma, under the overall direction of the founding managing director Mr. Dilip S. Shanghvi. Three executive directors and seven directors form the board of directors for the three major product

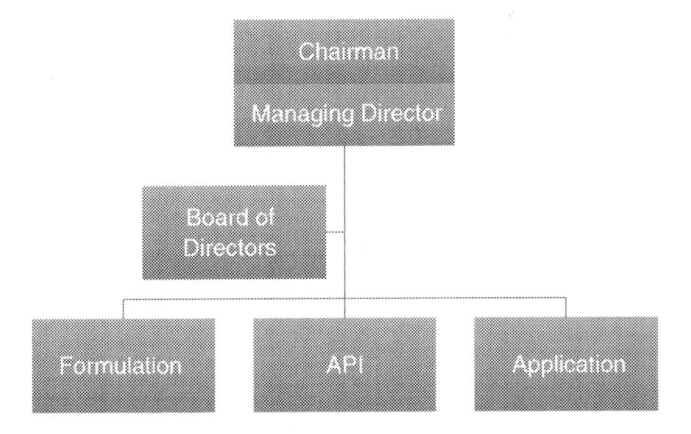

Fig. 2   Organisational structure of Sun Pharma

lines worldwide. "*Indian companies historically used to sell in unregulated markets. But increasingly now, a large part of the business is coming out of regulated markets. So, the understanding and assessment of requirements—structurally and organisationally are important transition points. I think the structure is important so that people within the organisation, those who manage these processes, have the requisite power and authority to ensure that changes are managed effectively*" said Shanghvi.

An effective supply chain strategy begins with a core business strategy that is established with its boundary conditions appropriately, according to Cohen and Roussell (2015). Therefore, in order to become a lead industry player, the business strategy must be effectively aligned with the core strategic vision. For Sun Pharma, such strategic positioning found is clearly articulated in terms of its vision, mission, and value proposition. This forms the first phase of Sun Pharma's supply chain strategy implementation process.

For many successful organisations, once thoughtfully aligned relationship gradually becomes disconnected as the organization's needs and priorities have changed was also seemed to be very much applicable to Sun Pharma as well. That was one of the reasons why Shanghvi eliminated some of the non-value added business lines as soon as the merger took place (*The Economic Times* 2015). Appendix 1 exhibits the vision, mission, and value statement of Sun Pharma as excerpted from the company handbook published in 2017.

Key Business Challenges of Ranbaxy Before Merging

Through the acquisition of Ranbaxy, Sun Pharma had managed to acquire strong R&D among its competitors, which include a state-of-the-art multi-disciplinary research centre located at Gurgaon in India consisting of dedicated facilities of 1200 scientists for Innovative & Generics API Research (Jayashree and Rajesh 2010). In addition, there are various categories of centers namely R&D centres I and II, focus on the development of generics and Novel Drug Delivery Systems (NDDS) research; whereas R&D centre III, is dedicated to New Drug Discovery Research (NDDR).

Ranbaxy has a major market share from BRIC countries, UAE and Europe; hence, brand is the global key success factor which determines the firm's scope of conduct from product expansion, manufacturing, shipping, and complaint handling (Meenakshi and Vinayshil 2010).

Global sales growth of Ranbaxy in which North America has a tremendous growth in 2011 through various acquisitions, increased R&D cost, and increased investment in various sectors. The major drivers of Ranbaxy which indicate the key success for firm's competition in the international market are product range, brand recognition, access to raw materials, technical capabilities, flexible production systems, and regulatory expertise (Rao 2008).

However, Sun Pharma also faced some of the challenges which are listed below and in Fig. 3:

1. Recession, regulatory issues, lack of laws, concerns on data protection, research skill sets, lagging infrastructure, and delay in approvals are among the many reasons given by sector experts for the decline of Ranbaxy.
2. Competition due to increased presence of generic players (e.g. Cipla) in developed market.
3. Ranbaxy was the largest foreign suppliers of generic drugs to the United States and hence the Food and Drug Administration (FDA) slapped with imports ban on it in the US market.
4. Drug price control order puts product prices under pressure thus affecting the profitability of Ranbaxy.
5. Stricter registration procedures with high entry cost in newer markets and high cost of sales and marketing.

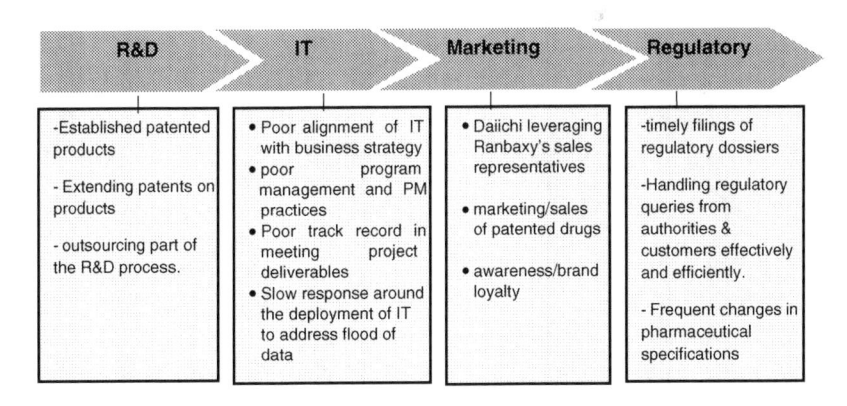

Fig. 3 Challenging sectors of Ranbaxy

6. Increased government regulation, declining economy, increasing R&D costs, and a decrease in the global population are other challenges.
7. Very-complex supply chain, with manufacturing presence across 7 countries caused due to lack of end-to-end integration.
8. Poor alignment of IT, marketing functions with business strategy in which the supply chain architectures are not well articulated.
9. Managing cultural diversity and to keep different product specifications and packaging requirements to different regions.

QUALITY MANAGEMENT OF RANBAXY BECAME THEIR KINGPIN

Ranbaxy has a high quality asset for branded medicines compliance focussed on internalization in which quality is measured based on strict quality policies and guidelines that are executed at all manufacturing locations all over the world. Ranbaxy has been using statistical process control and process capability analysis as a tool for implementing operational excellence which can be performed by a cross-functional team through commercialization. The Quality Control or the Quality Assurance Department (QAD) of Ranbaxy did always ensure the desired quality standard for the processing or manufacturing of material. In addition, the set of corporate guidelines on Goods Manufacturing Service (GMP) are deployed by the cross functional quality teams to reduce the risk for competition with the global market. Process Analytical Technology (PAT) and risk-based techniques are used to develop the firm's product safety and rigorously mitigate risks associated with the quality issues.

SUN PHARMA CONSIDERS SUPPLY CHAIN AS STRATEGIC ASSET

Supply chain and distribution channel of Sun is the path that products follow on their way from the manufacturers to the consumers or industrial users. Figure 4 depicts the supply chain stages as well as their omni-channel for electronic ordering. In the case of pharmaceutical supply chain, clinical doctor is not considered as part of distribution channel because he only influences the patients. The industry is highly structured based on functional silos and fragmented which leads to a critical level of mis-coordination.

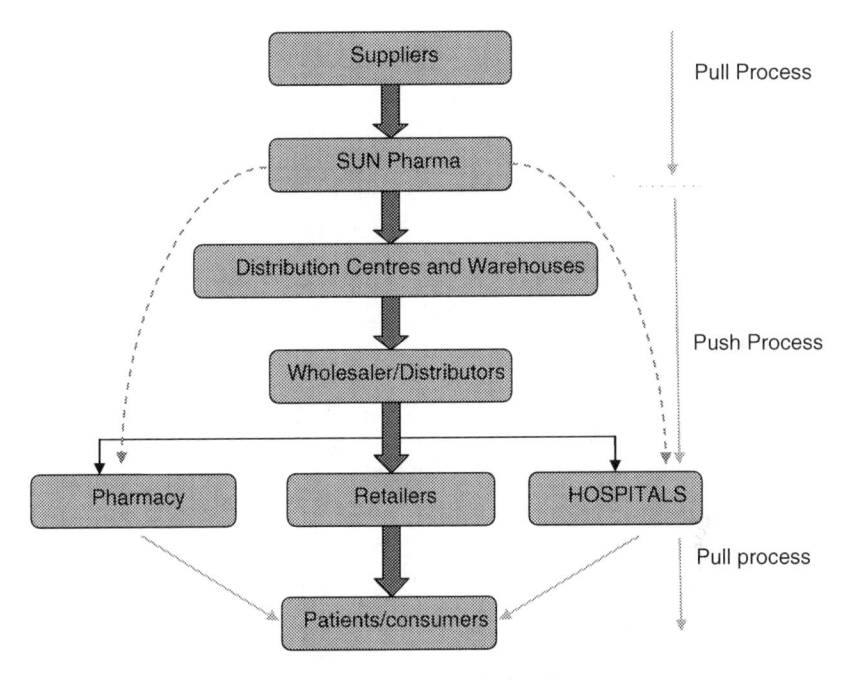

Fig. 4 Supply chain of Sun Pharma (*Source* Authors)

Even though there were many initiatives taken in the modern closed loop economy to integrate the fragmented supply chains together, different stakeholders conflicting priorities challenge the integration.

THE SUPPLIERS

Traditionally, Sun Pharma is one of the key overseas suppliers of generic drugs to the United States. Moreover, Sun Pharma is the sole distributor of a range of drugs including generic and patented drugs. Supply orders for the medicines are given by the production units based on raw materials or Active Pharmaceutical Ingredients (API) from various global vendors and local vendors using Sun's ethical purchasing generic operating procedures (Shah 2004). Sun provides biological suppliers resources such as Chemicals, Farm products, Growth media, cell cultures, Test organisms, and Non-biologic suppliers such as Computers, software, Databases (e.g., target molecules, DNA sequences).

The Manufacturing Facilities

Sun Pharma operates in all six continents with its establishment of various manufacturing sites consisting of generics, branded generics, and a major provider of its series of API globally. Figure 5 exhibits its global footprint after the mergers and acquisitions of Ranbaxy in 2014. Earlier, Ranbaxy had manufacturing facilities only in eight countries namely Ireland, India, Malaysia, Morocco, Nigeria, Romania, South Africa, and USA; where their overseas facilities are considered to supply to the requirements of the local regulatory bodies. However, their Indian facilities meet the requirements of all International Regulatory Agencies for safety, quality, and efficacy.

After the takeover, Sun pharma is having 28 finished dosage manufacturing sites and 14 API manufacturing locations across worldwide. They are very much vertically integrated in their supply chain enabling high quality, low cost, and a quick market entry across the geographies. Many of the plants have received approvals from US FDA, UK MHRA, and various other regulatory authorities.

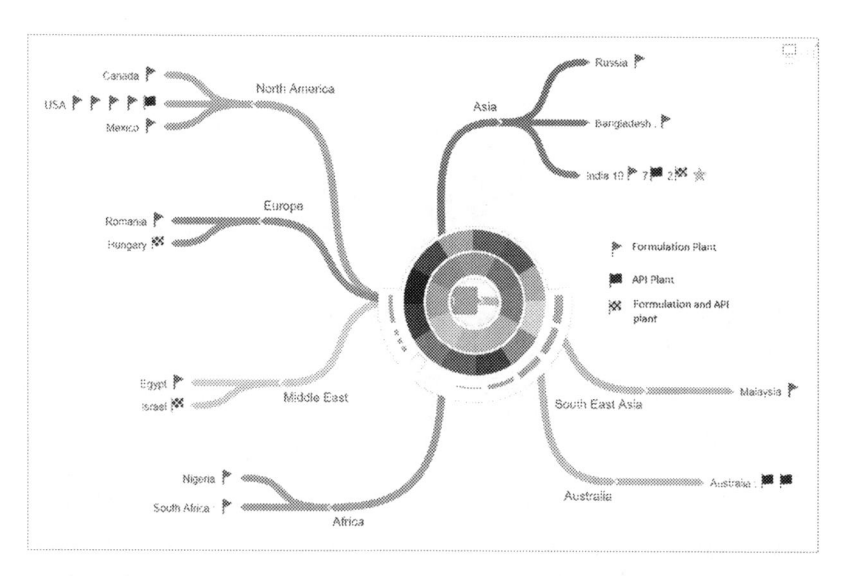

Fig. 5 Sun Pharma manufacturing footprint worldwide (*Source* Adapted from Sun Pharma)

India has a global pharmaceutical outsourcing worth US$58 billion in 2009 with an expected growth of US$32 billion in 2012 which indicates an annual growth of 15%. US FDA-approved manufacturing facilities, is one of the most preferred locations for outsourcing manufacturing services in India by the multinationals and global pharmaceutical companies.

CENTRAL WAREHOUSE

The warehouses of Sun Pharma directly supply the medicines to the Hospitals and other medical institutions on bulk orders. It also absorbs all the stocks manufactured at the production units based on the space availability and the demand from the marketing units. There are two categories, namely, depot and the carry and forward (C&F) agent. The depot is responsible only for storing the products from the manufacturing unit to the stockist; whereas the C&F agent has the facility of cold storage for injections and other drugs which need cold storage.

DISTRIBUTORS

The distributors also known as super-stockist normally places the order with the C&F agents and in some cases buys directly from the firm which uses various communication strategies to make them aware of the products. Distributors generally give order on e-mail and through sales agent, where the agent comes to the distributors place and note down the order in a company supplied format, the format consists of drug code, name of the drug and the quantity. After the order is being supplied the company generates the invoice and thereby, payment is made.

WHOLESALERS, HOSPITALS, AND RETAILERS

Wholesaler or stockist place an order on call or through a salesman of the distributor and the delivery is done or the same or next day morning. After the order is served, the invoice is being generated by the company and in cases of regular wholesaler the order is given on credit. They also use various tools to build up relations with the retailers and especially with the hospitals, as this is a more profitable deal. It is a win-win situation for both the supplier and the buyer as hospital gets more

Table 1   Various levels of profit margins of Sun Pharma

Sl. No	Various levels	Margins
1.	C&F agents/Warehouses	1–7% on the total turnover and other expenses
2.	Distributors	4% on scheduled drugs
		8% on nonscheduled drugs
3.	Wholesaler	3% on scheduled drugs
		7% on nonscheduled drugs
4.	Hospitals	12% on scheduled drugs
		16% on nonscheduled drugs
5.	Retailers	12% on scheduled drugs
		16% on nonscheduled drugs

discounts and the supplier, the wholesaler, gets high sales. Hospitals can place the order directly with the Distributor or through Wholesaler. They act as a retailer and also supply the drugs to the patients directly which are there in the hospitals for the treatment. However, the Retailers are the Chemists, Pharmacies (e.g. Apollo) and mixed product departmental stores. Chemists and Pharmacies get the same benefits from the wholesaler products whereas the mixed product departmental stores provide some lesser discounts given because they are not the regular buyers and they order only on need basis (refer Table 1). They supply the drugs directly to the customers. They use tools like discounts and home delivery to attract the customers. The retailers give timely orders to the marketing representatives for their stocks replenishments and maintain a safety stock to avoid the supply exigencies.

SUPPLY CHAIN COMPLEXITY

The supply chain is very complex, as lot of accountability are needed to ensure the delivery of right drug, at the right time and place, in the right condition to the people in need of such drugs for fighting against the diseases. Another discerning feature of the company is their product nature in which products, such as vaccines and biologics, require cold chain management in the entire process of transportation, beginning from the manufacturing site till the final delivery of the product, in order to maintain the conditions and quality of the products. Due to these challenging aspects, the logistics cost accounts a significant cost as they account for 25–35% of the total landed costs.

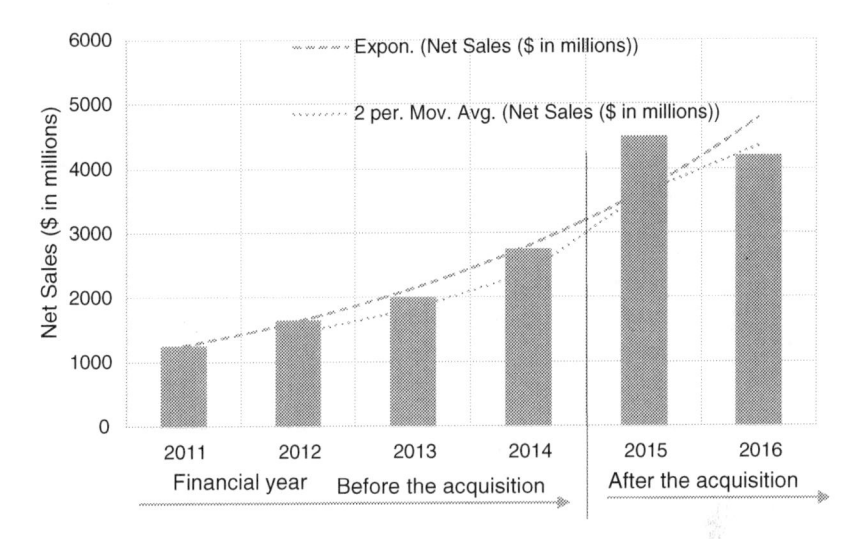

Fig. 6 Sun Pharma's annual sales revenue before and after the acquisition of Ranbaxy (*Source* Drawn from the data of Sun Pharma investors book 2017)

As the company consist of large quantities of exports and imports of medicines, and hence, it requires extensive warehousing facilities. The degree of complexity grew much after the acquisition of Ranbaxy global network. Figure 6 exhibits the net sales of Sun pharma before and after the merger of Ranbaxy.

Before merge, Ranbaxy used Aqua Logistics services to track and trace the shipments in order to avoid distribution centers at various overseas and domestic locations by keeping track of the current position of the shipment dispatched by it. Thousands of Ranbaxy customers from more than 104 countries are served more than 4000 Stock Keeping Units (SKUs) manufactured either at Ranbaxy's manufacturing facilities or at various other outsourced sites but coordination is found to be difficult among their supply chain stages. After the acquisition, Sun pharma introduced, supply chain integration system provided by SAP, which acts as the digital backbone of the chain providing on line information to the customers and the organization. To enhance global supply chain capability, Sun Pharma used Radio Frequency Identification (RFID) technology replacing their bar coding system in order to track the stocks automatically.

COMPETITORS

The top 10 major competitors of Sun pharma are Dr Reddey's Laboratories, Cipla, Nicholas Piramal, Aurobindo Pharma, GlaxoSmithKline, Lupin Laboratories, Sun Pharmaceutical Industries, Cadila Healthcare, and Wockhardt. The major drivers of Ranbaxy gained by Sun Pharma's is its International market presence in terms of its product range, brand recognition, access to raw materials, technical capabilities, flexible production systems, regulatory expertise (Jocelyn et al. 2006). Despite these competitions, India's business environment will remain highly challenging for innovative pharmaceutical firms. Despite the challenges involved, the Indian market continues to hold significant potential as the third largest in Asia Pacific, epitomized by India's status as a high-risk high-reward pharmaceutical market for innovative drugmakers. The potential behind India's pharmaceutical sales will be the country's large population which has a sizeable and growing elderly segment.

CONCLUSION

In general, pharmaceutical industry plays a significant role in India because of high revenue associated with the product and likely demand. With the scale of pharmaceutical drugs production, consumption, and trade investments, Sun Pharma is one of the top pharmaceutical manufacturers who established a strong position of brand, specialized in the production of drugs and medicines, developed a strong R&D for product regime worldwide. Moreover, Sun Pharma faces high competition from domestic players such as Cipla and Dr. Reddy's Lab who hone their competitive advantages as well. However, the analysis of their strategic supply chain reveals that they sustained their competitive advantage by aggressive mergers and acquisition and market expansion in the global scale thus providing a powerful edge in the domestic market. Could Sun Pharma survive this in longer run despite its current challenges? Could Shangvi's vision of becoming a global lead player in five-year time horizon be achievable?

Appendix 1: Mission, Vision, and Values of Sun Pharma

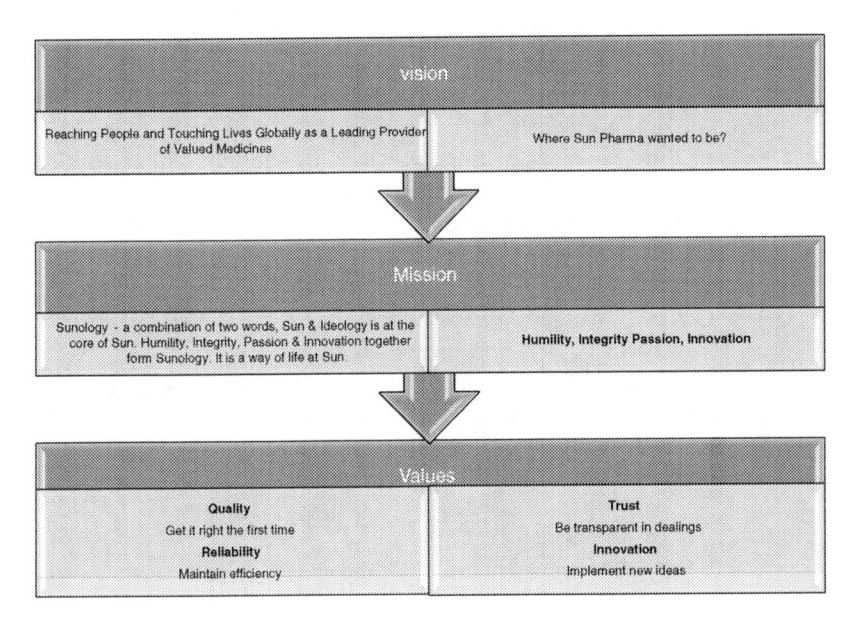

(*Source* Sun Pharma 2017)

Teaching Note

Synopsis of the Case
The case study critically examines the supply chain strategy of 'SUN pharma' company and its acquisition strategy of Ranbaxy. The case illustrates the story of the mergers and acquisition from a supply chain theory point of view and thereby states how SUN has moved forward from its regional presence to global expansion.

Teaching Purpose and Objectives
The case aims to aid teaching concepts and applications of subjects such as Supply Chain strategy, Operations strategy, and Strategic Management and to enrich concepts related but not limited to business Strategy, supply network expansion strategy, competitive analysis and omni-channel strategy.

Discussion Questions and Analysis

1. Assess the supply chain strategy development process for Sun Pharma and justify their alignment.
2. Propose an appropriate supply chain strategy that Sun Pharma should play for their products.
3. Should Sun Pharma focus more on a pull supply chain strategy rather than the current push strategy?
4. Should Sun Pharma have a cultural adaptation for the expansion of business for the new markets?
5. Using the theory of 'Bottom of Pyramid' by C.K Prahalad, Debate how should Sun Pharma target the Indian rural market by opening up company owned stores in the rural areas?
6. Did Dilip Shanghvi manage to turn around Ranbaxy after the take over?
7. What was Sun Pharma's rationale for acquiring Ranbaxy, despite the troubles faced by Ranbaxy in foreign markets?

1. Assess the supply chain strategy development process for Sun Pharma and justify their alignment.

   Supply chain strategy of any company must be developed in consistency with an organizational strategy and its functional strategies. This process starts from developing the core vision and mission of a company and relate them with the operational implementation aspects. In theory, it consists of strategy formulation, strategy implementation, and strategy evaluation as exhibited in Fig. 7. The essence of strategy formulation is an assessment of whether an organization is doing the right things and how it can be more effective in what it does. Regular reappraisal of strategy helps management avoid complacency.

   Students are expected to apply the strategy development theoretical framework of Fig. 7 in the context of Sun Pharma. This can be assessed in terms of Sun Pharma vision, mission, and value proposition statement to be able to see how realistic they are. Once the organizational strategy is generated, this must be translated into its functional strategy in order to evaluate the performance outcomes of its generic and specialty medicines. For sun pharma, its 'sunology' idea fits very well to their core value and, therefore, can sustain their competitive advantage very much.

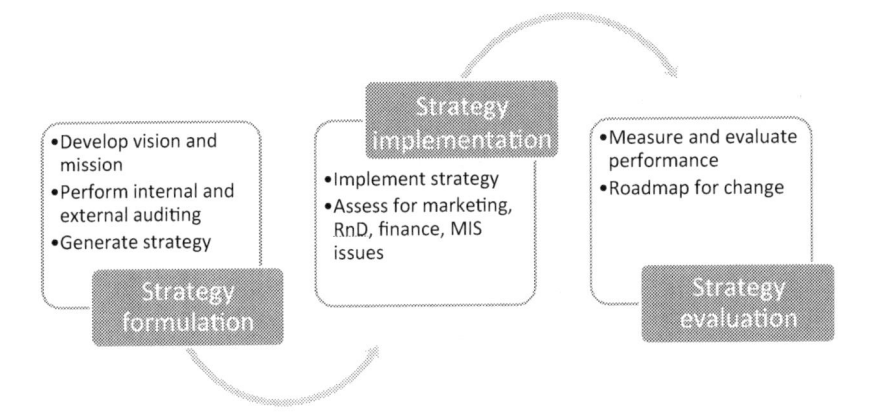

Fig. 7 Supply chain strategy formulation and implementation framework (*Source* Authors)

2. Propose an appropriate supply chain strategy that Sun Pharma should play for their products.

   Supply Chain strategy development process starts from identifying the nature of product through product uncertainty and then comparing with the supply chain capabilities as proposed by Chopra and Meindl (2017) framework. For pharmaceutical products, the uncertainty is somewhat moderate to high and, therefore, the recommended supply chain strategy is to play with a highly responsive supply chain together with little degree of efficiency embedded in the pharma supply chain processes as illustrated in Fig. 8.

3. Should Sun Pharma focus more on pull supply chain strategy rather than the current push strategy?

   Theoretically, the push supply chain process involves supply delivery in anticipation to any customer order whereas the pull supply chain process is of reacting to the customer order. For pharma company industry in general, pull supply chain strategy ensures 'just in time' delivery and this mechanism require distribution capital investment and or 3PL outsourcing. In the case of Sun pharma, the stages are very much into pull from supplier to manufacturer and push from Manufacturer to retailer and pull again from retailer, pharmacies, and clinics to patients as end users. Since supplier orders the medicines to the production units based

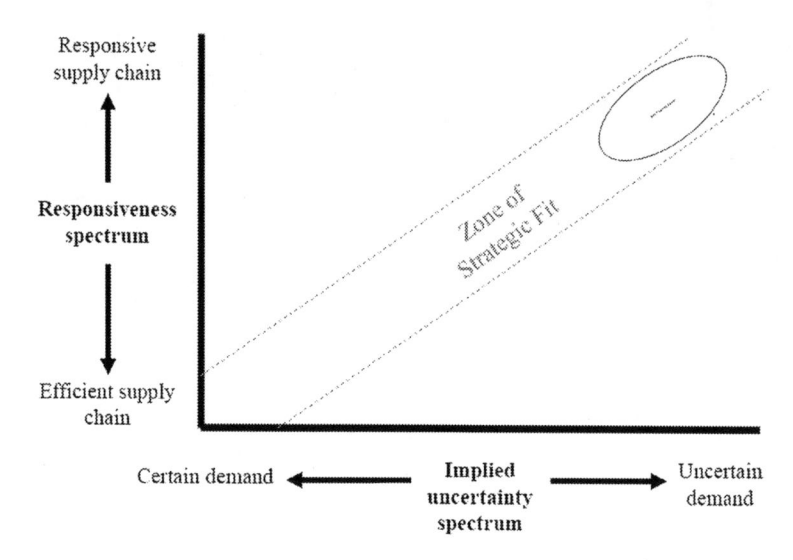

Fig. 8 Supply chain strategy alignment with product uncertainty (*Source* Chopra and Meindl 2017 framework)

on raw materials or Active Pharmaceutical Ingredients (API) from various global vendors and local vendors with their ethical purchasing generic operating procedures, pull supply chain ensures more responsiveness and thus lead to a very high supply chain cost. However, for industry leader such as Sun Pharma cost pressures can offset supply chain speed.

4. Should Sun Pharma have a cultural adaptation for the expansion of business into any new markets?
   Yes, very much likely Sun should have a cultural adaptation for any new market such as Africa, Middle East, and South America where cultural requirement place very dominant role for any business's success. Students, therefore, should be able to relate the cultural differences of these countries or any new markets while proposing recommendations.

5. Using the theory of 'Bottom of Pyramid' by C.K Prahalad, Debate how should Sun Pharma target the Indian rural market by opening up company owned stores in the rural areas?

Students can be suggested to research about the 'Bottom of Pyramid' population through BMI Research, World bank data and Sun Pharma industry performance. According to BMR Research (2017), Fig. 9 below details the population pyramid of Indian in 2017 and the change in the structure of the population between 2017 and 2050. Table below shows the key metrics such as population ratios, the urban/rural split and life expectancy between 1990 and 2025, which needs to be considered to target tapping the bottom of the pyramid demand. Since the purchasing power of the rural segment is less as compared to Urban population, Sun should devise a more Integrated health care services while opening up stores in the urban areas. Perhaps, partnerships with Government, Medical Colleges, Educational Institutions, association of Indian Industry, and other like agencies, Sun Pharma could reach out to the bottom of the pyramid (see Table 2).

6. Did Dilip Shanghvi manage to turn around Ranbaxy after the take over?

Yes, very much successful through the takeover. For example, before merge, Ranbaxy used Aqua Logistics services to track and trace the shipments in order to avoid distribution centers at various overseas and domestic locations by keeping track of the current position of the shipment dispatched by it. Since customer

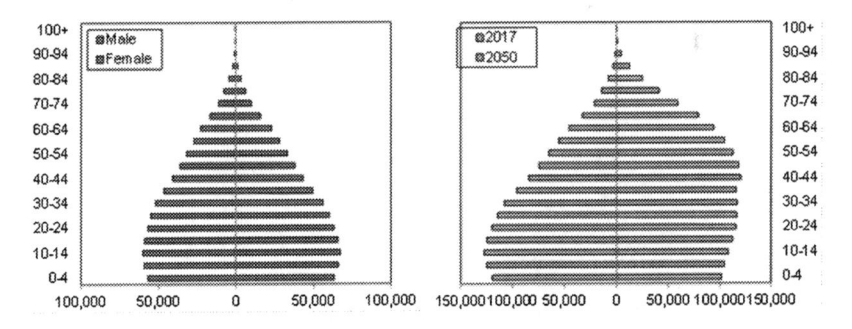

Fig. 9 India population pyramid, 2017 (LHS) versus 2050 (RHS). *Source* World Bank (2017) and BMI (2017)

Table 2   India's Urban and Rural population and Life expectancy

Urban/Rural population and life expectancy (India 1990–2025)

	1990	2000	2005	2010	2015e	2020f	2025f
Urban population, '000	222,293.0	291,347.6	334,483.1	380,742.3	428,675.9	481,117.7	537,713.9
Urban population, % of total	25.5	27.7	29.2	30.9	32.7	34.8	37.0
Rural population, '000	647,840.5	761,703.3	809,635.6	850,238.4	880,378.1	902,080.1	914,115.1
Rural population, % of total	74.5	72.3	70.8	69.1	67.3	65.2	63.0
Life expectancy at birth, male, years	57.6	61.8	63.7	65.5	66.9	68.0	68.9
Life expectancy at birth, female, years	58.3	63.4	65.4	67.8	69.9	71.2	72.3
Life expectancy at birth, average, years	57.9	62.6	64.6	66.6	68.3	69.5	70.5

e=Expected population
f=BMI forecast
Source World Bank, UN, BMI

is the King or the key success of Ranbaxy in which thousands of Ranbaxy customers from more than 104 countries served more than 4000 Stock Keeping Units (SKUs) manufactured either at Ranbaxy's manufacturing facilities or at various other outsourced, but coordination found to be difficult among their supply chain stages. After the acquisition, Sun pharma introduced, supply chain integration system provided by SAP, which acts as the digital backbone of the chain providing on line information to the customers and the organization. To enhance global supply chain capability Sun Pharma, used Radio Frequency Identification (RFID) technology replacing their bar coding system in order to track the stocks automatically (Rossetti et al. 2011).

7. What was Sun Pharma's rationale for acquiring Ranbaxy, despite the troubles faced by Ranbaxy in foreign markets?

The prime factor behind the acquisition was to gain more control on the Indian pharma manufacturing market and thus to become an industry leader in this segment. Other factors for the takeover include impact of low levels of patent protection, price cuts, a preference for generic medicines and low per capita pharmaceutical and healthcare spending will pose headwinds to innovative drug maker like Sun Pharma to capture opportunities in India. While there is an increased prevalence of chronic diseases, the focus on cost-efficiency within the healthcare sector has aided the acquiring process of Ranbaxy. On the other hand, Ranbaxy had faced tough regulatory challenges due to export ban, very low pricing strategy and stringent regulatory requirements moved the company to 'bearish' market performance (Cook and Hagey 2003). Ranbaxy's idea of 'Putting people first' approach did not work very well. As said, In order to sustain its success and renew its products, Ranbaxy focused on the people behind its products and not on the products. Ranbaxy's strength was the people, i.e. both employees and customers. The strategy was to recruit locally in host countries who are culturally adopted within the short time in creating multicultural portfolio of human resource skills. As a result, the company had a challenging working environment and tall organizational structure. These are the trouble faced by Ranbaxy which are the rationale for selling the company to Sun pharma to be able to lead the company's future.

Suggested Websites:
The following websites are good places for students to get on overall understanding of the context.
Websites:
  https://markets.ft.com/data/equities/tearsheet/forecasts?s= RANBAXY:NSI.
  http://businessworld.in/article/Sun-Pharma-Acquiring-Growth/ 16-03-2016-91995/.
  http://www.thehindubusinessline.com/specials/pulse/case-study-sun-sets-on-ranbaxy/article7065610.ece.
  http://economictimes.indiatimes.com/industry/healthcare/bio-tech/pharmaceuticals/ranbaxy-integration-sun-pharma-may-drop-some-non-strategic-units/articleshow/49615336.cms.
  http://www.sunpharma.com/investors/annualreports.
  https://www.rankingthebrands.com/Brand-detail.aspx?brandID=5455.
  https://www.bmiresearch.com/india.

REFERENCES

BMI. (2017). *India Pharmaceuticals & Healthcare Report*. Available at https://www.bmiresearch.com/india. Accessed on July 24, 2018.

Chopra, S., & Meindl, P. (2017). *Supply Chain Drivers and Metrics. Supply Chain Management, Strategy, Planning and Operation* (6th ed.). Upper Saddle River, NJ: Pearson.

Cohen, S., & Roussel, J. (2015). Strategic Supply Chain Management, 2nd Edition. New York: McGraw-Hill.

Cook, M., & Hagey, R. (2003). "Why Companies Flunk Supply-Chain 101: Only 33 percent Correctly Measure Supply-Chain Performance; Few Use the Right Incentives", *Journal of Business Strategy*, vol. 24, no. 4, pp. 35–42.

Directorate General of Commercial Intelligence and Statistics. (2012). http://www.dgciskol.nic.in/data.asp.

IBEF. (2018). *Indian Pharmaceutical Industry*. Available at https://www.ibef.org/industry/pharmaceuticalindia.aspx. Accessed on July 24, 2018.

Jayashree, D., & Rajesh, D. (2010). "Pharmaceutical Innovation and Generic Challenge: Recent Trends and Causal Factors", *International Journal of Pharmaceutical and Healthcare Marketing*, vol. 4, no. 2, pp. 175–190.

Jocelyn, E. M., Andrew, D. T., Abdallah, S. D., & Peter, A. (2006). "Corporate Social Responsibility Strategies Aimed at the Developing World: Perspectives From Bioscience Companies in the Industrialised World", *International Journal of Biotechnology*, vol. 8, no. 1/2, pp. 87–89.

Meenakshi, K., & Vinayshil, G. (2010). "Innovation in the Pharmaceutical Industry: Study of Select Parameters", *Journal of Advances in Management Research*, vol. 7, no. 1, pp. 127–138.

Papert, M., Rimpler, P., & Pflaum, A. (2016). "Enhancing Supply Chain Visibility in a Pharmaceutical Supply Chain", *International Journal of Physical Distribution & Logistics Management*, vol. 46, no. 9, pp. 859–884.

Rao, P. (2008). "The Emergence of the Pharmaceutical Industry in the Developing World and Its Implications for Multinational Enterprise Strategies", *International Journal of Pharmaceutical and Healthcare Marketing*, vol. 2, no. 2, pp. 103–116.

Rossetti, C.L., Handfield, R., & Dooley, K.J. (2011). "Forces, Trends, and Decisions in Pharmaceutical Supply Chain Management", *International Journal of Physical Distribution and Logistics Management*, vol. 41, no. 6, pp. 601–622.

Shah, N. (2004). "Pharmaceutical Supply Chains: Key Issues and Strategies for Optimisation", *Computers & Chemical Engineering*, vol. 28, no. 6/7, pp. 929–941.

Singh, R., Kumar, R., & Kumar, P. (2016). "Strategic Issues in Pharmaceutical Supply Chains: A Review", *International Journal of Pharmaceutical and Healthcare Marketing*, vol. 10, no. 3, pp. 234–257.

Sun Pharma. (2017). Available at http://www.sunpharma.com/sites/default/files/annual/Sun%20Pharma%20Annual%20Report-FY17.pdf.

The Economic Times. (2015). Ranbaxy Integration: Sun Pharma May Drop Some Non-strategic Units. Available at http://economictimes.indiatimes.com/industry/healthcare/biotech/pharmaceuticals/ranbaxy-integration-sun-pharma-may-drop-some-non-strategic-units/articleshow/49615336.cms. Accessed on July 24, 2018.

World Bank. (2017). *India Population Pyramid Report.* Available at https://www.populationpyramid.net/india/2017/. Accessed on July 24, 2018.

Hope in Their Hands: Seeing Hands Nepal

Perry Haan and Malavika Desai

INTRODUCTION

Though we cannot see, our hands can see and we can perform better through our hands.

Chiran Poudel, Owner, Seeing Hands Nepal

Chiran Poudel sat on the front porch of his business, Seeing Hands Nepal (SHN), in the district of Thamel, Kathmandu. Over the previous 12 years, Poudel had gone from giving up his gig in a band in Pokhara, Nepal, where he went to University, to owning three massage therapy locations in the Kathmandu area.

'I am not sure what we will do next' he said. 'I have thought about more locations but I also have concerns that this business is becoming too dependent on only one service—massage.' He said he was considering other businesses to complement the successful massage business. 'I'm considering other things but for now I don't know what.'

P. Haan (✉)
Tiffin University, Tiffin, OH, USA
e-mail: haanpc@tiffin.edu

M. Desai
King's College, Kathmandu, Nepal

© The Author(s) 2019
A. Sikdar and V. Pereira (eds.), *Business and Management Practices in South Asia*, https://doi.org/10.1007/978-981-13-1399-8_12

THE BUSINESS

Seeing Hands[1] is a social enterprise offering massage services at three locations in the Kathmandu area. It is also known for providing training and employment opportunities in massage therapy for visually impaired people. Chiran's three massage clinics employ teams of professionally-trained blind therapists who provide massage to Guests. Part of the fees they earn is used to fund the training and employment of more blind masseurs so the organisation can grow and develop. Over 25 blind individuals have now benefited through employment with Seeing Hands and its professional sports-style massage services have a good reputation, with excellent ratings on TripAdvisor (ranked #1 among 'things to do in Kathmandu'), Lonely Planet, as well as other tourist websites and guidebooks.[2]

Poudel sees massage as a way for him, as an owner, to operate independently. 'Massage allows you to be on your own' he said. 'I wanted to run my own clinics in Kathmandu' he said of his move from working in Pokhara to owning his own location in Kathmandu in 2010. Poudel's goal in starting his own 'clinics', as they are referred to in the medical massage business was creating a self-sustaining social enterprise that could be run by the blind. Becoming an entrepreneur was something he decided to do to provide a way to help others. 'Being an entrepreneur is part of who I am now' he stated.

Today, the organisation is running independently, with minimal support from its international founders and volunteers who helped it get started. Since operations were localised, with support from Change Fusion Nepal, the team has successfully opened a second clinic in the Patan district of Kathmandu and began a training program with six more blind students. The latest location is near the Bouddha Stupa, one of the more popular tourist attractions in Kathmandu.

Change Fusion Nepal[3] is a non-governmental organisation founded in September 2008. It channels creative opportunities for aspiring change-makers in diverse fields within the social entrepreneurship framework. Change Fusion supports social ventures and individuals who create

---

[1] http://www.seeinghandsnepal.org/.

[2] https://www.tripadvisor.in/Attraction_Review-g293890-d12694454-Reviews-Seeing_Hands-Kathmandu_Kathmandu_Valley_Bagmati_Zone_Central_Region.html.

[3] http://changefusionnepal.org/.

value for 'People, Planet and Profit using four components: Mentorship, Knowledge, Funding and Networking', according to its website.

Poudel received the Surya Nepal Asha Award[4] for Social Entrepreneurship from Change Fusion for his work in training sight impaired employees as part of his Seeing Hands massage business. The Surya Nepal Asha Social Entrepreneurship Award was established in 2011 to recognise business owners in Nepal who challenge traditional thinking and approaches and are determined to bring about positive change in their communities. The main objective of the award was to identify, inspire, reward and support social entrepreneurs who promote the development of communities and contribute to nation building in Nepal.

In 2010, Chiran Poudel opened his first clinic in Thamel to provide jobs for a growing team of massage therapists. The clinic started with two blind therapists. With the success of the massage clinic in Thamel, SHN started with a second clinic in Lalitpur on 1 September 2014. Together, the clinics now cater to 35 people on an average in a day, 15–18 being a daily number, with 3 types of massage services currently being offered to Clients. The Seeing Hands clinics offer remedial and Sports Therapy, Swedish Relaxation Massage and Relaxation Foot Massage. The clinic currently has 8 masseurs, 3 office assistants and cleaners. With regard to income generation and management, a third of it is used to pay the therapists. After paying for overhead operating expenses, the rest is put on reserve for emergencies and possible expansion of the business.

The massage business in Kathmandu is very competitive. There are many clinics and other massage locations just in the neighborhood in which Poudel operates his clinic in Thamel, Kathmandu. Poudel attributes the success of the business to two reasons. First, he believes in the quality of massages. 'I was trained well and try to train my people well' Poudel stated.

Seeing Hands practices an Eastern style of massage. In Eastern massage, the therapist feels for the pulse in three positions on the wrist in an attempt to detect imbalances throughout the body. Special techniques are used to soothe very specific points on the body's energy meridians. This is believed to create healing effects in the patient's body. Quite akin

[4]https://asha2012.wordpress.com/2012/10/10/chiran-jeevi-poudel-snasea-2012/.

to Eastern medicine, the ultimate goal of Eastern massage is to locate the primary cause of a possible health issue or physical discomfort (like back pain or sprained muscles) and address them not merely at the symptomatic or superficial level. 'We can't be doctors but we can help other people be healthier through massage,' shares Poudel.

Second, Poudel attributed the success of the business to people (Customers) wanting to help. 'People believe in causes like training visually impaired people.' He estimated that about 90% of his business in the three Kathmandu locations comes from tourists. Word of mouth among travelers as well as favourable ratings on travel sites such as TripAdvisor and Lonely Planet have been his main promotional tools. Seeing Hands also has a website (http://www.seeinghandsnepal.org/) where it is possible to make reservations as well as get more information about the clinics. Poudel believes that being visually impaired does not come in the way of working as a massage therapist because the visually impaired have an extra sense of touch and can connect more with the body's pressure points. Besides, scientific massage focuses on the assessment and treatment of soft tissue ailments through manual manipulation.

Chiran Poudel

> What I like about my profession is that I can give health and happiness to people, even when I am blind.
>
> Chiran Poudel, Owner, Seeing Hands Clinic, Nepal

Poudel was born into a big family in Pokhara. He had 13 siblings, eight brothers and four sisters. Among his siblings, four are born blind (three brothers and one sister). Poudel was blind by birth. He graduated with a bachelor's degree in English. As he finished his bachelor degree, a British couple, Rob and Sue Ainley came to Poudel's college looking for candidates for massage training. Poudel was one of four chosen from the 40 interviewed for the positions. After the training, he worked with Seeing Hands Clinic Pokhara for five years to gain experience operating a massage clinic. In 2010, Poudel decided to set up his own venture. He received help from the Ainleys to start the business in Kathmandu. The first clinic in Kathmandu started on 1 November 2010.

History of Seeing Hands Kathmandu

I am happiest when therapists graduate and work at the clinics, because
I am reassured that more blind people are getting the jobs they need.
Chiran Poudel, Owner, Seeing Hands Clinic, Nepal

Seeing Hands Nepal imparts training to its blind students specialising in professional sports and remedial massage. The courses run for a year and are taught by overseas volunteer tutors, with some assistance from local personnel. SHN offers scholarships that cover the living expenses of the students during the training. It also conducts advanced training like Train the Trainers and other skill building sessions to make the students self-sufficient in running their own units. For the job seekers, the organisation assists in finding employments for its graduates in income generating clinics.

Seeing Hands was established in Pokhara in 2005 by the Ainleys with funding from private donors, charitable trusts, and companies. The project began with a small massage training program, initially with just four blind students. Their training course, following UK standards, was rigorous and delivered in 18 months by a team of experienced volunteer massage tutors. With support from local hotelier, Kul Bahadur Acharya, the first Seeing Hands Clinic was established in Pokhara, Nepal and the qualified students began working as sports massage therapists, treating tired trekkers and tourists.

Pokhara is one of Nepal's top tourist cities. Located on a lake, it is approximately 200 kilometres (125 miles) from Kathmandu and has a population of over 200,000. It is the gateway to the popular Annapurna trekking trails in Nepal. In Pokhara, tourists experience the best in trekking, boating, hiking, pony rides, paragliding or simply relax at one of the lakes near the city with the stunning Annapurna mountain range in the background.

Poudel was one of four students chosen from 40 applicants to be accepted to the first class of therapist trainees. He was playing in a band in a restaurant owned by Acharya, who provided the space to start the massage business. 'I was bored playing in a band'. At first, Poudel was reluctant to apply. Eventually, he applied and was selected. Poudel's fear was centered around working in the massage industry because of its reputation as being a front for prostitution and other criminal activities.

Founder Rob Ainly is a massage therapist and his wife Susan was the marketing manager for the business. They have been visiting Nepal since

1993. Rob, as a masseur, had realised the value and importance of massage in Nepal where so many tourists came for trekking and looking for a professional massage. But nobody had done this to this point.

In 2003, Ainlys went for a vacation to Cambodia where they received a massage from visually impaired people in Seeing Hands Cambodia and came to realise that sense of touch with visually impaired people was far better than that of sighted massage therapists. After returning to Nepal from Cambodia, the couple did some research concerning the situation of the visually impaired. They found out the situation was poor in terms of employment opportunities.

Ainlys sought funding from several non-profit organisations to start massage training for the visually impaired. None of these organisations initially responded to their appeal. Finally, they decided to start the training program themselves and raised some support from their family and friends.

Seeing Hands is widely used and popular name in the blind massage businesses around the world. The name was used in several other countries before it was used in Nepal. The name was used by Ainlys in Nepal, after seeing the name at a massage clinic operated by the visually impaired in Cambodia (Fig. 1).

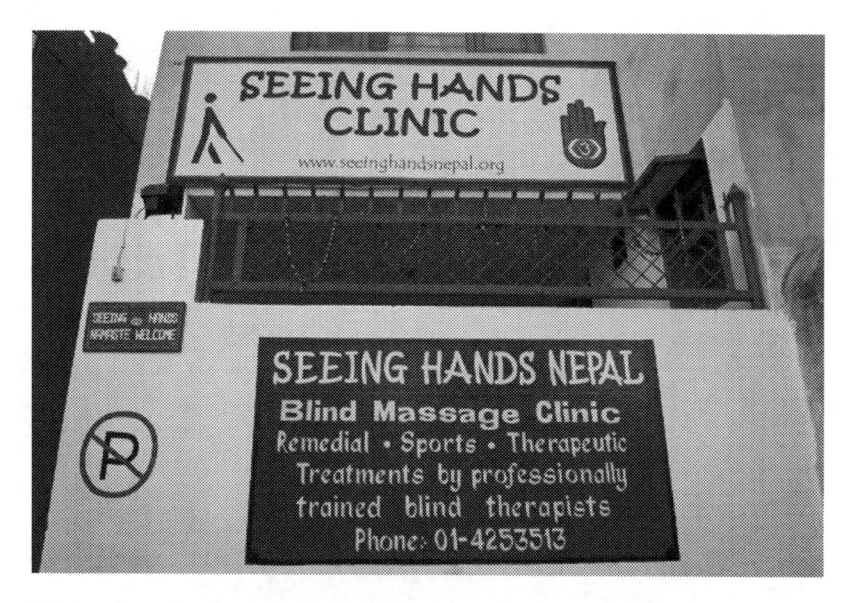

Fig. 1   Front facade of Seeing Hands Clinic, Kumari Marg, Kathmandu

NEPAL

Nepal is a landlocked central Himalayan country in South Asia. It has a population of 26.4 million. Nepal shares borders with China in the north and India in the south, east, and west. It is the largest sovereign Himalayan state. As a nation, Nepal has enjoyed total autonomy through history, never having to celebrate an Independence Day. Yet, till date, because of the conflicting coexistence of Communism and monarchies, the country stands in economic isolation. In an era of globalisation, when the rest of the world was busy seizing opportunities to reap the benefits of worldwide proliferation and integration, Nepal was struggling with political instability, corruption, poverty, natural disasters, lack of industry and outdated farming practices. It is only since 2005 when two events, first, King Gyanendra bowing down to foreign pressure and lifting emergency and reinstating parliament; and second, the Maoist insurgents agreeing to join hands and restoring democracy, that the country has witnessed some mention of worthy entrepreneurial activity.

To the traveller, Nepal appears as a romantic and picturesque holiday and a trekker's paradise.[5] The picture-perfect image hides the scars that has racked Nepal for ages. Nepal's turbulent history can be traced back to three decades, which according to C.K. Lal, a columnist, can be referred to as 'history on steroids'. During all these years, the Nepalese people had to live through a decade long bloody insurgency that got thousands killed, a gun spraying infuriated Crown Prince who murdered the entire royal family, a 'musical chair' government that was constructed and 're' constructed under 25 different Prime Ministers, oppression by Maoist guerrillas, a massive earthquake, destructive floods and a life halting economic blockade, to name a few.

Known to be among the most beautiful places on Earth, Nepal is still a country where more than one fourth of the country's population lives below the poverty line. An Asian Development Bank survey ranked Nepal as the poorest country in South Asia after Bangladesh and one among a dozen poorest countries in the World. A significant percentage (nearly 12.5%) of the working class Nepalese gets to earn less that USD 1.90 per day. Mount Everest, or Sagarmatha, as it is fondly addressed locally, is the highest mountain on Earth and is shared between Nepal and Tibet. Because of political reasons, the mountain is better accessible

[5]https://www.welcomenepal.com/.

Table 1   Change in international Nepalese tourism 2014–2017

Year	Number of international tourists arriving in Nepal	% change from previous year
2014	790,118	−0.9
2015	538,970	−31
2016	753,002	+40
2017	940,218	+24.8

Source Department of Tourism, Government of Nepal

from Nepal and remains a signature tourist attraction till date. About 1000 people attempt to climb the Everest each year with about half reaching the summit. Though Nepal is among the top three destinations out of the 10 best places, listed by the National Geographic that attracts travelers, tourism is not a significant part of the economy, only accounting for about 7% of its Gross Domestic Product (GDP).[6]

However, Nepal is catching up with better days. For the first time, in 2017, the number of visitors to Mount Everest was a swelling 900,000 plus. Footfalls in Nepal jumped 41.50% (460,237 visitors) in the first two quarters of 2017, leaving the travel and hospitality business with the expectation that the total figure will hit the 1-million mark by the end of the year. It missed the target by a mere 6% closing at a figure of 940,000 visitors. Encouraged by a good start, Nepali people resolved to shed the despair and move forward with a renewed dose of optimism, planning to showcase its uniqueness to the international market as one of the places on Earth to visit 'before one dies'. This advancement was long awaited and justified as for a country with a population of 30 million people, with larger countries like China and India as neighbours, the scope for a thriving tourism industry is obvious (Table 1).[7]

According to the Department of Immigration, Nepal received 134,988 more tourists in the first six months of 2017 out of which +200,000 were trekkers. Undoubtedly, Nepal's foreign exchange earnings from tourism have been on the rise (Table 2).

Despite the encouraging statistics in tourism business, agriculture continues to be Nepal's main economic activity, employing nearly 65% of the population and contributing to 31.7% of GDP. The country's

[6] https://www.adb.org/countries/nepal/poverty.

[7] http://kathmandupost.ekantipur.com/news/2017-08-25/tourism-earnings-hit-record-rs5852b-last-fiscal-year.html.

Table 2   Tourism earnings[a]

Year	Earnings (in NPR)
2016–17	Rs. 58.52 billion
2015–16	Rs. 41.76 billion
2014–15	Rs. 53.42 billion
2013–14	Rs. 46.37 billion
2012–13	Rs. 34.21 billion
2011–12	Rs. 30.70 billion
2010–11	Rs. 24.61 billion

[a]Foreign exchange calculated by adding the tourist service charge collected at the airport and revenue earned by hotels and travel agencies, among other establishments. The calculation is also based on data received from money changers
Source Nepal Rastra Bank

GDP is also dependent on remittances (29.1%) of foreign workers. Nepal's travel and tourism industry's direct contribution to the GDP is a mere 3.6%, as an outcome of the economic activities in the tourism sector that generated 800 million USD (Table 3).[8]

One of the problems of the trekking business, as it is known in Nepal, has caused is an increase in the level of pollution on Mt. Everest and other mountains in the area. People climbing the mountains often leave trash along their way. The country is facing a dilemma that it would like to attract more tourists but is also concerned about the additional environmental issues the industry can create.

Agriculture constitutes 36.1%, while services and industry account for 48.5 and 15.4% of Nepal's GDP, respectively. Though an agrarian country, agriculture in Nepal is crippled with lack of quality research and non-availability of inputs, services and technology for the crop bearers. With the current state of affairs, the future looks bleak as Nepal is likely to face greater food scarcity and poverty, especially for those 66% of people whose means of survival is agriculture, predict analysts. Lack of capital, infrastructure and non-availability of skilled manpower allows industries to employ only 3% of the population. While the scenario in agriculture and industry is grim, service sector contribution to the country's GDP seems to be looking up. Agriculture engages 76% of the population, 18% is hired

---

[8] https://www.wttc.org/-/media/files/reports/economic-impact-research/countries-2015/nepal2015.ashx.

Table 3   Nepal 2017 tourism annual research: key facts

GDP: Direct contribution	The direct contribution of Travel and Tourism to GDP was NPR 85.2 billion (USD 0.8 billion), 3.6% of total GDP in 2016 and is forecast to rise by 6.8% in 2017, and to rise by 4.3% pa from 2017 to 2027 to NPR 138.9 billion (USD 1.3 billion), 4.0% of total GDP in 2027
GDP: Total contribution	The total contribution of Travel and Tourism to GDP was NPR 177.9 billion (USD 1.6 billion), 7.5% of GDP in 2016, and is forecast to rise by 6.2% in 2017, and to rise by 4.3% pa to NPR 287.6 billion (USD 2.7 billion), 8.3% of GDP in 2027
Employment: Direct contribution	In 2016, Travel and Tourism directly supported 427,000 jobs (2.9% of total employment). This is expected to rise by 6.0% in 2017 and rise by 2.9% pa to 604,000 jobs (3.2% of total employment) in 2027
Employment: Total contribution	In 2016, the total contribution of Travel and Tourism to employment, including jobs indirectly supported by the industry was 6.4% of total employment (945,000 jobs). This is expected to rise by 5.4% in 2017—996,000 jobs and rise by 2.9% pa to 1,325,000 jobs in 2027 (7.1% of total)
Visitor exports	Visitor exports generated NPR 48.6 billion (USD 449.8mn), 17.7% of total exports in 2016. This is forecast to grow by 9.0% in 2017, and grow by 6.8% pa, from 2017 to 2027, to NPR 102.1 billion (USD 945.0mn) in 2027,25.9% of total
Investment	Travel and Tourism investment in 2016 was NPR 16.5 billion, 3.0% of total investment (USD 0.2 billion). It should rise by 0.3% in 2017, and rise by 5.5% pa over the next ten years to NPR 28.3 billion (USD 0.3 billion) in 2027, 3.6% of total

All values are in constant 2016 prices and exchange rates
Source World travel and tourism council

by services while manufacturing and craft-based industry employ around 6%. Agricultural produce that are mostly grown in the Terai region around the borders of India, includes buffalo meat, rice, tea, corn, sugarcane, wheat, root crops. Industry in Nepal primarily comprises of agricultural products, like sugarcane, jute, tobacco and grain.[9,10]

Nepal's economy is heavily dependent on remittances of foreign workers. Almost a third of the GDP comes from those individuals who leave the country and send money back to their family inside Nepal.

[9] https://www.britannica.com/place/Nepal/The-economy.

[10] World Bank. 1964. *Nepal—The economy (English)*. Asia series; no. AS 101. Washington, DC: World Bank. http://documents.worldbank.org/curated/en/337531468324853642/Nepal-The-economy.

For this and other reasons, economic development in social services and infrastructure has not progressed as quickly as some other nations.

However, poverty in Nepal seems to be on the decline. A study conducted by Oxford Poverty and Human Development Initiative (OPHI) confirmed that poverty in Nepal is fast reducing at a rate faster than that of India (37.2% in 2004–05 to 21.9% by 2011–12).[11,12] Since 2003, the percentage of poor people in Nepal seem to have reduced to a significant extent. Between 2006 and 2011, Nepal's poverty rate had shown an impressive decline from 64.7 to 44.2%. People living below the international poverty line (earning less than US$1.25 per day) were reduced to half in last half decade. Nepal has also made noticeable progress in areas like child mortality, nutrition, energy and assets. The country commendable stride in controlling poverty making it 21.6% in 2015 from 25.2% in 2011. More than 50% of the poverty alleviation that took place between the years 1995–2010 was on account of the growth in labour incomes and service business, which are non-agricultural in nature. With the current rate of reducing poverty, it is predicted that the middle class in Nepal will grow and flourish (see Footnote 11).

The spectacular landscape and diverse, exotic cultures of Nepal represent considerable potential for tourism, but growth in the sector has been stifled by political instability and poor infrastructure. Though in 2017, Nepal's rate of unemployment dropped to 3.20% from 3.40% in 2016, the Foreign Permit department is reported to receive as many as 1500 applications per day from Nepali citizens aiming for jobs with higher remuneration. In 2017, the Labour Force participation rate in Nepal was as low as 84.21%.[13] Despite confirmed news about the unhealthy working conditions and blatant abuse of workers' rights prevalent in certain countries such as Qatar, Nepali youth still choose to flock to such countries. They also move to the United States, Canada, United Kingdom, India, Thailand, Japan, Brunei, Darussalam, Australia and Saudi Arabia, clearly signaling the absence of opportunities in their home land (Table 4).

---

[11] http://ophi.org.uk/ophi_stories/nepals-poverty-halved-in-less-than-a-decade-new-official-index-reveals/.

[12] http://planningcommission.nic.in/news/pre_pov2307.pdf.

[13] https://www.ceicdata.com/en/indicator/nepal/labour-force-participation-rate.

Table 4   Unemployment rate in Nepal: year 2017

Last	Previous	Minimum	Maximum	Unit	Frequency	Range
3.20	3.40	1.80	4.50	%	Yearly	1991–2017
2017	2016	1999	1996			Updated on 1 January 2017

Source World Bank

THE HISTORY OF DISASTER INCIDENTS AND ITS IMPACT ON TOURISM IN NEPAL

The people of Nepal have been exposed to a series of local disaster events and exhibit a serious vulnerability to natural calamities. Over and above loss of precious human lives, damage to infrastructure and resources, these catastrophes have hit the tourism industry hard making them lag behind a few years.

The hard profile of Nepal, obtained from the DesInventar Disaster Information System (DesInventar 2011),[14] points out that Nepal is susceptible to a large number of disasters, both natural as well as human induced. Nepal's proneness to disaster is quite complex and varies across different states across the country resulting in sharp increase or decrease in World decision to visit Nepal. There is an apparent rise in the incidents of disasters in Nepal that can be linked to factors like political instability, relations with neighboring countries, rapid urban expansion etc.[15]

THE FATAL EARTHQUAKE OF 2015

On 25 April 2015, a 7.8 magnitude twin earthquake ravaged Nepal. In a matter of few seconds, more than 9000 people were killed and people were made homeless. With a total damage of 1000 crores USD (50% of Nepal's nominal GDP) the ravaging calamity destroyed the stability that the Nepali people had garnered post the royal massacre and civil war.[16,17,18]

---

[14] https://www.nset.org.np/nset2012/images/publicationfile/20111220153002.pdf.

[15] Aryal, K.R. (2012). The History of Disaster Incidents and Impacts in Nepal 1900–2005. *International Journal of Disaster Risk Science*, 3(3), 147–154.

[16] https://www.britannica.com/topic/Nepal-earthquake-of-2015.

[17] https://en.wikipedia.org/wiki/Nepalese_royal_massacre.

[18] https://en.wikipedia.org/wiki/Nepalese_Civil_War.

The earthquake also triggered an avalanche that left large numbers of climbers dead, missing, injured and trapped. In another incident in 2014, the climbing season came to an abrupt end when a fierce snowstorm resulted in the deaths of at least 43 people of various nationalities, including at least 21 trekkers.

The sever aftershocks gave a huge blow to Nepal causing an estimated 43 billion rupees ($405 million) damage to its tourism industry, according to a report by the Ministry of Culture, Tourism and Civil Aviation. Tourism figures took a nosedive and plummeted to a low of 300,000 from 800,000 tourists in 2014. These figures however, mostly included people who travelled by air to reach Nepal, mostly foreigner and presumably, trekkers. Nepal government labored hard to change the narrative post the disaster, but the results were not encouraging. Now in 2018, in its third year after the destruction, the country has been gathering momentum into recovery and reconstruction.

The setback, fortunately, was short-lived. Nepal was up on its feet again, making a steep 40% jump in revenue (58.2 billion) from the previous fiscal year. The country received 845,147 tourists in the last fiscal year (2016–17). This remarkable progress towards recovery is a proof of the global attention and partnership that Nepal receives aiding its speedy progress and recovery. Funding from Australia, Denmark, the European Union, Finland, Germany, Japan, Mauritius, Nepal, Norway, Republic of Korea, Sweden, Switzerland, the United Kingdom, the World Bank and other partners poured into support the Government of Nepal through several recovery programs.[19]

THE 2015 NEPAL BLOCKADE

As a landlocked nation, Nepal imports all of its petroleum supplies from India. Besides petroleum, Nepal also relies heavily on imports, especially food, medicines and fuel, from India, which is its largest trade partner.

This economic and humanitarian crisis began on 23 September 2015, which severely affected Nepal and its economy. Nepal accused India of

---

[19] http://www.undp.org/content/dam/undp/library/crisis%20prevention/UNDP_NP_supporting-nepal-to-build-back-better-key-achievements-in-undps-earthquake-response.pdf.

imposing an undeclared blockade. India on its part denied all allegations, and stated that the supply shortage was a man-made emergency situation doctored by the agitating Madheshi community in Nepal. However, despite Indian denials, minimal border entries even from peaceful border points fueled allegations that it was indeed an India enforced border blockade. Over and above a strained Indo-Nepal relation, the blockade crippled the economy of Nepal, as it dissuaded travelers to stay away for a reasonable period of time.[20]

TRIBUBHAN AIRPORT

Undeniably Nepal's growth and economy depend to a large extent on foreign aid and tourism. However, the state of affairs at Tribhuban International Airport (TIA), the country's sole international airport raises alarm in the minds of overseas travelers. Judging on the criteria of comfort, services, security and immigration, in 2016 'Sleeping In Airports', an international airport review agency ranked TIA as the second worst airport in Asia. The rankings are based on comfort, services, security and immigration.[21]

'According to the voters, the Kathmandu's international airport is chaotic, crowded and corrupt. The airport greets visitors with disorganised and spawned by a lack of flight information, signage, or any semblance of a logical layout,' the report said.

It also said,

The staff does little to organise the crowds, making the terminal feel more like a rugby scrum than anything else. Of course, we do recognise that Nepal has had a difficult few years and we can understand that airport enhancements aren't at the top of the national priority list.

With corrective action that is slow to be visible, in a time span of eight years TIA has witnessed 10 fatal accidents. As recent as on 12 March 2018, a US-Bangla Airlines plane crashed killing 49 people on

[20] https://en.wikipedia.org/wiki/2015_Nepal_blockade.

[21] https://www.sleepinginairports.net/community/reviews/kathmandu-airport-reviews.htm?review-page=3.

board when the aircraft made a surprise turn while trying to land in Kathmandu. Tourism entrepreneurs have voiced their concern over the appalling conditions in TIA, fearing that it is sure to create fear in the minds of the tourists and affect their arrivals.[22]

Demonetisation of the Indian Rupee

The Indian demonetisation has hurt Nepali nationals. I will raise this in my meetings with Indian leaders and request them to resolve the issue,

KP Sharma Oli, Nepalese Prime Minister

Indian currency is widely accepted in Nepal. On 8 November 2016, the Government of India announced the demonetisation of all ₹500 and ₹1000 banknotes of the Mahatma Gandhi series. This created a ripple effect in neighbouring Nepal with an almost instantaneous impact on its economy, trade, remittances and visitors. Soon after Indian government's demonetisation exercise, mass tourist group cancellations took place.

BMI Research, a group company of the Fitch rating agency, commented that demonetisation could dwarf down Nepal's growth to 2.2% for the year 2016–17 from an earlier estimate of 2.5% (see Footnote 21). The World Bank too, predicted a heavy weighing down of Nepalese economy as an immediate after-effect of the Indian demonetisation. In 'Global Economic Prospects—Weak Investment in Uncertain Times', the World Bank Group's flagship report commented, 'Spill overs from India to Nepal and Bhutan, through trade and remittances channels, could also negatively impact growth in these neighbouring smaller economies.'[23]

India's scrapping of high value notes caused a significant disruption in Nepalese economy and its banking system. As of date, with no facility to exchange demonetised notes, Kathmandu is still looking for a mechanism to return $146 million (Rs. 950 crore) of demonetised Indian rupees lying useless in Nepal.[24]

---

[22] http://www.dhakatribune.com/world/south-asia/2018/03/23/tribhuvan-international-airport-hellish-gateway-himalayan-havens/.

[23] https://www.bmiresearch.com/nepal.

[24] https://www.news18.com/news/india/troubled-with-rs-950-crore-demonetised-indian-notes-nepal-pm-to-raise-issue-during-visit-1708343.html.

CHINA—A REALITY?

The editorial column in Global Times, a State run tabloid daily in China put forth the question outright in an article titled, 'Will Kathmandu swing to Beijing and stay away from New Delhi?' The editorial analyses the 'dual wooing' by India and China of Nepal and describes it as a 'competition between new complexities of the legacy of colonialism and Cold War logic, and the new global dynamics based on connectivity.'[25]

Historically, on account of its geographical position, Nepal always had to live under the shadow of its two powerful Asian neighbors, India and China. As geo political allies and nuclear rivals, both the powers have abundantly gifted aids to Nepal, with the objective of improving ties and exerting greater influence. However, a sudden surge of Chinese investments seems to have taken the Nepalese people off-guard which they fear could take a toll on its sovereignty.

An explicit political dimension makes the Nepal China India triangle dynamics interesting. India, as a neighbor, is known to have played a key role in Nepal's fight for democracy—aiding to oust the Rana reign in the early 50s; supporting the democracy movement in 1990, facilitating the peace accord between democratic parties and Maoists in 2006. Though Nepal is maintaining a stance of 'equidistance' which is in essence is a fine balancing act between a former important protector and a recent (and wealthier) investor, the comfort between Nepal and its second benefactor, China, is still at a formative stage. Nepal has shown larger preference to the cultural, social and political closeness with India recognising the common language that is shared between the two countries. Aditya Adhikari, in his book, 'The Bullet and the Ballot Box: The Story of Nepal's Maoist Revolution' writes, 'The Indian influence far exceeded the Chinese and various leaders in Nepal dreamed—and continue to dream to this day—of using Chinese support to counterweight Indian domination'.[26]

The gigantic earthquake and the economic blockade that crippled Nepalese economy in 2015, created a perfect opportunity for China to make a grand official entry. Beijing's successful experiment with Africa

[25] http://www.globaltimes.cn/content/1062240.shtml.

[26] Adhikari, Aditya. (2014). *The Bullet and the Ballot Box: The Story of Nepal's Maoist Revolution*. London and New York: Verso.

was well orchestrated and massive investments in infrastructure followed. Quite expectedly, soon after a struggle ridden 2015, 2016 witnessed China breezing past India to the list of top aid providers to Nepal. Having shown interest to invest over \$8.3 billion, there are indications enough that China is speeding to further supersede India, who has been the principal Foreign Direct Investor so far (Nepal Investment Summit Kathmandu 2017).[27]

The following facts are indicative enough of China's aggressive stance

- In 2015/16, total exports to China were US\$181 million.
- Import from China has been growing at the rate of 39% per year since 2006. Nepal's import value from China has gone up 17 times since 2006. From a mere US\$421 million in the year 2009–10 to it rose to 1247 million in 2015–16. To enhance these ties, China has offered zero-tariff treatment to 60% products of Nepal.
- There is a visible surge to boost Nepal–China cultural relations. Simultaneously there is added emphasis on boosting cultural exchanges. As of now there are about 19 China Study Centres (CSC) and Confucius Institutes in Nepal aiming to promote Chinese language and culture.
- In 2015, during the undeclared blockade of fuel and necessary supplies near Birgunj, on the India–Nepal border, a month long stand—off started by local Madhesis, Beijing came forward to give 1.3 million litres of petrol to Nepal as aid, and promised to follow up after a memorandum of understanding was signed between Nepal Oil Corporation (NOC) and its Chinese counterpart companies.
- China has solemnised Nepal as the 'official destination' and declared 2018 as the 'Visit Nepal Year'. The town of Pokhara became a hot attraction for Chinese nationals on 31 January 2018 when they thronged the lake in thousands to celebrate the lunar year on 31 January 2018. Shops in Pokhara flaunt signboards written in Chinese with more than a dozen hotels run by Chinese owners.

---

[27] http://www.ibn.gov.np/nepal-investment-summit-2017.

- Chinese are the second largest population to visit Nepal. Over 1,500,000 Chinese tourists are expected to visit Nepal by air in 2018, according to Nepal Tourism Board.
- In 2016–17, according to reports, China is funding 108 active projects worth NPR 29.8 billion. In comparison, India only has eighteen projects amounting NPR 8 billion.

The structural economic development is visible in Nepal. From an agricultural country, Nepal is turning to a consumer driven nation. Cheaper and attractive goods from China flood the markets luring those buyers who have suffered years of economic instability due to adverse balance of payments.

Blind Massage in China

Blind Massage goes a long way back in the history of China. The eighth century Buddhist monk Jianzhen, practiced massage after he lost vision. More than 12 million people in China are visually challenged and have been compelled to restrict their career choices to a mere two, music or massage. It was around 1996 when the Chinese Massage Association of Blind Practitioners came into existence and professional trainings were offered. As on date there are more than 100,000 blind massage therapists across China. The streets of Beijing are flooded with blind massage parlors flaunting the sign 盲人按摩 (pronounced: mángrén ànmó).[28]

Indo Nepalese Relation

India is known to have contributed extensively to the economic, cultural and social development in Nepal though achieving it has not been an easy task for the Indian Government. Despite the geographic closeness, cultural commonness, economic interdependence and shared political values with Nepal, India's attitude is perceived as that of 'highhandedness' by a section of the Nepalese people. The Nepal India bilateral Peace and Friendship Treaty that was signed in 1950 got a jolt when an economic blockade was imposed on Nepal and continued for five long months beginning September 2015. The blockade came at that critical

[28] https://kungfuprincess-on-the-road.com/blind-massage-in-beijing/.

moment when Nepal was trying to rise from the devastating earthquake of 2015. The blockade resulted in an economic and humanitarian crisis as Nepali citizens had no access to basic commodities like fuel, food, medicines and cooking gas. The hashtag GoHomeIndianMedia topped the social media trend in Nepal, with tens of thousands of tweets. Nepalese citizens also complained that the coverage by Indian television was insensitive and jingoistic.

Another nagging point of friction that looms large in the Indo Nepalese relation is Indian demonetisation. India being Nepal's biggest trade ally and the provider of most of the consumer items, Indian rupee is freely used by Nepali businesses and individuals. When Prime Minister Modi announced scrapping of high value notes in 2016, individuals and the informal sector were in possession of a large sum of Indian currency notes. The Reserve Bank of India was not in a position to take back and exchange the old currency notes in Nepal as no alternate arrangement was made prior to or at the time of demonetisation.[29]

Nepal Rastra Bank, the central Bank of Nepal on the other hand, prohibited the new Indian currency notes of Rs. 500 and 2000 denomination, issued by the Reserve Bank of India, post demonetisation. The central bank labeled these currencies as 'unauthorized and illegal' (see Footnote 7) till FEMA notification comes into force. This backlash has caused great inconvenience to the Indian traveler and small and medium sized business owners.[30]

SOCIAL ENTREPRENEURSHIP

A charity dollar only has one life. A social business dollar can be invested over and over again.

Muhammad Yunus, Nobel Laureate

Though a joke, the saying that goes in Nepal is that the birth of a politician takes away 100 jobs whereas the arrival of an entrepreneur brings 100 jobs. Absence of commitment from people who matter and the

---

[29] https://www.news18.com/news/india/troubled-with-rs-950-crore-demonetised-indian-notes-nepal-pm-to-raise-issue-during-visit-1708343.html.

[30] https://timesofindia.indiatimes.com/india/New-Indian-notes-of-Rs-500-2000-illegal-in-Nepal-for-now/articleshow/55605024.cms.

resulting unemployment compelled young Nepali men and women to turn entrepreneurs and fulfill their personal and professional aspirations. In July 2017, Nepal's Gross National Product was recorded at per capita 91,488.16 NPR (see Footnote 11). To be upgraded from Least Developed Country (LDC) to Developing Economy, Nepal's per capita income needs to be $1245, a goal that the Government aims to attain by 2022.

Kathmandu's TIA is witness to a daily Nepali muscle drain to the Gulf countries. On an average more than 1750 would-be migrant laborers travel daily for foreign employment, according to data available at the Department of Foreign Employment (DoFE). The number is on a perennial rise. Compared to a total of 418,713 in the year 2015–16, a total of 639,167 aspirant youth flew to various countries in the fiscal year 2016–17.

The challenging work conditions abroad are also a motivating factor that has given rise to the entrepreneurial spirit among the youth of Nepal. Tired with the brutal working conditions in the Gulf but richer with foreign cash in their wallets, a significant number of Nepali youth return home and start an enterprise of their own. The skills acquired overseas is also making the Nepali youth confident to explore a variety of businesses. Thus, the experience foreign employment is fostering young entrepreneurs in many SMEs ventured like farming, recreation, tourism, technology and retail.

The standardisation of credit channels too encourages the Nepalese people to start their own independent ventures. Banks and financial institutions are seen coming forward to allocate a certain percentage of their corpus to be invested in SMEs. This has encouraged small business owners to muster the courage and emerge as entrepreneurs. The spread of cooperatives in rural Nepal is also a major motivator for entrepreneurs. Entrepreneurs in the villages are relying on banks to invest in agricultural farming, animal farm and daily supplies.

Social entrepreneurship in Nepal is a fairly recent phenomenon, where people start businesses not just with the objective of making a profit but also wanting to contribute to society. Social entrepreneurs champion social innovation and aim to bring visible transformation in the fields of health, education, enterprise development and the ecosystem as a whole. A social entrepreneur, is quite like a business entrepreneur, he is a mix of capitalism with a philanthropic attitude, one who creates strong, robust and sustainable business organisations, which can be exclusively Not for Profit or a hybrid of Profit with Not for Profit.

There is an emphasis on social entrepreneurship in Nepal. Many young people are establishing socially conscious businesses through the length and breadth of the country. Institutions of higher learning in Nepal such as King's College in Kathmandu have established degree programs and business incubators specialising in social entrepreneurship.

The digital platform seems to be the strongest weapon of the social entrepreneur. The internet has scaled up the promotion of social entrepreneurship where the entrepreneur tells his story and instead of he selling the story, the story 'sells' 'for the entrepreneur.' Through a choice of carefully selected websites the social entrepreneur can reach out to a larger population of individuals who may not be close in physical proximity but happen to share similar passion. Through the use of social media, these like-minded individuals can collaborate, brainstorm learn about trending issues, circulate news about an organisation's activities, and raise funds through crowdfunding and other methods. According to the Nepal Association of Tour Operators, social media seems to have changed the face of tourism marketing. Though traditional marketing still forms an integral part of the tourism business, it is the 'hashtag' that has changed the industry.

Seeing Hands Nepal as a social enterprise that works hand in hand with the Nepal Association of the Blind, a local grassroots NGO. The organisation is managed by the visually impaired whose main objectives are lobbying with Government besides creating awareness and advocacy. Very recently the organisation earned and secured voting rights for the blind and access to jobs in Government schools.

Besides collaborating with the association for the Blind, SHN also acts as an enabler in arranging schooling and training scholarships for the Blind. With this mission, SHN has been able to help around 100 blind Nepalese students pass the SSC examination. However, with 50% unemployment in Nepal, the vast majority of this 'specially-abled' population is unable to make use of its education to find gainful employment and a respectful life.

The lack of formal support creates a culture of 'survival and dependence' among the Blind in Nepal. People from this population not only compete fiercely for the Seeing Hand scholarships but they also expect special care from the organisation. SHN has discouraged and undone this pattern by not providing the blind with food and shelter. The organisation, on the other hand, has strived to bring up a group of visually challenged people who are able to live independently, manage their daily chores and commute to work by public transport.

The Future

As of 2018, the population of blind people in Nepal is nearing 117,623 (0.84 per 100 population), with an additional 223,612 persons blind in one eye (1.66 per 100 population). The blind community in Nepal is closely knit and functions with a set of unique and self-regulating mores and norms that makes it distinctive from the mainstream society. Inter-blind (love-based) marriages are common and the visually challenged individuals make a decent living by working hard that enables them to support not just their own families but also sustain, mentor and guide their lesser privileged peers in the community.

Over and above the intimidating landscape, erratic weather, shifty politics and indelible bureaucracy, Nepal is a country that struggles to advocate the rights of its disabled citizens, fight urban-rural inequality, and punish culprits who commit sexual violence on these 'specially-abled' people. Blindness is met with a lot of social stigma and prejudice in Nepal. It is perceived as a punishment from the Supreme and the Blind is viewed as a helpless person who is nothing but a burden for the family who eventually is left to care for himself. Women who are visually impaired are cruelly marginalised on account of their gender, and get deprived from their right to education, employment and a respectable livelihood. According to Nepal Blind Association only 134 women are employed out of a projected population of 100,000 visually impaired.[31] This apathy and lack of social support for the blind creates a negative impact on the self-esteem of the individual rendering him further helpless.

Each year, on an average, a total of 70–80 visually challenged students pass the school leaving examination (SLC). Most of these students are not able to avail college education because of lack of specialised literature, and poor means to relocate to Kathmandu or Pokhara, where most institutions for the blind are situated. Poor accessibility to higher education makes it even harder for the visually impaired to find employment. Traditionally, the employed visually impaired people are found to work as teachers, musicians or telephone operators. It is only in 2006 that that the Cricket Association of the Blind formed a blind team that made its debut appearance in the Blind T20 World Cup tournament 2017.[32]

[31] http://www.nabnepal.org/.

[32] http://www.cabnepal.com/.

Customised vocational training programs for visually impaired that offer a bouquet of career options needs to be implemented at a policy level in Nepal. With the above realisation, non-governmental organisations have come forward to train the visually challenged in sustainable skill building programs like Barista Training Program, waste management, and other community-based solutions that make best use of local resources in energy management, hygiene, healthcare and literacy.

For the future of Seeing Hands, Poudel plans to continue training for more blind massage practitioners. 'Just pleasant manners and professional skills are not enough when interacting with a client, but massage business also needs people who understand their responsibilities as a therapist. That's the only means to safeguard the precious Seeing Hands brand with our own hands,' foresees Poudel.

Poudel is not sure yet if he will open new branches. He is seeking certification for his therapists from the Nepali government. Currently, they are certified by the Institute of Sports and Remedial Massage in London but would like to add the Nepal approval to his staff's credentials. The earthquake in 2015 motivated Poudel to consider other ideas. 'The earthquake hurt business. It took a long time for business to return.'

This is one of the main reasons he is considering other income streams for the business. Should he continue to grow his massage business or look for other opportunities beyond massage? What might be other types of business that make sense for Poudel to get involved? What challenges could he encounter if he decides to venture into other businesses? What are the risks of staying only in the massage business in the Kathmandu area?

Conclusion

During my early years in 2010, the industry of massage clinics itself used to be taken negatively, as unprofessionalism was rampant, and the name 'massage' had a polluted scene in Kathmandu

Chiran Poudel, Owner, Seeing Hands Nepal

Since the establishment of the new Democratic Republic, Nepal has a great opportunity to remake and rejuvenate itself, despite the sluggish post-earthquake reconstruction and disruptions in Indo Nepalese trade transactions. Data from the Global Competitiveness Report indicates that Nepal's competitiveness has been on the rise over the last decade especially in areas like education, institution building, macroeconomics and infrastructure.[33]

Blind massage is a new profession in Nepal. It is a rewarding vocation for the visually challenged not just because the community is in desperate need of employment but also massage therapy a route to enable the visually challenged an access to the mainstream. As professional masseurs, the visually impaired can lead a life of dignity and independence and be a contributor to family income. With Government intervention and active participation from NGOs, it is feasible to bring to life a robust and self-sustaining massage training and employment program for the blind in Nepal. The corpus of funds earned from clients can be meaningfully used to support relevant vocational training for many more blinds in the remote parts of the country.[34]

Guilt, negativity, judgment and stigma, all are associated with the word 'massage' in an orthodox country like Nepal. Across the World and over centuries, massage therapy has had a rich, intricate and complex narrative. With this background, massage therapy has evolved from being a part of conventional medicine and is now admissible to being complementary to other lines of treatment. Surprisingly, even till date massage is associated with pleasure and remains marginalised as an industry. To overcome the societal mindset associated with massage therapy, the industry needs to gain social and professional legitimatisation as certified by health professionals within Nepal. Creating professional associations, creating awareness by defining scopes of therapy, active lobbying with government, and raising education standards are some of the critical strategies by which the value of massage as a profession in Nepal can be established. This can be administered in the form of sustainable locally-run projects and can pave the way forward for many blind individuals in Nepal.

The United Nations designated 2017 as the International Year of Sustainable Tourism for Development. Lonely planet too, named Nepal the World's 'best value destination' for the year 2017. Though the country has stepped into another New Year, the magic still lingers. The prestigious listing encouraged stakeholders a great lot and soon thereafter, the Nepali Government declared to mark 2017 and 2018 as 'Nepal Visit

---

[33] http://reports.weforum.org/global-competitiveness-index-2017-2018/.

[34] https://www.changemakers.com/economicopportunity/entries/sustainable-training-employment-program-for-blind.

Year'. It is a positive move because being the largest revenue earner in the globe, Travel and Tourism is an ocean of opportunities that creates jobs, encourages exports and creates prosperity and wealth across the planet.

Surely it can bring smiles on the lips of the blind masseurs in Nepal.[35,36]

[35] https://thehimalayantimes.com/nepal/lonely-planet-crowns-nepal-worlds-best-value-destination-2017.

[36] http://archive.nepalitimes.com/article/Nepali-Times-Buzz/touching-and-feeling-seeing-hands,4105.

Doing Business in South Asia: Critical Issues and Future Opportunities

Arijit Sikdar and Vijay Pereira

INTRODUCTION

As editors of this book, we have carried out a cross case analysis of the eleven cases and the teaching notes to identify common threads that seem to run through all or most of cases. Based on this analysis, four key themes emerge that could be considered to provide contribution to teaching and practice in the context of South Asia. Each of these key themes is discussed subsequently in this chapter.

REPUTATIONAL LEGACY

South Asian countries could be classified as developing or emerging economies that are growing economically but characterised by underdeveloped institutions that are required to carry out efficient transactions. These 'institutional voids' (Khanna and Palepu 1997) cause market

A. Sikdar (✉) · V. Pereira
Faculty of Business, University of Wollongong, Dubai, UAE
e-mail: arijitsikdar@uowdubai.ac.ae

V. Pereira
e-mail: vijaypereira@uowdubai.ac.ae

A. Sikdar and V. Pereira (eds.), *Business and Management Practices in South Asia*, https://doi.org/10.1007/978-981-13-1399-8_13

307

failures as firms are not able to transact in the market due to lack of business facilitation institutions. For example, lack of proper credit rating agency would cause difficulties in assessing the credit worthiness of supply chain partners leading to inefficiencies in transaction due increased cost of information search or additional compliance. This present a challenge of doing business in developing countries and data show that multinational try to avoid such markets due to the difficulties caused by institutional voids (Khanna et al. 2005).

Research by Gao et al. (2017) have identified that firm reputation built through prominence, perceived quality and resilience acts as a meta-resource that allows firms to activate conventional resources to help overcome potential transactional uncertainty. Thus reputation ensures the long run survival of the firm in emerging markets. The case studies of Aditya Birla Financial Services, Sun Pharma and Reliance Jio do highlight this leveraging of the firm reputation to expand business opportunities in the face of changing competitive dynamics. The case study of Aditya Birla Financial Services Group (ABFSG) focuses on a business model decision on how to leverage the existing brand reputation. ABFSG is a part of the iconic Aditya Birla group, a $42 billion behemoth. In the context of the changing nature of financial services industry in India, the case grapples with the issue of how the existing brand reputation can be leveraged best between business models of having a 'house of brands' or 'branded house' or 'house blend.' The case of Reliance Jio presents the leveraging of existing reputation of Reliance Group in launching the Reliance Jio Infocomm Limited (RJIL) to tap into the growing telecom market of India. Reliance Group is a leading diversified business group in India having presence across multiple sectors leveraging the reputation of creating value amongst the investor community. The launch of RJIL is an attempt to leverage that reputation by offering a new business model and take on the existing competition. The case focuses on how can that reputation be leveraged effectively in the face of the intense competition and the drastic changes in the demographics, needs and wants of the Indian consumers. Similarly, the case of Sun Pharma focuses on the acquisition of Ranbaxy to enhance the international expansion of Sun Pharma by leveraging Ranbaxy's global supply chain. The case discusses how Sun Pharma leverages Ranbaxy's reputation in research, quality production and brand name in international markets to achieve its vision of becoming a leading global player in the pharma industry. The case focuses on building supply chain as a strategic asset for developing reputation in the pharmaceutical industry.

In summary, the three case studies focus on leveraging the existing reputation to overcome the challenges. This theme provides the learning of the importance of creating firm reputation to overcome potential transactional uncertainty while operating under conditions of institutional voids. The theme also opens up opportunities for future research and case studies to understand how durable the firm reputation is in the face of undergoing institutional change. Also, future research can unfold how new established companies have built up firm reputation to overcome potential transactional uncertainty.

APPLICATION OF TECHNOLOGY

Developing markets like South Asian countries are characterised by infrastructural voids such as poor road network, frequent power outages, lack of electricity and internet connectivity in rural areas, etc. Overcoming these infrastructural challenges increases the cost of doing business as firms would have to invest in creating the required infrastructure (e.g. power, road, etc.) on their own. Example, the participation of many private players in acquiring coal mines through auction in India was to assure coal linkage for their in-house power plants due to lack of assured power supply. According to Arnold and Quelch (1998), such infrastructural as well institutional voids provide an opportunity for technological leapfrogging by surpassing conventional infrastructure requirements in marketing their products.

The case studies of Pakwheels.com, MakeMyTrip and bKash do highlight this aspect of technological leapfrogging used by firms to leveraging their business opportunities. The case study of Pakwheels.com focuses on the use of the internet to develop an online portal for buying and selling of cars. The case highlights the use of technology to overcome the problems associated with conventional car trade options like visiting numerous showrooms, sifting through thousands of advertisements with no proper categorisation to find the desired car, visiting weekly car markets, and paying a higher price or selling the car than the actual market value. Also these issues were compounded by the lack of transparency and reliability as no rating or review system existed for dealers or individual sellers. The creation of the portal, Pakwheels.com, provided the necessary transparency in the car buying market thus leapfrogging the infrastructural and institutional voids that existed in the used car market. The case of MakeMyTrip from India similarly focuses on the use of technology to create a travel portal that would help customers plan and book for their travel and stay through the click of a mouse. Here also the travel portal,

MakeMyTrip, overcame the problem faced by customers while booking their travel like visiting travel agents and not always being provided with the right support and price. Here again, internet technology was used to create convenience for customers by leapfrogging the conventional system of booking reservations. The case of bKash from Bangladesh focuses on the use of mobile network to develop mobile financial services that provided financial inclusion to the people who could not be covered by conventional banking. This case also highlights the use of technology to overcome the infrastructural challenges faced by bank to spread their network across the country.

In summary, all the three case studies focus on leveraging the technology solution to create opportunities to market products/services that provide higher efficacy against the conventional form of marketing. This theme provides the learning of how technology solutions can be used to develop business models relevant for the context of South Asia and similar developing countries to overcome conditions created by infrastructural and institutional voids. This theme also opens up opportunities for future research and case studies to understand how durable this business model is, as there is increasing evidence of followers using similar business model across industries like in e-tailing. Future research can also unfold whether similar business models can exist in both rural and urban regions, as there is wide disparity between rural and urban regions in South Asia. Similarly, new research could look at the importance of linkage between customer preparedness and the implementation of the technology-enabled business model.

Developing Social Connections

Developing economies like South Asia have a large segment of low income population wanting to improve their economic status. Such customers would appreciate products/services that improve their lives. An example of such practice can be seen in the growth of sachet packaging of shampoo in India that allowed low income customers to enjoy the use of modern cleaning without having to pay a large price to acquire the product. This requires a deeper understanding of the customer's culture which is supported by Letelier et al.'s (2003) focus on penetrating emerging economies: "The key is it understand the particular value created for the end-user, which often can only be found through a deep cultural understanding of the issues faced by end-users in these markets."

The case studies of Mobile Banking in Bangladesh and Weaving Clusters in India highlight this aspect of creating local cultural connections as a part of the business model. The Bangladeshi Banking Innovation case study discusses the customer's perception that influences the adoption of mobile banking in Bangladesh and revealed that perception to security, cost and convenience, and complexity in using mobile banking service influences mobile banking adoption amongst the low income segment of the population. The case of Weaving Clusters in India discusses how a sustainable business model was created for the weaving cluster, driven by financing, marketing and distribution, without multiple layers between the weaver and end user. Both the case studies illustrate the attempt to create a connection with the low income customer by developing a deeper cultural understanding of the issues faced. In the case of Bangladesh's mobile banking, the earning level of major portion of the population (students, housewives and small businessmen) is low and most of the people are still uneducated about mobile banking service, so they need assurance for their small amount of saving. Thus mobile banking service providers need to be concerned about the customers' security, cost, convenience and flexibility issue in designing mobile banking service. Similarly, in the case of Weaving Clusters of India, the domination of much cheaper mass-produced power looms, led to the erosion of 'local produce, local consumption models,' and thus ambiguity regarding predictability of supply and demand considerations for the weaving clusters, and the near death for the local weavers. The Spandan and Spoorthi movements to support the local weavers was started to provide an alternative business model such that weavers had more autonomy and were informed and empowered enough, leading to a supply chain that connected the weavers directly with the connoisseurs of handloom saris. This case also highlights the importance of building a business model based upon the deep cultural understanding of the issues faced by the weaving community as well as the customers.

In summary, both these case studies focus on leveraging the deep cultural understanding of the issues faced by end-users in the markets to create value for the end-user. This theme provides the learning of how the development of successful business models relevant for the context of South Asia needs to be integrated with the cultural understanding of the issues faced by the end-user. This theme also opens up opportunities for future research and case studies to understand different types of social movements to create business models based on deep understanding of cultural issues in South Asia, e.g. the Mumbai Dabbawallas. Future research can also unfold whether in a culturally and disparate region such as South Asia, would a pan national business mode would work or there needs to be different variations of the core business model to satisfy local cultural contexts. Similarly, new research could look at how to bring together various societal stakeholders required to achieve success in creating value based on cultural issues of the society and thus the role of the social entrepreneur.

RESOURCE RECOMBINATION

Developing countries like South Asia are hampered by availability of quality resources such as finance, managerial talent, assets, etc. This lack of quality resources hampers a business' expansion strategy as business needs to address trade-offs between business opportunities and availability of resources. According to Verbeke (2013), "resource recombination is critical to creating value and satisfying consumer demand." Firms in South Asia need to effectively utilise their existing resources through recombination to address the value creation.

The following case studies of Internationalisation of Bangladeshi Banks and Overseas Courier Services' (OCS) Logistics Operations provides illustration of the challenges faced in business expansion strategy. The case of Internationalisation of Bangladeshi Banks illustrates the balancing the dilemma of expanding internationally to increase economic potential vis a vis the managerial challenges faced related to lack of international experience and quality human resources, social and management cultural differences, and operational complexity during the process of internationalisation by the banks. As the case study showed the negative impact on internationalisation performance due to managerial challenges faced, understanding the challenges and their role in obstructing the internationalisation process would provide perspectives to the learners on generic difficulties faced by banks in an emerging economy. Similarly, the case of OCS illustrates managing the conflicting objectives of operational cost and customer service while designing and managing the logistics network. Here, also the firm is needed to address the route planning of transport fleet and selecting headquarter location to create value for their customers. Here, the challenge is to deal with the existing infrastructural and human resources to develop a strategy to compete effectively. In both the cases, the business opportunities cannot be effectively exploited due to challenges posed by the existing firm resources and called for resource recombination to create value. In the case of bank internationalisation, this would require banks to rationalise their managerial independence, human resource management and policy orientation to effectively serve the international markets. In the OCS case, there is need to rationalise the route plan to achieve the objective of cost saving.

The case Seeing Hands Nepal deals with the start-up and development of an entrepreneurial venture. The case provides the perspective of the entrepreneurial challenges of dealing with dilemma balancing social entrepreneurship goals of providing employment to blind massage therapists against whether enough qualified blind therapists are available to expand the business. This is a classic challenge that business in developing regions like South Asia would encounter as adequate quality resources are not available for business expansion. In such context, there is a need for resource recombination to create value. This case also presents such resource recombination challenge of how to fulfil the mission of employing blind people while identifying new opportunities of business expansion that could create value through employing blind people. The case is apt in the context to understand the role of entrepreneurial leadership in creating a sustainable model of social entrepreneurship.

In summary, all these three cases focus on addressing the management of existing resources to create value for addressing business opportunities. This theme opens up opportunities of future research directed towards understanding different approaches of management and optimization of existing resources to create value.

Conclusions

The four themes identified and their depiction in the case studies does provide a useful focus on the possible positioning of the case studies and their application in teaching. It also provides a useful knowledge for practitioners to understand the key challenges that are present while operating in South Asia and points to practical approaches that have been taken by businesses to address such challenges. In addition, each of the case studies do focus on different managerial and functional issues that are being performed. This open up opportunities in each case to understand how the key managerial issues are being addressed to address the challenges of doing business in South Asia.

The following table illustrates how the ten case studies address the key themes of doing business in South Asia through the application of managerial and functional issues (Table 1).

Table 1   Key themes emerging from this book of doing business in South Asia

	Themes			
Managerial roles	*Reputational legacy*	*Application of technology*	*Developing social connections*	*Resource recombination*
Strategic decision making	Aditya Birla Financial Services Group			Internationalization of Bangladeshi Banks
Entrepreneurial leadership			Weaving Clusters in India	Seeing Hands Nepal
Market expansion	Reliance Jio	Pakwheels. com, MakeMyTrip		
Operational planning	Sun Pharma			Overseas Courier Services
Product development		bKash	Bangladeshi Banking Innovations	

The table provides an easy reference for the reader and case teacher to understand the key positioning of each case for targeted teaching and understanding of relevant managerial concepts/practices. In addition, the interaction of the themes with the managerial issues do also open up opportunities for future research that can be directed to explore each theme and uncover how different managerial roles issues could be addressed to achieve the theme but have not been explored in these case studies.

REFERENCES

Arnold, D.J., & Quelch, J.A. (1998). "New Strategies in Emerging Markets", *Sloan Management Review*, vol. 40, pp. 7–20.

Gao, C., Zuzul, T., Jones, G., & Khanna, T. (2017). "Overcoming Institutional Voids: A Reputation-Based View of Long-Run Survival", *Strategic Management Journal*, vol. 38, no. 11, pp. 2147–2167.

Khanna, T., & Palepu, K.G. (1997). "Why Focused Strategies May Be Wrong for Emerging Markets", *Harvard Business Review*, vol. 75, pp. 41–51.

Khanna, T., Palepu, K.G., & Sinha, J. (2005). "Strategies That Fit Emerging Markets", *Harvard Business Review*, vol. 83, pp. 63–76.

Letelier, M.F., Flores, F., & Spinosa, J. (2003). "Developing Productive Customers in Emerging Markets", *California Management Review*, vol. 45, pp. 77–103.

Verbeke, A. (2013). *International Business Strategy*. London: Cambridge University Press.

INDEX